GLOBALISATION OR COLONISATION ?

GLOBALISATION OR COLONISATION ?

KALYAN RAY
IAS (Retd.)

DEEP & DEEP PUBLICATIONS PVT. LTD.
F-159, Rajouri Garden, New Delhi-110027

GLOBALISATION OR COLONISATION?

ISBN 81-7629-560-4

Typeset by S.S. COMPOSERS,
3190, Mohindra Park, Shakur Basti, Delhi-110034.

Printed in India at ELEGANT PRINTERS,
A-38/2, Maya Puri, Phase-I, New Delhi-110064.

Published by DEEP & DEEP PUBLICATIONS PVT. LTD.
F-159, Rajouri Garden, New Delhi-110027.
Phones: 25435369, 25440916
E-mail: ddpbooks@yahoo.co.in • deep98@del3.vsnl.net.in
Showroom:
2/13, Ansari Road, Daryaganj, New Delhi-110002 • Telefax: 23245122

DEDICATED

To the Memory of my Parents
Dr. Parimal Ray, Ph.D. (London),
whose collection of books over a lifetime,
helped me in my research

and

Mrs. Chhaya Ray, B.A.

Contents

Preface

Today we are told that globalisation is inevitable and any body not prepared to jump on the bandwagon will be left high and dry. For the major part of the twentieth century, the refrain was 'socialism is inevitable'. Anybody intent on a political career had to publicly declare his faith in socialism. Great merit was attached to votaries of socialism. Even in the academic field, hold of socialism was near absolute and few could challenge its inevitability. Those who opposed it, like Fredrich Hayek and Milton Friedman were banished to the economic fringe, till they were rehabilitated as champions of New World Order, under Reagan and Thatcher. The inevitability theory has an element of fatalism and is opposed to rationalism. This is clear from the writings of Hayek, particularly his, 'The Fatal Conceit: The Errors of Socialism'. The book is a throwback on primitivism and law of the jungle, with everybody for himself and the devil take the hindmost. Naturally, a civilised society cannot accept such a dictum and must wage a war against such inevitability. The theory that man is not the master of his destiny and is a tool in the hands of socio-economic forces, is being increasingly touted to the third world countries, who are facing crisis of development, after the euphoria of earlier years. This also promises a convenient alibi for politicians and the power brokers. The theory of 'natural rate of unemployment' by Milton Friedman, is a call for institutionalization of poverty. Natural rate of unemployment is not specified. With the progressive integration of the economies of the developed and developing countries, the latter countries will have the worst of the bargain. World unemployment is increasing with the progress of globalisation and in the developing countries, this is increasing exponentially. The concept of inevitality in economics, which has been introduced by Hayek and Friedman, spells danger for mankind. No doubt, these two long marginalised economists suddenly found favour and became the ideological soulmates of powerful leaders like Ronald Reagan and Margaret Thatcher.

New International Economic Order proposed by Brandt Commission in its report released in 1979 and sought to be debated in Cancun world economic meet gave way to New World Order of President Reagan. NWO has come to mean U.S.-centric development. Free trade imperialism has strong political overtones, as economics and politics overlap. Economic interdependence also promotes political dependence, as economic decisions of governments control the lives of the people. Elections are decided on the economic agenda of the parties. Economic issues are not independent of political issues and cannot be separated. Globalisation is as such both economic and political, in which security dimension is also covered. As major armament industries are controlled by the West, free trade globalisation with international division of labour, is also leading to globalisation of security. In such a scenario of U.S.-centric economic globalisation, international security will also be U.S.-centric. After the end of Cold War bi-polarism, this trend has become more and more pronounced. With an unipolar world, U.S. has become the dominant world power, alongwith its close ally Britain. This has created tensions in Europe, with major European powers like France, Germany and Russia having different views on world matters. The very concept of globalisation has come under challenge in the developed countries. Many of them do not accept the substitution of the British-centred world economy with American-centred one, through the intervention of two world wars and the Cold War. Thus, economic globalisation, as is being understood today is development of other countries, as a periphery of U.S.A. and U.K. An understanding of economic factors in the development of a country through a broader time span, is vital to the understanding of the process of globalisation. Economic and political history of a country are closely interlinked and one cannot be fully understood without an understanding of the other. A repetition of history should be avoided, at least by the countries, which have been under foreign domination.

Loss of political sovereignty is more apparent than loss of economic sovereignty and involves lot of emotions and rhetorics, whereas loss of economic sovereignty is more subtle. Gokhale had pointed out in 1907, 'The industrial domination is less visible and does its work in a more insidious manner. . . . Human feelings often matter more to humanity than human interests'*. Earlier R.C. Dutt, Dadabhai Naoroji and M.G. Ranade were the pioneers amongst the Indians in pointing out the adverse effects of Britain's economic domination of India. Colonial imperialism is basically economic and the political aspect of it is like the proverbial tip of the iceberg. Economic domination comes in attractive package, which caters to our senses and dulls the mind. Barter in trinkets, which led to earlier colonisation, still constitutes the basis of New World Order. More and more import of puerile luxury goods and redundant foreign technology, have made us welcome such domination, quite forgetting that these are intended to 'Win us with honest trifles, to betray's in deepest consequence'. (Shakespeare, Macbeth).

Globalisation has serious implications on world's poverty. As it means basically globalisation of the rich and powerful. Small islands of prosperity are being carved out even amidst severe poverty and destitution. These islands of affluence are linked up in the name of globalisation. Call for globalisation has not only sounded the death knell of Communism, it has also stood Marx on his head, as Marx had supposed to have stood Hegel on his head. Globalisation call is for the rich of the world to unite and assert their power. Industrial Revolution in Britain of the eighteenth and nineteenth century led to colonialism and imperialism. This aspect has been analysed in the book. Colonialism was also

---

* Speeches of G.K. Gokhale, p. 959.

justified as a policy of mutual benefit to the colonies and the colonial power, as the former was getting the benefit of international division of labour through import of technology and finished goods from the latter and export of primary goods. The balance of trade was heavily loaded in favour of the goods produced by the colonial power. Industrial Revolution led to British-centric world capitalism, which did not go unchallenged, as we have seen through various wars in Europe and colonial wars in the eighteenth and nineteenth centuries, leading to two major world wars and cold war, which led to unprecedented military expenditure during peace time, through stock piling of armaments.

Experiments with socialism and communism have run out of their steam, as the promised utopia of the workers did not materialize. With the failure of these experiments, the intellectual movement, which had sustained these social philosophies and over a period of time acquired a stridency of its own also died down. These philosophies, which are the products of British Industrial Revolution and a reaction to the same, found themselves lacking in the next phase, when the concept of industrial worker became blurred and got merged with a huge army of clerical workers, which the next phase of industrial revolution generated. Socialism and communism were targeted at industrial workers, who were the most visible part of the system. With the electronics revolution and gradual decline of heavy and factory-based industries, the industrial worker became a smaller element in the work-force. The traditional concept of workers in conflict with management did not work, as the State had become the major employer, even in non-communist countries. The conflict situation led to world capitalism shifting to a new economic pattern with electronic and information-based industries, where the jobs can be outsourced. The concept of factories with a huge work-force, became outdated, as machines displaced men in work site and even in supervisory jobs. When unemployment became the main problem, socialism and communism could not be sustained. The result is that we find ourselves back to the old fashioned liberal capitalism, which is an euphemism for colonialism.

World Bank, I.M.F. and GATT (re-designated as WTO) have been the main agencies of this neo-classical policy of economy, which had been recommended by the League of Nations in 1945 in their document, Economic Stability in the Post-War World, to keep the world safe for democracy. According to this document, 'Nationalistic economic policies aggravated the situation after the war (First World War). . . Efforts to combat the depression by expanding purchasing power also contributed to this end by creating a domestic demand which made it profitable to establish local manufacturing industries in certain non-industrialised states'. The document has also recommended an active policy of foreign lending by the industrially developed states to the under-developed countries to prevent growth of economic independence and development of an economic system more suited to their needs. The document warns that the ultimate stability of the world economic system will depend mainly on the extent to which policies designed to maintain full employment are successfully applied in the great industrial states.* Report of the Delegation on Economic Depressions, 'The Conditions of Prosperity After the Transition from War to Peace', published by the League of Nations, was the result of deliberations, held during 1938-45, leading to the formation of International Bank for Reconstruction and Development (World Bank) and International Monetary Fund. Two institutions, which have controlled the world financial system in the non-communist world, since the end of the last world war. It was feared that with the granting of political independence to the under-developed countries, these countries will slip away from the economic grip of the colonising countries. The fact was well realised that the economic nexus which has been worked out over the colonial years, is vital for the economic survival of the colonising countries.

The World Bank policy of loaning to the developing countries has strictly followed the colonial policy of tying up loans and grants with transfer of technology, which was not

---

* Report of the Delegation on Economic Depressions, pp. 37-40, 190-92.

the technology appropriate for developing countries. With the free flow of tied loan and aid, developing countries had no choice over technology. The World Bank loan packages came in attractive garbs, which promised a complete transformation of the economy of the developing countries. The packages were too attractive to resist and the governments of developing countries, which had promised too much to the electorate, fell for them in a big way to redeem their promise and win another term of governance and power. The international loaning agencies cashed in on the psychology of developing countries to show development in a short period. Life of a democratically elected government is five years or less and within that time it has to show some startling economic miracle to win another term in office. What best away to achieve this, than through foreign loans, whose burden will fall much later? World Bank loaning policy marketed proposals, which promised short-term benefits at the cost of long-term loss. I.M.F., which was the brain-child of Keynes, encouraged such a policy, in accordance with the Keynesian precept of 'in the long-run, we are all dead'. No doubt, the World Bank experiment was a big failure in the developing countries, whereas it was a big success for the loaning countries, in finding a profitable outlet for its surplus capital. Even according to Bank's narrowly defined economic criteria, the World Bank projects have been failures. According to an internal study conducted by the World Bank, 37.5 per cent of Bank-funded projects completed in 1991 were failures at the time of completion.*[1] In an earlier post-completion report after four-to-ten years, it was found that half of the projects, rated to have been completed successfully were failures. In a study conducted by Baum and Tolbert of forty years' experience of World Bank, since its inception, it was found that Bank financed projects failed due to application of inappropriate technology.*[2] Foreign financed projects have been failures due to mismatch of technology and the local economy. Technological innovation is a product of particular socio-economic conditions. Super imposition of technology does not yield the desired result and may prove

*1. Korten, When Corporations Rule The World, p. 171. *2. Seitz, Global Issues, p. 191.

counter-productive, with other parameters being different. Such projects with sudden and sporadic rise of economic activity, fails to take roots in the surrounding economy and only helps the speculators and economic adventurers, who are able to corner most of these resources. The initial economic activity is not sustainable and the projects only succeed in creating socio-economic and environmental imbalance. Technology, which had been used as a tool of imperialism during the colonial years, continued to serve the same purpose through World Bank and other smaller multilateral development banks and bilateral loans and aids.

The promised generation of resources through World Bank projects hardly materialised and huge foreign debt burden was loaded on the country. With a huge foreign debt, developing countries became a part of the global financial system and came under the direct control of IMF, which dictated the financial policies of these governments, under the aegis of its main shareholders. IMF directed policy of sharp devaluation of the Rupee and complete reversal of economic policy by the Indian government in 1992; picture of IMF Managing Director, Michel Camdessus rebuking the humiliated President of Indonesia, General Suharto; are some of the more glaring of such instances. This, after India had been praised sky high by World Bank-IMF combine as model of economic development with World Bank assistance. General Suharto, under whose regime Indonesia became one of the Asian Tigers; the person who prevented communist take over of Indonesia and prevented it from being another Vietnam in the 1960s, suddenly became a fall guy in the wake of south-east Asian financial crisis. World Bank-IMF, duo do not take any responsibility for its own errors and are adept at passing on the same to the loanee countries.

The first priority of any government in India, should be to bring down the external debt to manageable limits. Main justification of foreign loan and aid, is lack of investible resources within the country. With a high saving rate within the country and a low interest regime, there is no reason why the government should not mobilize internal resources for its development programmes, instead of continuously depending on foreign loans and aids. The old justification of cycle of poverty due to lack of investible resources, has ceased to be valid for a long time, with India being one of the high saving economies. It may be of interest to recollect that the entire capital of setting up Tata Iron and Steel Industry in 1907 was raised within India. This, after attempt to raise funds for the project in London money-market in 1906, was a failure. Indian funding of TISCO was entirely a product of the Swadeshi movement of encouragement of indigenous enterprises, which motivated the Indians to raise the entire capital within three weeks.* If at that time funding for a major steel factory, which was a novelty, could be done in India, there is no reason why we require loans for road projects, railways, steel mills, where we have adequate expertise.

Technological bondage is the main reason for our constant dependence on foreign loan packages with tied technology. Unless, we are able to achieve technological independence, it is unlikely that we should be able to break through the technology control regime. It is the control over technology, which is the key to the dominance of the third-world countries by the developed countries. With the advance in technical education, India has adequate technical manpower and should be in a position of not depending on foreign technology. We should develop technology suited to our own socio-economic conditions, instead of going in for the so-called state of the art technology which comes in attractive packages with a huge foreign exchange bill and touch only the fringe of our economy. Moreover, state of the art technology of today becomes outdated tomorrow and the mismatch between technology and economy, hardly gives the desired result. Technology control regime has further been strengthened by a Patent Control regime introduced through 'Agreement on Trade-Related Aspects of Intellectual Property Rights', which has necessitated a change in Indian patent laws favouring a patent control regime by developed

* Life of J.N. Tata, by F.R. Harris, pp. 184-203.

countries. This has great potentiality of hindering the development of any independent technology by our own industrial research and development organisation. In fact, during the last decade, since the signing of the IPR agreement, there has been little progress in industrial innovation in India.

'The process of industrialisation of the under-developed countries will, in our view, take place with or without assistance from outside in the form of foreign lending . . . If no outside assistance is forthcoming, it is likely that many of the economically under-developed countries will aim at producing at home the industrial equipment of all types they require for their industrialisation. On the other hand, if the economic development of economically under-developed areas is assisted by foreign investment, it can proceed more quickly and with smaller risk of fostering autarkic (economic independence) tendencies inimical to the healthy, development of a world economic system'*. These were the guidelines under which institutions like World Bank, IMF and GATT were set-up to control the world economic structure. While political independence of the colonies could not be prevented, economic control was vital for the maintenance of full employment 'in the great industrial states'. Unlike, the General Assembly of the United Nations, these bodies are weighed in favour of developed nations, with greater voting power. These institutions have been remarkably successful in working over half a century in accordance with the mandate laid down for them.

Industrially under-developed countries did not succeed in establishing an independent industrial system and remained dependent on foreign technology. 'The international division of labour' envisaged an one-way traffic from the industrialised countries, with complete control of technology by these countries. In the history of industrialisation, since the Industrial Revolution in Britain, no country has been successful in industrialising itself by replicating the industrial

* Report of the Delegation on Economic Depressions (1945), League of Nations (p. 191).

development pattern of the other. Germany is the only major country in Europe, which has been nearest to the British model of industrialisation. This had put her in a collision course with Britain, resulting in two major world wars, although these two countries have been traditional allies for centuries against the other major European country, France. The two world wars have their origin in the struggle for economic supremacy. The system devised under the New World Order, has created serious differences in the West, as we have seen in various WTO meetings and the latest Iraq War. Even in the case of the war, the differences are basically economic, as can be seen in the exclusion of major industrial countries like France, Germany and Russia from the project contracts in post-war Iraq. India has to be careful in not aligning with any economic power bloc. Now with ideological linkages gone, India has a greater chance of coming within the ambit of Anglo-American power bloc, due to the colonial historical relations, particularly in the field of economy.

A study of industrial revolution in the industrialised countries will show that countries, which have industrialised successfully have followed their own pattern suited to their socio-economic conditions. In fact, a social revolution must precede industrial revolution. France, is perhaps the only country, where a social revolution preceded industrial revolution. This delayed the industrialisation process, but could be achieved at lower social cost than the others. Industrialisation of France has been also the most successful in balancing agricultural and industrial development. In other industrialised countries, the basic feudal structure remained and it only took a different form with industrial revolution. The newly independent countries in a hurry to achieve industrialisation did little to bring in a socio-economic transformation, before launching on an industrialisation drive. It was thought that industrialisation would bring in a socio-economic transformation. This has not happened, as industrialisation does not take place in a social vacuum and has to be integrated with the socio-economic structure. Industrialisation process releases forces, which tend to break up the existing socio-economic structure, without creating an alternative viable one. Due to lack of social dynamics in most of the societies, the new emerging socio-economic structure tends to combine the worst features of both the systems. Feudalism of the past is combined with the rapacity of a market-oriented society. It is difficult to achieve any lasting economic development, with a feudal structure of society.

KALYAN RAY

1

Linkage of Industrial Revolution and Colonisation

The key to Great Britain being pioneer in Industrial Revolution lies in their early realisation of a colonial policy of acquiring captive markets and siphoning off, the population made redundant by the grinding wheels of industrial revolution. R.C. Dutt's 'The Economic History of British India' quotes William Pitt, who was the British Prime Minister in the mid-eighteenth century "I am sure that I can save the country, and that no one else can." Having said that, he pursued an active colonial policy during his Prime Ministership from 1757 to 1761. 'The whole of Canada was conquered from the French in 1760. Clive won the battle of Plassey in 1757, and Eyre Coote crushed the French power in India in 1761. Within 5 years England's greatness as a world-power was assured, France was humbled in Europe, and effaced in Asia and America.'[1] This coincided with the time, when Britain was vigorously searching for distant markets for its mass-produced goods, particularly textiles. Pitt's family background in colonial trade, must have made him realize the powerful potentiality of colonialism. The fortunes of the Pitt family, were the products of the East India trade. 'The most successful East India family was unquestionably that of Pitt. Founder of the Pitt fortunes was Thomas (1653-1726) who began his career as an interloper in the East Indies trade but ended as Governor of Madras. His fortune sufficed to make his son Earl of Londonderry and his grandson became Prime Minister and Earl of Chatham'.[2] If a personal fortune and consequent power could be built-up from such humble beginnings, through colonial trades, an impoverished island nation could aspire to great wealth and power through pursuit of an aggressive policy of colonialism.

It is no accident of history that 'the Industrial Revolution set in England about the time when the Company gained its first foothold in India as a territorial power'.[3] There is enough historical evidence to show that before the advent of the Britishers, India basically was an economically balanced country between agriculture and industry. India was no worse of than Britain at the beginning of the Industrial Revolution, but the position changed with the advent of the machine age. 'The awful result, according to one calculation, was that whereas the British and Indian peoples had roughly similar per capital levels of industrialisation at the on set of the Industrial Revolution (1750), India's level was only one hundredth of the United Kingdom's by 1900'.[4] This benefits, however did not percolate to the bulk of the British people, who were if anything, worse of than before. Toynbee has noted in his lecturers, delivered in 1880s that one-half of the land in the United Kingdom is owned by 2512 persons. Industrial Revolution led to decimation of British peasantry, whereas industialisation of Britain led to systematic de-industrialisation of India. 'By 1840 an observer already warned against the disastrous effects of turning India into the agricultural farm of England; she is a manufacturing country, her manufactures of various descriptions have existed for ages, and have never been able to be competed with by any nation wherever fair play has been given to them. . . . To reduce her now to an agricultural country would be an injustice to India'.[5] We have on the authority of Adam Smith, 'Bengal, accordingly, the province of Indostan, which commonly exports the greatest quantity of rice, has always been more remarkable for the exportation of a great variety of manufactures than for that of its grain'. Adam Smith also says, 'The great extent of Indostan, too, rendered the home market of that country very great, and sufficient to support a great variety of manufactures'.[6] Industrial Revolution in Britain should not be treated as a mere economic phenomenon powered by technical knowledge. It should be treated more as a socio-economic process, in which numerous factors are involved, primary of which is colonialism. Close linkage between colonialism and industrial revolution needs to be understood for a true understanding of the changing world economic structure set in motion under colonialism.

INDUSTRIALISATION AND NEED FOR CAPTIVE MARKETS (ECONOMIC COLONIES)

Colonialism was the first attempt at Globalisation with colonies working as hinterland for mass produced consumer goods. In the beginning of the nineteenth century, Great Britain had a colonial population of 126.4 million, as against France's 0.5 million, whereas other European countries were yet to emerge as major colonial powers.[7]

The Industrial Revolution was both a cause and effect of the colonial policy pursued by Great Britain in the eighteenth and the nineteenth centuries and was not a result of the policy of *laissez faire*, as commonly assumed, but a policy of active State capitalism through colonisation of distant markets. The creation of the colonies in the eighteenth and nineteenth centuries was primarily motivated by the necessity of having assured markets for the large-scale production generated by the Industrial Revolution. The direct intervention by the colonial Government in the economy of the colonies to make it a subsidiary of the economy of the former was not taken into account by the majority of the British School of classical economists. The continental economists, specially of the Austro-German school of thought were very clear about this paradox of development. The gap between theory and practice in British economic thinking was expressed by Friedrich List in his book, 'The National System of Political Economy', which first appeared in Germany in 1840. Friedrich List (1786-1846) who was an academician and also political activist, representing German merchants, could see through the difference between the economic thinking and practical policies in the economic sphere in Great Britain.

British Government was first to understand that commercial supremacy depended on supremacy in the sphere of production of manufactured goods. The colonial policy of England was mainly establishing her supremacy in the sphere of manufacture and utilise the colony for supply of raw materials. 'England was unwilling to found settlements in Asia in order to become subservient to India in manufacturing industry. She strove for commercial supremacy, and felt that of two countries maintaining free trade between one another, that one would be supreme which sold manufactured goods, while that one would be subservient which could only sell agricultural produce. In the North American colonies, England had already acted on those principles in disallowing the manufacture in those colonies of even a single horse-shoe nail, and still more that no horse-shoe nails made there should be imported into England. How could it be expected of her that she would give up her own market for manufactures, the basis of her future greatness, to a people so numerous, so thrifty, so experienced and perfect in the old systems of manufacture as the Hindus'. List goes on to say that the British Government acted not according to the theory of value of the classical economists, according to which England should have bought what she required where she could buy them cheapest and best. 'The case is quite the contrary, according to our theory, which we term the Theory of the Powers of Production, and which the English Ministry, without having examined the foundation on which it rests yet practically adopted when enforcing their maxim of importing produce and exporting fabrics. The English Ministers cared not for the acquisition of low priced and perishable articles of manufacture, but for that of a more costly and enduring manufacturing power'.[8]

Adam Smith, held that, 'unless perhaps, we give credit to the wonderful accounts of the wealth and cultivation of China, of those of ancient Egypt, and of the ancient State of Indostan. Even those three countries, the wealthiest, according to all accounts, that ever were in the world, are chiefly renowned for their superiority in agriculture and manufactures'.[9] This was the situation in 1776. India, from a trade surplus country 'was systematically deindustrialised and became in turn a market for Lancashire cottons: in 1820 the subcontinent took only 11 million yards; but by 1840 it already took 145 million yards'.[10] Hobsbawm goes on, 'It was a major landmark in World History. For since the dawn of time Europe had always imported more from the East than she had sold there'. Colonialism, coupled with factory system of production, changed all that and the economic balance started tilting in favour of West, particularly Britain, which kept India in a subtle economic bondage.

'Still, as late as the beginning of the seventeenth century, India was "the respiratory organ for the circulation and distribution of moneys and commodities of the commercial system of the world; it was the sea wherein all the rivers of trade and industry flowed and thus profusely enriched its inhabitants." Even "up to the eighteenth century the economic condition of India was relatively advanced, and Indian methods of production and of industrial and commercial organisation could stand comparison with those in vogue in any other part of the World." But before many years elapsed, India presented to the world a picture just the reverse of what we have portrayed above'.[11] There is enough evidence of superiority of Indian manufactures over British goods. 'It was stated in evidence (in 1813) that the cotton and silk goods of India upto the period could be sold for a profit in the British market at a price from 52 to 60 per cent, lower than those fabricated in England. It consequently became necessary to protect the latter by duties of 70 to 80 percent on their value, or by positive prohibition. Had this not been the case, had not such prohibitory duties and decrees existed, the mills, of Paisley and Manchester would have been stopped in their outset and could scarcely have been again set in motion, even by the power of steam'.[12] Industrial revolution and gradual colonisation of India changed the position completely and India ceased to be a manufacturing country by the beginning of the nineteenth century. With the Industrial Revolution in Britain, Company gained its first foothold in India as a territorial power. 'There fell on the country the full force of its impact and the old economic structure began to crumble down to pieces before the remorseless, rising tide of English competition, armed with the ever-growing mastery of the forces of nature and of technique'.[13] Prosperity of Britain during the nineteenth and early twentieth century was entirely due to a captive colonial market, aided by factories of mass production. Strangely, the workers did not share in the benefit of this loot from the colonies. The factory system brought in untold misery to the British working class, who lost their traditional occupation. Adam Smith's 'Wealth of Nations' clearly reveals that the great economist was well aware of the adverse effects of colonial policy on the countries, which are subject to the same. To him colonialism was the natural extension of the policy of towns exploiting the country. To quote Adam Smith, 'every town draws its whole subsistence, and all the materials of its industry from the country'. Adam Smith had also this to say about the East India Company. 'Such exclusive companies (British and Dutch East India Company), therefore, are nuisance in every respect, always more or less inconvenient to the countries in which they are established, and destructive to those which have the misfortune to fall under their government.'[14]

Adam Smith is portrayed as the presiding deity of *laissez faire* capitalism. A careful reading of Adam Smith's 'Wealth of Nations' shows that the economic system pursued by Britain and other dominant European countries in his time was a highly restrictive system. Towns were exploiting the countryside by municipal laws which were favourable to them. 'The superiority which the industry of the towns has everywhere in Europe over that of the country is not altogether owing to corporations and corporation laws. It is supported by many other regulations. The high duties upon foreign manufactures and upon all goods imported by alien merchants, all tend to the same purpose.'[15] The economic power, which the town has over the country, is due to the ability of the town's people to combine in their economic interest, as compared to the country, where the people are dispersed and cannot easily combine. This is the anatomy of colonialism, which Smith explored in his thesis on 'Wealth of Nations'. In the early chapters, 'The Wealth of Nations' analyses how towns as colonies of people who are able to combine in their economic pursuits, were exploiting the country side, where the people are dispersed in distant places. British colonialism of the eighteenth and nineteenth centuries is an extension beyond national boundaries of the process, which began with towns colonising the countryside. The creation of the colonies in the eighteenth and nineteenth centuries was primarily motivated by the necessity of having assured markets for the increase in production brought about by the transformation of the production process of industrial goods, with capital becoming more and more a dominating factor, instead of labour.

According to all accounts of the British Industrial Colonialism, cotton industry had the pioneering role in the transition of the British industry. Textile industry was originally a cottage industry and was a subsidiary occupation to agriculture. 'In 1775, the cotton manufacture in England was ranked amongst the humblest of the domestic arts, the production of this branch were then almost entirely for home consumption, in 1797, it took the lead of all other manufactures in Great Britain, and in 1809 gave employment to 800,000 persons'.[16] Peter Kriedte while tracing the transition of British economy from proto-industrialisation to capitalist industrialisation stages writes, 'There was only one way out of the crisis of the proto-industrial mode of production: mechanisation coupled with centralisation. It was the latest branch of English textile industry, the one most closely connected with the colonial trade, namely, the cotton industry, which embarked upon this course, starting in the 1760s. The cotton industry became the 'pacemaker' (E.J. Hobsbawm) of the first phase of the Industrial Revolution. The invention of the spinning machines of the 1760s and 1770s, Hargreave's 'Jenny,' Arkwright's water frame, Crompton's mule, and their installation in central building made it possible not only to control part of the production process, but also to eliminate the disequilibrium between yarn and cloth production.'[17] Machine weaving followed machine spinning 'Due to the increasing supply of yarn and the immensely growing demand for cotton goods, domestic looms multiplied at the end of the eighteenth and the beginning of the nineteenth centuries'.[18] Mechanisation of textile industries created large-scale unemployment amongst the handloom weavers in Great Britain. 'The handloom weavers and others who were starved out were not simply "survivals from the middle age", but a class multiplied, and largely created as part of capitalist industrialisation in its early phases just as the factory workers were'.[19]

DETERIORATING CONDITIONS OF BRITISH PEASANTRY

It is of some interest to consider a point raised by M. Fores in 'The Myth of a British Industrial Revolution'. 'Instead of having experienced an industrial revolution, England experienced an urban evolution, as part of an age-old process of a shift of population to the towns. This change was accompanied by changes in wealth, skill, commercial practices and transport facilities. It was part of a process which can first be observed to have occurred in the Sumerian cities of 3000 BC, in which some people got much richer, and other people got poorer (slaves in the earlier case, wage-slaves latterly)'.[20] The period from 1750 onwards saw a shift of working population from the countryside to cities. Farmers with small holdings, who were dependant on cottage industries with local markets, to supplement their farm incomes, gradually became non-viable. This class of peasant farmers, when they found themselves economically non-viable, had to surrender their holdings to the landlords and became a part of the urban wage-slaves. In the nineteenth century, Great Britain was the most urbanised country in Europe. 'Between 1776 and 1811, for example, roughly 60 per cent of the increase in the population resident in British urban areas consisted of immigrants from the rural areas of Great Britain and Ireland.'[21]

Arnold Toynbee in his Lectures on the Industrial Revolution in England (1884), published posthumously, laments, 'The destruction of the old bonds between employers and workmen was not peculiar to manufactures; it came to pass in agriculture also. An agrarian as well as an industrial revolution had taken place.'[22] Toynbee had in mind probably a state of feudal dependence, transformed into an impersonal relation in the machine age. 'Between the individual workman and the capitalist who employed hundreds of 'hands' a wide gulf opened; the workman ceased to be the cherished dependant, he became the living tool of whom the employer knew less than he did of his steam-engine.'[23] In Britain, there was both an industrial revolution and an agrarian revolution. As in the case of industry, in the case of agriculture, big farms replaced small holdings. The push of peasant proprietors away from their holdings, due to forces unleashed by organised industry, which resulted in small holdings, dependent on agriculture and cottage industries becoming non-viable, resulted in big estates grabbing small holdings of the peasant proprietors. Such big agricultural estates were not more efficient. These estates became the playground of British aristocracy and were used more for fox-hunting and other leisure pursuits of the aristocracy, than for increasing agricultural productivity. It was thought prudent not to increase agricultural productivity, to keep the agricultural prices, particularly that of corn, high. British agriculture was protectionist till the middle of the nineteenth century and did not allow the import of foreign corn, through the draconian Corn Laws, enacted by the British Parliament, through the disproportionate influence of aristocracy in that body. We have the exposition of Adam Smith regarding the inefficiency of British agriculture, due to the disappearance of small holdings. 'Compare the present condition of those estates with the possessions of the small proprietors in their neighbourhood, and you will require no other argument to convince you how unfavourable such extensive property is to improvement'.[24] Adam Smith clearly mentions that small landholders were the backbone of agriculture. While French Revolution was asserting the rights of the peasantry over the aristocracy and the clergy, British phenomenon of industrial revolution was eroding the rights of the peasant proprietors and small holders.

In the pre-capitalist phase of industrialisation, rural industries had an important part to play. Even in Great Britain before the industrial revolution, the domestic industries played an important part in the industrialisation process. The theory of transition from feudalism to capitalism, is more a myth than reality, created by the apologists of industrial revolution. Small producers enjoyed considerable amount of freedom in production and the interdependence with the merchants was on equal terms. As the producers were spread out over a large area, merchant capitalists had as much difficulty in controlling production as the former had in controlling trade. Once the freedom of the work-place and the right to self-employment were lost, the producers were in much the difficult position and lost the power of decision-making. It is certainly difficult to have any effective control over a work force spread over a vast area, without the assistance of modern transport and communication facilities. This certainly give the work force greater freedom in decision-making regarding their economic activities. Herding the work-force in small work places has been the main characteristic of British industrial revolution in the nineteenth century, while the Continent, although slow in catching up with the march of so-called British industrial revolution, retained a large net work of cottage industries. 'Until well into the nineteenth century, in most European countries, more value was created and more people were employed in small workshops than in centralised and mechanised production units'.[25] Industrial Revolution was not a miraculous phenomenon, but a process preceded by several centuries of proto-industrialisation. The term 'proto-industrialisation' was used by Franklin F. Mendels in his article 'Proto industrialisation. The First phase of the Industrialisation Process'.[26] As industrialisation was basically studied as a technological event, rather than a socio-economic one, the latter aspect has received much less attention. In the early stages of industrialisation, greater emphasis was on dispersed industries spread throughout the countryside, rather than on centralised production. This phase disappeared with the setting up of the factory system. Factory system was a clear break from the domestic system of production. Earlier, during the proto-industrialisation phase, the work-force, as independent producers, had depended on the merchants for trade of their products but retained control of production. With the introduction of the factory system from the beginning of the nineteenth century, they lost their independence and became wage-employees of trader-industrialists. This completely destroyed the industrial guilds and labour organisations and later was replaced by labour movement. 'The process of pauperisation which seized the proto-industrial population began when the first cotton spinning factories were built'.[27]

Effect of the British Industrial Revolution was most adverse on the existing rural industry system in India. Beginning of the industrial revolution marked the de-industrialisation of India. But the position of the British peasantry was far from satisfactory and deteriorated sharply with the Industrial Revolution. Eric Hobsbawm in his 'The Age of Revolution' writes in his colourful way, 'India and Ireland were perhaps the worst countries to be a peasant in between 1789 and 1848; but nobody who had the choice would have wished to be a farm-labourer in England either.'[28] Economic forces released by the Industrial Revolution, made the position of small farmers and agriculture labour unviable. These categories of rural population had so far depended on domestic industries to make themselves economically self-sufficient. With the destruction of domestic system of industries, a large portion of rural populace who depended on cottage industries as a subsidiary occupation to agriculture, became redundant to the rural economy and had to migrate to urban areas in search of wage employment. Industrial Revolution released the twin forces of denuding the countryside of the rural peasantry by making them economically non-viable and creating an ever increasing class of urban job-seekers. The process of industrial revolution in England in the late eighteenth and early nineteenth century, separated the ownership of the means of production from the actual producers and large-scale production methods were concentrated in the hands of a few industrialists and land-owners.

Studies of industrial revolution in Britain, have generally ignored its effect on the agrarian economy. The phenomenal growth of industries attracted almost all the attention. The actual linkage between agriculture, in all its aspects like land-ownership pattern, land-tenure has not been systematically analysed in the study of industrial revolution in Great Britain. Arnold Toynbee who is generally credited with coining the term 'industrial revolution' in English

Economic History, in his 'Lectures on the Industrial Revolution' advocated, historical method for a proper understanding of the Industrial Revolution in Britain. 'It has been a weakness of the science (Political Economy) as pursued in England that it has been too much dissociated from History'. Then further 'Without the aid of the Historical Method it would be impossible, for instance, to understand why one-half of the land in the United Kingdom is owned by 2512 persons'.[29] Toynbee goes on to say that there is too much of generalisation in Political Economy to find out universal law of Economics, when there are no such laws. It is the insufficient understanding of the history of British Industrial Revolution that has been made a model for Developing Economies, as if this model can be superimposed on other countries in other situations to experience the growth which Britain experienced in the nineteenth century.

Industrial Revolution in Britain was at the cost of major structural changes in the British agrarian economy, which brought untold misery to the British peasantry and agricultural labour. Small and marginal peasants were systematically driven out of the countryside to provide a steady stream of wage-slaves for working in the factories and living in urban slums. Industrial Revolution in Britain eliminated the peasantry. 'The classical British solution produced a country in which perhaps 4,000 proprietors owned perhaps four-sevenths of the land which was cultivated—I take the 1851 figures—by a quarter of a million farmers (three quarters of the acreage being in farms of from 50 to 500 acres) who employed about one and a quarter million of hired labourers and servants. Pockets of small holders persisted, but outside of the Scots highlands and parts of Wales only the pedant can speak of a British peasantry in the continental sense'.[30] The aristocracy and the gentry gradually increased their ownership of the nation's arable resources in England and the rest of Great Britain throughout the eighteenth and nineteenth centuries.

By the end of the eighteenth century 'England was overwhelmingly a land of tenant farmers and that the rural labour force was largely wage-dependant. It was an agrarian structure unique in contemporary Europe. On the continent the typical owner occupied peasant holding produced most of its basic subsistence needs'.[31] Commercialisation of British agriculture would not have been possible, had England been a land of cultivator owners. In England agricultural capitalism preceded industrial capitalism. Even in the beginning of the eighteenth century, the aristocracy and gentry owned more than 70 per cent of the nation's arable resources and increased their ownership to over 75 per cent by the end of the century. 'It would have been of fundamental importance 'if the England of the population explosion and industrial revolution had been a country of peasant owners'.[32] Such a socio-economic structure would not have produced population explosion, so necessary for cheap supply of wage-workers to support the forces of industrial revolution. The conservative spending and saving habits of the peasantry would not have also supported growing commercialization of the economy. Britain is the first and only European country, which commercialised land. The only other country, which was to do it later was the U.S.A. In almost all of the countries the traditional linkage of land with the peasantry continued with minor modifications till the end of nineteenth century. Britain was the only country, which was able to melt 'The great frozen ice-cap of the world's traditional agrarian systems and rural social relations that lay above the fertile soil of economic growth'.[33] England was the pioneer in the field of industrial revolution ahead of the European continent, primarily because of a policy of colonisation of the countryside by the British aristocracy, which made rest of the population destitute and pushed them to wage-slavery. In the seventeenth and the eighteenth centuries, the brunt of industrialisation in Great Britain was borne by the British peasants.

The condition of the working class, who were squeezed out of their small-holdings in the countryside was made miserable'. The industrial development of the period were bringing about the separation of textile employment from agricultural work and the aggregation of textile workers in towns. The increase of population led to a greater demand for food, and prices rose while wages remained stationery. Employment under the new conditions became less certain, and towards the end of the century (eighteenth), distress was widespread among the working classes.[34] The labouring class, whose ranks continued to multiply throughout the Industrial Revolution of the eighteenth and nineteenth century, were debarred from movement in search of employment from one place to another through Poor Laws and Settlement Laws, which were Acts of British Parliament. Adam Smith in his 'Wealth of Nations', published in 1776, writing on the obstruction of free circulation of labour writes, 'That which is given to it by the Poor Laws is, so far as I know, peculiar to England. It consists in the difficulty which a poor man finds in obtaining a settlement, or even in being allowed to exercise his industry in any parish but that to which he belongs . . . The difficulty of obtaining settlements obstructs even that of common labour'.[35]

The position of the poor deteriorated further in Great Britain by the passing of Gilbert Act of 1782, which severely curtailed the 'only means of relief open to the destitute poor under the Act of 1722, the shelter afforded by a workhouse'.[36] According to the new Act 'only the aged, the sick, the infirm and pauper children might be sent to the workhouse'. The situation was worsened by the poor Law Amendment Act of 1834, which was based on the report of the Royal Commission, appointed in 1832 to inquire into the working of the poor Law. 'The amount expended in poor-relief was substantially reduced during the next few years. The suddenness of the change, however, caused a great deal of suffering among the labouring classes . . . The ultimate effect of the change was to re-establish the principle that a man must maintain himself by his own exertions and that, if the community is compelled to assist him on account of his inability to support himself, it is entitled to do so in a way which offers no attraction to the idle.'[37] The Act reduced the amount of relief, which the tax-payers were paying. 'It did nothing to reduce the amount of poverty, and it failed to recognise any obligation upon the community to provide work for those who needed it and were willing to do it.'[38]

It is clear that throughout the eighteenth and nineteenth centuries in Britain, State and the society were trying to wash their hands of the severe poverty and lack of job-opportunities of those made redundant by the Industrial Revolution. Irony of the situation was that the State and the Society, after depriving the workers of their means of livelihood, which was earlier agriculture, supplemented by cottage industry, were reluctant to take upon any major responsibility of providing them any alternative employment or vocation or maintaining them in case they are unable to earn their living, due to lack of opportunity for the same. Condition of working classes particularly those who could not get regular employment, continued to remain precarious throughout the nineteenth century and another Royal Commission had to be appointed at the beginning of twentieth century to go into the causes of poverty and the administration of laws relating to the same. Royal Commission appointed in 1905 to deliberate on the question of poverty, reported after serious deliberations in 1909, 'Pauperism, in their opinion, was due to a variety of factors, including drunkenness, old-age, feeble-mindedness, improvident marriage, casual labour and the existence of 'blind alley' occupations.'[39] Thus, the causes of the poverty were put entirely at the doors of the working class, caused by their various misdemeanors and weakness of character. No attempt was made to analyse the causes of poverty, as a major by-product of the Industrial Revolution.

Even apologists of the British Industrial Revolution have not been able to come up with sufficient alibi about the deteriorating conditions of the workers throughout the eighteenth and nineteenth centuries. The Article by Peter H. Lindert and Jeffrey G. Williamson on 'English Workers' Living Standards During the Industrial Revolution: A New Look', which is part of a larger research project on 'British inequality since 1670', supported by grants from the U.S. National Science Foundation and the U.S. National Endowment for the Humanities, begins with the sentence, 'The politically charged debate over workers' living standards during the Industrial Revolution deserves renewal with the appearance of fresh data or new perspectives.' The concluding paragraph of the article reads 'Research inspired by the pessimists' allegations about the Industrial Revolution will now have to shift to social injustice and social disorder.

Reported crime, alcoholism, protest, and illegitimacy appear to have been on the rise in the first half of the nineteenth century. In addition, rising material inequality seems to characterise the period, and these trends were likely to have influenced social disorder. We know from related research for example, that common labourers failed to experience gains as rapid as those for better-paid employees. Earnings inequality statistics suggest the same between the 1820s and the 1880s. Our preliminary results on probated wealth and land rents also suggest rising inequality between upper and lower middle classes in the course of the first half of the nineteenth century.'[40] Critics of Industrial Revolution are at once classified as 'Pessimists, by those who want to show the Industrial Revolution as an unmixed blessing for mankind in general and Great Britain in particular. This line of argument takes the plea that peasants and workers were no better of before the Industrial revolution and some of the workers did benefit from the Industrial Revolution. This type of argument takes refuge in the lack of statistical data prior to the Industrial Revolution. 'The great majority of these human gains came after 1820. Pessimists must retreat to the pre-1820 era, where workers' net gains look as elusive in this essay as in past studies of single occupations.' 'Inequality between workers and the very poor may also have widened: we need far better information on the material condition of those below the working classes—vagrants and disabled paupers—than the large literature on poor relief has yet been able to supply. These issues, not trends in absolute living standards, are likely to mark the future battleground between optimists and pessimists about how workers fared under nineteenth century British capitalism.'[41]

In the pre-capitalist stage, industrial production in the countryside was a flourishing activity. 'It has long been known that industrial commodity production in the countryside for large inter-regional and international markets was of considerable importance during the formative period of capitalism. Contemporary travel accounts and geographies by authors interested in economics described the extent and variety of industrial activity in the countryside.' Classical examples are D. Defoe, A Tour through the Whole Island of

Great Britain, Ist edn. (1724-6) and the travel accounts by Arthur Young. Such writings often contain interesting general reflections about problems of rural industry, for example, J. Tucker, Instructions for Travellers (1757).[42] Adam Smith while analysing the growth of export industries in Britain since the Middle Ages, distinguished between a 'violent' way and a 'natural' way. Natural way consisted in development of export industries out of household 'manufactures'. 'Violent way' of industrialisation came about when the merchants and manufacturers introduced export industries through imitation of foreign crafts and usually based on imported raw materials. Adam Smith called these the 'offspring of foreign commerce'. The inequality brought about by the violent methods of industrialisation, which Britain adopted, was clearly brought out by Adam Smith, who has been regarded as the Presiding Deity of Capitalism. 'Wealth of Nations', has this to say about the violent methods of industrialisation of Britain, 'But what all the violence of the feudal institutions could never have effected, the silent and insensible operation of foreign commerce and manufactures gradually brought about. These gradually furnished the great proprietors with something for which they could exchange the whole surplus produce of their lands, and which they could consume themselves without sharing it either with tenants or retainers. All for ourselves and nothing for other people, seems, in every age of the world, to have been the vile maxim of the masters of mankind. As soon, therefore, as they could find a method of consuming the whole value of their rents themselves, they had no disposition to share them with any other persons. For a pair of diamond buckles, perhaps, or for something as frivolous and useless, they exchanged the maintenance, or what is the same thing, the price of the maintenance of a thousand men for a year, and with it the whole weight and authority which it could give them. The buckles, however, were to be all their own, and no other human creature was to have any share of them; whereas in the more ancient method of expense they must have shared with at least a thousand people'.[43]

Conspicuous consumption, which started in a big way with the advent of industrial and commercial revolution deprived the common people of the necessaries of life. The surplus from agriculture was diverted for conspicuous consumption due to the market forces let loose by the forces of industrial revolution, which was brought about by the vanity of the landlords and the greed of the merchants. 'A revolution of the greatest importance to the public happiness was in this manner brought about by two different orders of people (landlords and merchants) who had not the least intention to serve the public . . . . Neither of them had either knowledge or foresight of that great revolution which the folly of the one (landlords), and the industry of the other (merchants and artificers) was gradually bringing about.'[44] Adam Smith had the foresight to see the agricultural surplus being siphoned-off, to fuel the industrial revolution driven by the twin motors of vanity and avarice. Draining away of agricultural surplus from the countryside, atrophied agriculture in Britain, which declined proportionately to the growth of industry, resulting in turning of fertile agricultural land to pasturage. In their recent book about the problems of present day American Capitalism, Robert Heilbroner and Lester Thurow, while analysing the emergence of market economy of which Great Britain was pioneer, writes, 'In England the process bore with particular severity on the peasants who were expelled from their lands through the enclosure of common grazing lands. This enclosure took place to make private pasturage for the lord's sheep, whose wool had become a profitable commodity. As late as 1820 the Duchess of Sutherland evicted 15,000 tenants from 794,000 acres, replacing them with 131,000 sheep. The tenants, deprived of their traditional access to the fields, drifted into the towns, where they were forced to sell their services as a factor of production: labour'.[45]

Adam Smith, the Great Scottish Economist, who never pretended to any socialistic leanings and during his six years' stay at Oxford 'found much of which he did not approve',[46] could see through the hypocracy of the British ruling and industrial class towards their own people, gave effect to the same in his Magnum Opus, composed in his native Kirkcaldy in Scotland. If this was the situation, when Industrial Revolution was just taking shape, the position throughout the later eighteenth and nineteenth centuries could only have been much worse for the working class. That some members of the working class, became high wage earners, does not in any way mitigate the distress of the huge number of others who were marginalised and found themselves in the periphery of the society. It is clear that the Industrial Revolution was a bane rather than boon to the British working class. Throughout the nineteenth century, the conditions of the vast majority of the British people continued to decline and through various Acts of British Parliament and strict enforcement of the same their life was made intolerable. The Law of settlement prevented mobility of labour and workmen were unable to leave their homes in search of work elsewhere. 'A new kind of serfdom was imposed on the poor. They were compelled to remain in their place of settlement, not because they were forbidden to leave it, but because no other place would receive them'. Settlement Act prevented the practice of squatting, where poor people put up huts on wasteland and managed a precarious living. Poor Laws of 1782 and 1834 were designed to deprive the poor of the security of the workhouse, which they were getting by virtue of various laws of local Counsels and traditions coming down from the middle ages. Enclosure laws deprived the small free-holders of their cultivable land. 'The small free-holders and copy-holders were still numerous in 1793. By 1815 the large enclosed farm had become the normal unit in English rural economy, and open-field cultivation was exceptional'.[47]

The argument that Industrial Revolution raised the standard of living of the working class in Britain is a misconception. Certain sections of the working class, who became skilled workers and small entrepreneurs could benefit from the Industrial Revolution but vast majority of people suffered. Pauperism, which became a major problem for the poor throughout the period of Industrial Revolution did not exist in the Middle Ages. The march of Industrialisation in Britain during the heydays of Industrial Revolution helped a small portion of the working class to rise above their previous stations, while condemning the large majority to poverty and destitution. 'Such cases of destitution as occurred in the Middle Ages were relieved without recourse to State action. Gild members who fell into poverty were assisted by the fraternity, whose interest extended to the care of the widows and orphans of deceased brethren. Monastic charity was exercised towards all who needed it, and many great lords and great ecclesiastics kept open house to all comers. Hospitals and lazar-houses existed for the sick.'[48] Problem of destitution was taken care of by the community, prior to the Industrial Revolution, which turned man into a commodity and destroyed the protection provided by parish counsels and communities by getting various poor laws enacted by Parliament, as encouraging idleness and inefficiency. To borrow a phrase of Abraham Lincoln in a different context, Industrial Revolution was 'Of the rich, by the rich and for the rich'.

COLONIES OF EMIGRATION

It may very well be argued that if the Industrial Revolution did so much harm to the British working classes in general, how Britain prospered throughout the late eighteenth and the whole of nineteenth century, as well as the first quarter of the twentieth century. The reason lies in the colonial policy of expansion followed by Britain throughout this period. We have the following quotation from Cecil Rhodes, the arch British Imperialist. "I was in the East End of London (working-class quarter) yesterday and attended a meeting of the unemployed. I listened to the wild speeches, which were just a cry for 'bread', 'bread' and on my way home I pondered over the scene and I became more than ever convinced of the importance of imperialism. . . . My cherished idea is a solution for the social problem, i.e., in order to save the 40,000,000 inhabitants of the United Kingdom from a bloody civil war, we colonial statesmen must acquire new lands to settle the surplus population, to provide new markets for the goods produced in the factories and mines. The Empire, as I have always said, is a bread and butter question. If you want to avoid civil war, you must become imperialists."[49] There is no doubt that British Industrial Revolution could not have been sustained for any length of time without an active policy of Colonisation, which was necessary for rehabilitating the British poor displaced by the process of industrialisation, which deprived them of their existing vocations. Colonialism was also necessary for finding an assured market for ever increasing British industrial products.

British policy of active colonisation of Australia began in 1786, coinciding with the Industrial Revolution. 'The traditional view is that Britain thereby sought to relieve the pressure upon its prisons—a pressure intensified by the loss of its American colonies, which until that time had accepted felons. Convicts went to the settlement from the outset, and official statements put this first among the colony's intended purposes. . . . By 1830 about 58,000 convicts, including almost 50,000 men, had come to Australia (the rate increasing rapidly after 1815). Many were more or less habitual urban thieves. There were a few political prisoners, while a substantial proportion of Irish convicts (at least a third of the total) had become offenders through sociopolitical unrest.'[50] This clearly shows that the Industrial Revolution had made the socio-economic conditions untenable for the British poor, who had no other alternative than to turn to crime. Britain did not suffer from civil war because of an active policy of colonisation.

British colonial policy can be broadly divided in two distinct stages. The first stage of colonialism was an active pursuit of foreign markets to provide captive markets for the manufacturing industries. This stage was the first essential stage of development of capitalism. The fact that this destroyed the industries and the socio-economic structure of the colonial countries did not bother the practitioners of Industrial Capitalism. Economic subjugation of the colonies could be possible only after their complete political domination. In the early stages economic interest of capturing foreign markets for items of mass consumption was the primary factor in the policy of colonisation. 'The British manufacturer, in the words of the historian, H.H. Wilson employed the arm of political injustice to keep down and ultimately strangle a competitor with whom he could not have contended on equal terms, millions of Indian artisans lost their earnings, the population of India lost one great source of their wealth.'[51] Great Britain realised before the Industrial Revolution that an Island Nation cannot prosper without an active colonial policy. The dominance over colonies is key to the economic prosperity of Britain. British policy of gaining control over the colonies started from the eighteenth century. In this, they were ahead of other European nations by more than a century. According to the data provided by Henry Morris in the History of Colonisation, New York, 1900, Great Britain between 1815-30 had a colonial possession of about 2.2 million sq. miles with a population of 126.4 millions, against France's 0.02 million sq. miles with a population of 0.5 millions. Germany, the other major European country had no colonial possession at that time.

'J.A. Hobson, in his work on Imperialism, marks the years 1884-1900 as the epoch of intensified expansion of the chief European state's.[52] Even in this, Great Britain did not leg behind other European powers. According to Hobson, as quoted in Lenin's Imperialism, Great Britain during this period acquired 3,700,000 sq. miles of territory with a population of 57,000,000, whereas France which earlier had 0.2 million of sq. miles of colonial possession against England's 2.5 million sq. miles acquired 3,600,000 sq. miles with a population of 36,500,000. During these years Germany and Belgium opened their account of colonial possession with an area of 1,000,000 sq. miles and 900,000 sq. miles respectively. Colonisation increased the operational area of the European countries several times of their size. Colonisation has been defined as 'taking possession of territories unoccupied, or occupied by so-called uncivilised peoples'.[53] Basis of colonialism is pushing the frontiers of a country beyond its geographical border. Cecil Rhodes, the great advocate of imperialism has been quoted as saying 'wherever there is room there is hope'. (*Ibid.*) There is need for greater room for the colonial country to pursue its ambitions, which can be only at the cost of others. Wherever colonialists see new space, there is hope for them and despair for others. New inventions and technology require space for their development for the benefit of their inventors. The philosophy of colonialism towards the end of the nineteenth

	Area of the home country in sq. kms.	Area of the Colonies	Relation
British Isles	315,000	30,000,000	1 to 95
Belgium	30,000	2,500,000	1 to 83
Holland	33,000	2,000,000	1 to 60
Portugal	89,000	2,000,000	1 to 22
France	536,000	9,500,000	1 to 18
Germany	540,000	2,800,000	1 to 05

century was, 'who knows what wealth some new invention or new need may cause to spring from the soil or the sub-soil? We take when we can: we find out later.'[54] Gide in his Political Economy has quoted from Principes de Colonisation by M. Arthur Girault to show the area of the major European colonial countries in relation to the area of their colonial possessions at the beginning of the twentieth century.

Great Britain was the predominant colonial country, with a colonial possession of an area nearly hundred times its own area. Economics of such huge colonial empire with total control over territory and populace has not been properly analysed by the Anglo-Saxon School of economic thought.

Gide has divided colonisation into two broad types—colonies of exploitation and colonies of settlement. 'Colonies of exploitation are commercial, the natural wealth of the country, which is destined solely for export, being exploited and even monopolised by trading companies. These Companies have played a great part in colonisation, we have only to call to mind the famous East India Company.'[55] India has obviously been a colony of exploitation. Colonies of settlement are established to siphon-off the overflow of population from the colonising country. 'The object of colonies of settlement is to receive the overflow population from the mother country, the swarm from the hive. The climatic conditions in such colonies must not differ too much from those of the home country, or the immigrants can neither live there, nor, what is more difficult, perpetuate their race. England is almost the only country that has been able to lay hold of regions where the white man finds a familiar soil and a friendly sky'.[56] Great Britain's colonies of settlement consisted of the entire continent of Australia and New Zealand, continent of North America, besides South Affrica, Rhodesia (Zimbabwe) and some other pockets in the African continent. During the period 1820-1910, 16.8 million Britishers (including 4.1 million Irish) migrated to the U.S.A. and Canada. Two million Britishers migrated to Australia and New Zealand, which were exclusive British settlements. Besides, there were British Migrations to South Africa and Rhodesia, where the climate was favourable, as well as to favourable parts of South America. (*Source*: The Times Atlas of World History, depicted in Hobsbawm, The Age of Empire).[57] This out of a total population of 35.3 millions estimated in 1880. A large portion of the globe for a small island nation. This is the second stage of British colonialism, i.e., the acquisition of colonies of emigration for settlement of her population rendered surplus by industrial revolution. During this period, Britain experienced a population explosion.

CONTINUITY OF COLONIALISM

Spanish colonisation was the most horrible of colonisations, marked by greed and ferocity of the conquerors, whereas English colonisation was undoubtedly humane in its methods. But the result has been paradoxical. 'Spanish colonisation has left behind a large part of the native population in the Spanish-American colonies, while English colonisation has ended in the complete disappearance of the native population of North America and Australia'. Gide analyses the situation 'The fact is that economic competition between a strong race and a weak one is much more deadly than are individual acts of cruelty'.[58] Competition between unequals is always loaded with advantage in favour of the economically stronger and in the long-run will cause serious damage to the economy of the weaker nation. We have seen that in the case of India, monopolistic trade policies of Great Britain ruined the economic infrastructure of the country and turned it into a completely agrarian economy. 'Ernest Mandel estimated the European colonial booty between 1500 and 1800 at 1000 million gold pounds sterling, of which 100 to 150 million reached Britain from India alone between 1750 and 1800. This inflow of capital facilitated if not financed Britain's investments in the new industrial revolution, especially in steam engines and textile technology'.[59] Then again, 'For as Braudel well put it, Europe was able to consume beyond its means and invest beyond its savings. However, it did and was able to do both primarily as a function of the structure and development of the entire world economy as a whole'.[60]

It is a mistake to assume that the days of colonialism are over and that colonisation ended with the colonial countries gaining their independence after the Second World War. Colonisation is basically an economic process and the political process is only a more visible part of the system of colonisation. Globalisation is the new phase of colonialism, which is a continuation of the process of industrialisation, which began with the industrial revolution and its precursor proto-industrialisation. 'Proto-industrialisation contributed, at an early stage, to the development of a world-wide economic network of asymmetric relationships, which later—after the core had changed over to the factory system—made it inevitable that the backwardness of the periphery was continuously and massively reinforced by the economic progress of the core.'[61] Western economy constitutes the core of globalisation and the developing countries constitute the periphery. The development of the core is proportional to the decline of the periphery. Economic colonialism has survived the demise of political colonialism and the western countries are able to continue their economic network of asymmetric relationships, with economic globalisation. The forces of globalisation let loose after the break-down of the socialist system in Europe, have led to increased marginalisation of third world countries. 'The most sustained critique of the globalisation thesis is that offered by Hirst and Thompson. Their argument points out that the pre-1914 system was in many respects as open and integrated as the present; the transnationals are not genuinely transnational but depend critically on home-base markets and infrastructural supports; FDI is highly concentrated within the Triad (USA, Western

Europe and Japan), and the extent of globalisation is thereby limited; and there are serious restrictions on labour migration (especially for the poor and unskilled)'.[62] With the erosion of national autonomy by the process of globalisation, the developing countries will face increasing difficulty for standing up for their poor and dispossessed, who will increase in number. Developing countries are being gradually reduced to a position of 'a weak periphery to a strong capitalist centre'.[63] The days of colonialism seem to be coming back with a vengeance, with the erosion of governmental power in the developing countries and the control of levers of economic power by the developed countries.

Notes and References

1. R.C. Dutt, Economic History of British India under Early British Rule, Second Edition (1906), p. 1, Dutt, who held high administrative posts in British India and was also aware of the developments in contemporary Britain, made a detailed study of Indian economic conditions, *vis-a-vis*, British policies.
2. C. Northcote Parkinson, The Rise of Big Business (1977), p. 16.
3. Parimal Ray, India's Foreign Trade since 1870, First Edition (1934), pp. 2-3. Ray was one of the first to co-relate the lop-sided development of India's Foreign Trade with Britain and India's economic decline.
4. Paul Kennedy, Preparing for the Twenty-first century (1993), p. 11. Kennedy, in a historical perspective, synthesises the forces released by the Industrial Revolution in Britain with the forces controlling the present world economic scenario.
5. Eric Hobsbawm, The Age of Revolution (1789-1848), 1995, p. 165. By all accounts, India was an industrial country, before the British industrial revolution of iron and steel.
6. Adam Smith, An Inquiry into the Nature and Casues of the Wealth of Nations, (1776), Encyclopedia Britannica Edition, p. 298.
7. V.I. Lenin, Imperislism, The Highest Stage of Capitalism (1917), Selected Works of V.I. Lenin (Vol. I, Part 2), pp. 511-12. Figures quoted from Henry C. Morris, The History of Colonisation, New York, 1900.
8. Friedrich List, The National System of Political Economy (1885), p. 42. List was a powerful advocate of German economic nationalism, which brought about the unification of Germany, under Bismarck.
9. Adam Smith, An Inquiry into the Nature and Casues of the Wealth of Nations, p. 158.
10. The Age of Revolution, p. 35.

11. India's Foreign Trade, p. 2.
12. Mill's History of British India; Wilson's continuation, Book-I, Chapter VIII, note. Quoted in *Economic History of British India under Early British Rule*, p. 262.
13. India's Foreign Trade, p. 3.

14-15. Wealth of Nations, pp. 53, 279, 55. Adam Smith has been portrayed as the high priest of *laissez faire* capitalism. This does great injustice to Adam Smith, who highlighted the evils of mercantilist policies, which translated into rules and regulations, were hitting the common man hard. Smith was also against any form of traders or merchants organisation, as it was directed against the consumers, who had no such forums, in view of their dispersion. 'People of the same trade seldom meet together, even for merriment and diversion, but the conversation ends in a conspiracy against the public, or in some contrivance to raise prices' (Wealth of Nations, p. 55). The concept of universal free trade, was hardly in existence at that time.

16. Harold Underwood Faulkner, American Economic History (p. 200), quoted from Adam Seybert, Statistical Annals of the United States, 1818, p. 92.

17-18. Peter Kriedte, *et. al.*, Industrialisation before Industrialisation, pp. 137-38.

19. *Ibid.*, p. 138, quoted from E.J. Hobsbawm, History and "The Dark Satanic Mills" in Hobsbawm, Labouring Men. Studies in the History of Labour (1964), p. 116, Industrial Revolution thrives on constant redundancy of different classes of workers, it has created. Human cost of march of technology is enormous.
20. M. Fores, 'The myth of a British Industrial revolution', History, 66 (1981), pp. 181-98, quoted in the *Industrial Revolution in National Context* (1996), edited by Mikulas Teich and Roy Porter p. 3.
21. Phyllis Deane, The British Industrial Revolution in the *Industrial Revolution in National Context*, p. 27.

22-23. A. Toynbee, Lectures on the Industrial Revolution in England (1884), p. 191, quoted in the *Industrial Revolution in National Context*, p. 8.

24. Wealth of Nations, p. 167.
25. Industrialisation before Industrialisation, p. 1.
26. Journal of Economic History, 32, (1972), p. 241.
27. Industrialisation before Industrialisation, p. 156.
28. The Age of Revolution, p. 166.
29. Toynbee, Lectures, pp. 27-32, quoted in Introduction by Mikulas Teich in the *Industrial Revolution in National Context*, p. 6.
30. Age of Revolution, p. 150, These figures, obtained from various authentic sources, point out the same picture of concentration of land-holdings in the hands of a few and elimination of peasantry, during the early period of British industrial revolution.
31. Phylis Deane, The British Industrial Revolution, in the *Industrial Revolution in National Context* (1996), p. 30.
32. F.M.L. Thompson, The social distribution of landed property in

England since the sixteenth century, *Economic History Review*, 19(1966), p. 516. Quoted in (*Ibid.*), p. 30.

33. Age of Revolution, p. 149.
34. George W. Southgate, English Economic History (1960), p. 282.
35. Wealth of Nations, p. 59.

36-39. English Economic History, pp. 283-87. Southgate gives a detailed picture of the poverty created by industrial revolution in England and the indifference of society and Government to the conditions of the poor, who were increasing in number.

40-41. Peter, H. Lindert and Jeffrey G. Williamson, English Workers' living Standards: During the Industrial Revolution: A New Look (1983). Reprinted in the *Economics of the Industrial Revolution* (1985) edited Joel Mokyr, pp. 177-99.

42. Industrialisation before Industrialisation, pp. 1, 201.

43-44. Wealth of Nations, pp. 177, 179.

45. Robert Heilbrner and Lester Thurow, Economics Explained (1998), p. 15.
46. Biographical Note on Adam Smith in Great Books of the Western World, Vol. 39, p. V.

47-48. English Economic History, pp. 279, 282.

49. V.I. Lenin, Imperialism, the Highest Stage of Capitalism (1920), pp. 513-14, quoted from M. Beer, *Modern British Imperlialism* (1918).
50. The New Encyclopaedia Britannica (1997), Vol. 14, pp. 440-41.
51. Economic History of India Under Early British Rule, Preface, p. VIII.
52. Ref. Imperialism, pp. 511-12.

53-56. Charles Gide, Political Economy (1914), pp. 90-94. This is an English translation of Charles Gide's 'Course d' Economie Politique' (1913) in French. In this translator's preface, constance H.M. Archibald say, 'It has been thought good for the student of Political Economy to see the fundamental and familiar questions of his science pose themselves in slightly different forms under the influence of another race and another traditions. So he is reminded of the human element which is at one time main difficulty and the main interest of Political Economy'.

If the perceptions of English and French differed so widely in 1914, how can we expect the same solutions to economic problems will be applicable to different pople under different conditions to day? This is the fundamental question, the economists must address themselves to.

57. E.J. Hobsbawm, The Age of Empire (1987), p. 354; *Source*: The Times Atlas of World History.
58. Political Economy.

59-60. Andre Gunder Frank, Re Orient (1998), p. 296.

61. Industrialisation Before Industrialisation, p. 9.
62. Ian Clark, Globalisation and Fragmentation (1997), p. 184.
63. B. Buzan, The Interdependence of Security and Economic Issues in the New World Order (1994), quoted in *Ibid.*, p. 189.

2

Adverse Results of British Industrial Revolution

During the period when Britain was going through the stages of Industrial Revolution, France was going through the socio-economic upheaval of the French Revolution. The period from the mid-eighteenth century to mid-nineteenth century marks the growth of industrial revolution through various stages. This period also marks the various stages of French Revolution. French enlightenment, which followed the end of absolutism with the close of the reign of Louis XIV in 1715, preceded the French Revolution of 1789. The intellectual climate of French Revolution was created by 'les philosophes'. This School of thought was a broad-based intellectual movement, which used nationalism and empiricism against traditional ideas about religion, society and culture. They used empiricism to develop popular theories based on an appeal to science. 'The philosophes shared a conception of philosophy as action-oriented activity and united in their hostility to superstition, to the irrational and intolerant policies of the church, and to the cruelty of the State authorities who tried to secure conformity by force'. The Philosophes produced 'no great original thinkers like Descartes, Spinoza, Hobbes or Locke, but was rather the second stage of the Age of Reason'.[1] French enlightenment was the only intellectual movement, without being biased by dogma, brought reason and science to the common man. This great University of learning in France, broke the elitism of knowledge and learning, intellectually enabled the common man to think for himself and dare challenge the accepted beliefs, so essential to the dominance of religion and state. 'The philosophes broke down the censorship of thought by church and state, and opened and broadened a million minds, they prepared for the triumphs of science in the nineteenth century, amid the turmoil of revolution and war'.[2] The greatest strength of the Philosophes was that they were not weighed down by dogmas and did not believe in an intellectual master. 'The philosophes were more divided in their opinions than is commonly supposed. They were all humanitarians, committed to reform'.[3] One cannot, but remark in passing that the present age with its intellectual arrogance and intolerance, solely needs a school of thought like 'les Philosophes'.

SOCIAL REVOLUTION PRECEDES INDUSTRIAL REVOLUTION IN FRANCE

While Great Britain was going through the process of so-called Industrial Revolution, a social and Intellectual Revolution was taking place in France. This social Revolution was not only confined to France and French-speaking areas of Europe, but had its impact on different parts of Europe. The intellectual message of social revolution, which had already reached the continent through social reformers, was carried forward by the marching armies of Napoleon. The Intellectual and social Revolution in France and to some extent in the continent had a major role in the economy of these countries. While Britain passed from serfdom to Industrial Capitalism, which reduced the peasantry and the general populace to a commodity—merely one of the factors of production, the peasantry in France was able to ascertain its rights over the land released by the church and the big landowners. During the period when the British peasantry was thrown out of their traditional occupations by the process generated by the Industrial Revolution, we see a completely different picture in France. 'France as a whole therefore became neither a country of landlords and farm-labourers nor of commercial farmers, but largely of various types of peasant proprietors, who became the chief part of all subsequent political regimes which did not threaten to take away their land'.[4] French agricultural system transformed from the control of church and noble, to peasant proprietorship. During the same period British peasantry became rootless labouring class. The relation between peasant and landlord, which had been worked out over the centuries and which sustained the peasants during the crisis, was destroyed without any viable alternative.

French Revolution brought about a fundamental change in land ownership pattern in the continent. With the growth of individualism and equality before law, the land ownership pattern became more equitable. The peasantry was the main supporting base of the Government of the day, particularly in France and could not be ignored, as in Great Britain. 'The growth of individualism and of civil equality, and the disappearance of the feudal system, particularly in countries which came under the influence of the French Revolution, brought about a fifth phase, that which marks our own epoch. It is characterised by the final establishment of free ownership of land, with all the attributes which the right of ownership implies.' The attributes of individual ownership of land are firmly recorded in Code Napoleon. However, the ownership of land, as set forth in Code Napoleon is not the same as ownership of movable property. 'It differs from the latter in numerous features familiar to jurisconsults (lawyers): but the essential difference consists in the difficulties put in the way of transfer'.[5] This clearly shows that the French land laws were strict enough to ensure that the peasant does not lose his main factor of production, i.e. land. This has undoubtedly been a gift of the French Revolution to the French peasantry.

Let us contrast the situation in Britain, where most of the land was in possession of a small group of people. These people controlled, not only the entire land in the country, but also the British Parliament. 'It will be found that sixty families supply, and for generations have supplied, one-third of the House of Commons, one-third of the ultimate governing power for an empire which includes a fourth of the human race'.[6] This shows the power structure of the British Government and the British concept of democratic Government. Political power and big business were closely inter-linked and one supported the other. 'The peculiar strength of eighteenth century Britain lay in the close alliance of the peerage with the gentry, with the professions and the City. . . . . Men who mattered usually (not always) agreed with each other in the main purposes of trade and war. Big Business in eighteenth century Britain was represented, in the first place, by families whose wealth gave them power and whose power served to enhance their wealth'. Regarding ownership of land, Parkinson has this to say, 'When the 'New Doomsday Survey' of 1873 was compiled the fact emerged that four-fifths of the Kingdom belonged to seven thousand people. It also appeared that sixteen people in England and Scotland had rentals of over 100,000 a year'.[7]

Industrialisation in France was different from that of Britain and at a much less social cost. There was no major redeployment of resources away from agriculture, as was in the case of British Industrial Revolution. 'France had a dual economy, with agriculture and industry having roughly the same weight in gross national product'.[8] Average incomes in France throughout this period were not much lower than that of Britain, although the pace of industrial development in the latter country, was much faster particularly relating to the output of coal and iron. This leads one to conclude that industrial development in France was different than Britain and more humance. There was limited transfer of resources in terms of labour from agriculture to industry. 'Several historians are impressed by the fact that French average incomes were never much below the British, despite the country's poor showing in terms of iron output, have suggested that French development should not be characterised as slower than the British but different'.[9] Pollard also cites a version 'that it was France that was the pioneer, starting her industrialisation by the mid-eighteenth century and proceeding with relatively little social costs thereafter, and it was Britain, as the follower, which had to turn to hasty methods of catching up at a great cost to the generations which lived through the industrial revolution. The British sequence, far from being the model, would then be an aberration'.[10] British industrial development was basically a development pattern based on a huge captive colonial market. Britain's industrial development was based on production and marketing of mass-produced goods in colonies. In the industrialisation of France, 'The tradition and instinct ran toward individual design rather than mass production. . . . But with their own technique, with their preference for the modest sized establishment, the individual workbench, the French worked with a zeal that fell little short of genius'.[11]

In France transmission of British technology, in the field of cotton manufacturing, was not successful, as virtually the whole of world trade in cotton had been monopolised by Britain after the Napoleonic wars. British innovations had been answers to specific British problems, appropriate to British market colonialism and comparative advantage brought about by cheap supply of raw materials from the colonies. French industrial revolution was different from Britain, in that it did not depend on colonial markets for marketing of its products or procurement of cheap raw materials from dependencies. 'It was impossible for France to base a major industrial impetus upon foreign markets at least for cotton, and iron; France had to rely only upon her home market'.[12] France adopted the path of quality production, instead of mindless quantity. Instead of copying British pattern of industrialisation, France built-up its industry on areas, where it had competitive advantage due to superior craftsmanship. 'Direct competition with the strengths of the British economy was evidently unpromising; instead, France built on her own strengths, supplying high quality and fashion goods to wealthier markets, rather than cheap mass-produced, commodities to low income groups and colonial areas'.[13] France could achieve industrialisation with a much more humane system within the country and outside it. 'The pace and nature of French economic organisation tended to favour a comparatively even distribution of wealth, a widespread holding of small properties and small savings'.[14] France went in for a social revolution before industrial revolution. This caused a gap between British industrial production and French industrial production, but not in growth of per capita income. 'Roehl maintains that, in per capita terms, the rates of the two countries are indistinguishable'.[15]

INDUSTRIAL REVOLUTION FOR ONE COUNTRY AT THE COST OF INDUSTRIAL REVOLUTION FOR OTHERS

Germany is another country, which industrialised rapidly without formal colonies. German industrialisation found its markets in less developed European countries. Industrially backward Eastern Europe was crucial to the industrialisation of Germany. 'Mirabeau noted that few countries are as favourable placed as Prussia for having manufactures, since it borders along its whole length on a barbarous country (Sc Poland) where they do not exist'. To which Otto Hinze's view might be added that 'from the trade point of view, Poland was then for Prussia what the colonies were for England; a large market for exports and for the supply of cheap raw materials'.[16] German industrialisation was based on colonisation of Eastern Europe . The rivalry for dominance over Eastern Europe was the main cause of two basically European wars, which have been termed World Wars. Even Japan, which was a major participant in the Second World War was motivated by its economic interest of dominance of British colonies in Asia. Industrial Revolution of nineteenth century Europe had been piggy-backed on the shoulders of weaker countries and unleashed tremendous amount of violence and unstable relations between nations throughout the twentieth century.

The industrial revolution in Britain took advantage of the backwardness in other countries in the sense that majority of population was engaged in agriculture in the countryside and urbanisation was low. The ratio of population engaged in agriculture to the total population in Britain at the initial stages of industrial revolution in 1790, was reached in major industrial countries of Europe, only in the middle of the twentieth century. Britain had turned its colonies and the newly acquired continents to its agricultural farm-land for supply of raw material and food. 'This ratio (low proportion of the population in agriculture) draws attention to the fact that British industrialisation was played out against a backward world, the British economy specialising into a kind of role in the world economy which was no longer open to the later comers'.[17] This model of industrial revolution, followed by third world countries have led to dead-end in economic development, as for them there are no other countries to colonise. It has only led to colonial pattern of development within the third world countries. There has been major transfer of resources from rural to urban sectors, with increased economic disparity. Unnatural transfer of resources brought about by trying to copy the Industrial Revolution of Britain, has brought about serious economic imbalances within the country. Colonial pattern of development has taken place with transfer of resources from poor to the rich. Only one economic indicator, Inflation is sufficient to show how resources have been transferred from the poor to the rich. The wages and remuneration of the working class have not gone up, whereas the control over resources by a few have gone up. Huge amount of non-performing assets in the portfolio of different nationalised banks and financial institutions, in the name of industrial development, which never materialised, also shows the unindirectional flow of resources to the rich and powerful, to indulge in unbridled consumerism. The super-imposition of the model of British industrial revolution on the Indian economy, in the name of industrialisation has further strengthened the process of colonisation in India. In fact in India and other developing countries, the urban organised sector is colonising the rural un-organised and urban un-organised sectors. In the usual colonial pattern the few who have access to the levers of power are colonising the vast majority, who have no such access. By its very nature, the process of colonisation ensures that access to the levers of power are limited to the few, whereas the vast majority are reduced to economic subjugation.

British Economists of the nineteenth century consistently avoided the historical approach to Economics, as that would have exposed British Industrial Revolution in its true colours. British Industrial Revolution was nothing more nor less than exploitation of the economies of the colonies and large-scale displacement of British peasantry, who had to be accommodated in the newly acquired colonies. Colonies of settlement had to be acquired to settle the population of the home country, rendered redundant by the movement of the wheels of industrialisation, whereas colonies of exploitation had to be acquired for drawing away the wealth of these colonies and make their economies subservient to the economy of the colonial country, by destroying its industrial and agricultural base and turning it into a consumer economy. There are two broad phases of British colonialism. The first phase starting from the early eighteenth century was mainly motivated by search for markets for the products of industrialisation, which had already been set in motion. India bore the brunt of this market colonialism. During 1750 and 1769 the export of British cottons increased by ten times. India, from a traditional exporter of cotton goods became a net importer of Lancashire cottons. Eric Hobsbawm has put the colonial element in the British industrialisation in a colourful sentence. 'The cotton industry was thus launched, like a glider, by the pull of the colonial trade to which it was attached'.[18] Rapidly expanding colonial market encouraged techniques of production which completely transformed industry from craftsman-oriented, to machine-oriented. Previously industrial production bore the mark of craftsmanship. The industrial revolution created an impersonal machine culture. Market for such cheap standardised products could be explored in poor and backward areas with aggressive support from the Government. 'For within these areas British industry had established a monopoly by means of war, other people's revolutions and her own imperial rule'.[19] Latin America and India played crucial role in providing ever expanding markets for the standard textile products of the British mills. Latin American markets were captured after the defeat of Napoleon and subsequent decline in the influence of Spain and Portugal over this continent. 'The British super power had conquered overseas markets by force during the wars and firmly held them (e.g. the former Spanish colonies, which had been vital for France in the eighteenth century); it had obtained virtually the whole of world trade in cotton goods'.[20]

There is enough evidence to show that textile manufacturing was prosperous business in India and was a major pillar of the economic structure. J.C. Jack, ICS, who was the District Magistrate of Faridpur in Bengal between 1905-10 and wrote a pioneering work on the economic life of a Begal district, observed on the decline of textile industry 'Weaving, which used to be a vigorous industry, has been killed partly by the importation of foreign or factory made cotton goods and partly by the revages of malaria, which has always made great in roads upon the colonies of sedentary weavers. A very large number of weavers have bought land and become ordinary cultivators'.[21] This, inspite of the fact that the book was written for the purpose to show that the British colonial policy was a beneficial one and did not exploit the colonies. In the Foreward of the book Jack writes, 'The work of the British in India has only one counterpart in recorded history, the Roman Empire, upon which historians have agreed to lay the blame that it sucked the orange of its provinces dry and left only the rind to its subjects. This work will not be written in vain if it proves that, in one corner of India at least, no such charge can be laid against the British Empire'.[22]

Manufacturing activities had been an integral part of the agricultural economy in most regions of India, as in many of the countries, 'Deindustrialisation made the peasant village itself more dependent on the single fluctuating fortune of the harvest'.[23] Throughout the ages industry had been a subsidiary occupation of agriculture. Destruction of the industrial base in the rural economy made agriculture non-viable and Indian economy became a gamble on the monsoons. It is also no accident of history that famines had been occurring regularly in British India, in spite of introduction of modern methods of transport and communication through Railways, Telegraph and an efficient postal system. 'By a moderate calculation, the famines of 1877 and 1878, of 1889 and 1892, of 1897 and 1900, have carried off fifteen millions of people'.[24] There are no recorded evidence of such large scale famines in India, in such quick succession in earlier times.

Romesh Dutt poses the question 'what are the causes of this intense poverty and these repeated famines in India?' He dismisses all superficial explanations like rapid population expansion, on the ground that rate of population expansion has been greater in England and for the last decade of the nineteenth century, there has been no increase in population in India. He dismisses the argument of carelessness and improvidence on the part of Indian cultivators on the basis of the fact 'it is known to men who have lived all their lives among these cultivators, that there is not a more abstemious, a more thrifty, a more frugal race of peasantry on earth'. The argument that the money-lenders were the proverbial Devil, who sucked the life blood of the Indian peasantry, was also refuted by Dutt. Dutt cites the evidence of the Famine Commission 'that the cultivators of India are forced under the thraldom of money-lenders by the rigidity of the Government revenue demand'. The argument that an agrarian country, where people depend entirely on their crops, will suffer from starvation in years of drought, was as much touted at that time, as it is today. Dutt forcefully argued 'the crops in India, as a whole, have never failed, there has never been a single year when the food supply of the country was insufficient for the people, and there must be something wrong, when failure in a single province brings on a famine, and the people are unable to buy their supplies from neighbouring provinces rich in harvest'.[25] R.C. Dutt went into great details to refute these arguments of British intellectuals and administrators. Today these arguments are too easily accepted under the influence of colonial intellectual hegemony.

Dadabhai Naoroji in his speeches, articles and letters before various forums and authorities had stressed the constant drain of resources from India to Great Britain and the destruction of indigenous system of manufacture as the main cause of stranglehold of poverty in India. Naoroji highlighted, how the constant drain of resources from the country, was leading to the shrinking of the capital base of the country. While the colonial power destroyed the earlier industrial base of the country, it ensured through its policies that India remains dependent on British industries and does not become a competitor. India was used as the farmland for supporting the industrial revolution and the colonial economic structure. Naoroji was one of the pioneers, who sought to draw the attention of public, the British Government and the British Crown to the large-scale drain of resources from India to England. The cost of supporting the colonial administrative and economic structure was entirely borne by the Indians. 'The whole misfortune at the bottom, which made the people of British India the poorest in the world, was the pressure to be forced to pay, roughly speaking, 200,000,000 rupees annually for European foreign services.'[26] The amount of Rs. 20 crore annual outflow in the nineteenth century at the existing price level at that time was indeed a staggering drain of resources. The various wars waged within India and outside like Burma, Nepal and Afghanistan had to be financed from Indian revenue. The cost of colonialism has to be borne by the subject nation. 'Nor does it make any difference whether the costs of imperialism are greater or less than the returns, for the simple reason that the costs are borne by the public at large while the returns accrue to that small, but normally dominant, section of the capitalist class which, has extensive, international interests'.[27] In this case public at large constituted the Indian tax payers, who constituted the Indian poor, as bulk of the taxes were on items of common consumption like salt, sugar and cloth. Naoroji has quoted extensively from British Governor Generals, top British functionaries connected with the affairs of India, to show the British administration was well aware of the exploitative policies of British Government and Industry towards India. 'It is an exhausting drain upon the resources of the country, the issue of which is replaced by no reflex; it is an extraction of the life blood from the veins of national industry which no subsequent introduction of nourishment is furnished to restore'.[28] We have already seen the comments of the nineteenth century British Historian, H.H. Wilson in this regard. It has been held by all impartial observers of Indian socio-economic scenario from the beginning of the British rule in the eighteenth century to at least the first few decades of the present century, that the

British system of Government and commerce as practised in India, has seriously damaged the economic structure of the country. 'It is, unfortunately, a fact which no well informed Indian official will ignore, that in many ways, the sources of national wealth in India have been narrowed under British rule. India in the eighteenth century was a great manufacturing as well as a great agricultural country, and the products of the Indian loom supplied the markets of Asia and of Europe. It is, unfortunately, true that the East Indian Company and the British Parliament, following the selfish commercial policy of a hundred years ago, discouraged Indian manufactures in the early years of British rule in order to encourage the rising manufactures of England. Their fixed policy, pursued during the last decades of the eighteenth century and the first decades of the nineteenth, was to make India subservient to the industries of Great Britain, and to make the Indian people grow raw produce only, in order to supply material for the looms and manufacturers of Great Britain. This policy was pursued with unwavering resolution and with fatal success, orders were sent out, to force Indian artisans to work in the Company's factories; commercial residents were legally vested with extensive powers over villages and communities of Indian weavers, prohibitive tariffs excluded Indian silk and cotton goods from England; English goods were admitted into India free of duty or on payment of a nominal duty'.[29]

This from the pen of Romesh Dutt, who was the first Indian ICS to rise to the rank of Commissioner and be kept in-charge of a division and was also Member of the Bengal Legislative Council, is strong indictment indeed of the British rule. This assessment of British policy on Indian economic and industrial development is not from the speeches or writings of a political agitator or an antagonist of British rule. Dutt was aware that it was an ungracious and painful task for him to criticise the administration, of which he was an important part, but call of duty and the need of putting forth the truth were much stronger for him. In the words of Dutt, 'I have undertaken this duty because at the present moment the economic story of British India has to be told and the deep seated cause of the poverty of the Indian people has to be explained. . . . A nation prospers if the sources of its wealth are widened, and if the proceeds of taxation are spent among the people, and for the people. A nation is impoverished if the sources of its wealth are narrowed, and the proceeds of taxation are largely remitted out of the country. These are plain, self-evident economic laws, which operate in India, and in every other country'.[30] This has been the major thesis of all impartial observers and writers of the Indian economy till the first decade of the twentieth century.

'Upto the eighteenth century, the economic condition of India was relatively advanced, and Indian methods of production and of industrial and commercial organisation could stand comparison with those in vogue in any other part of the world'.[31] The British industrial and commercial policy in India during the colonial rule changed the Indian economic structure radically. The Indian economy was turned upside down. India became a producer of raw material for British industries and an agrarian-based economy. 'But these changes brought about a peculiar interdependence between India and the West, whereby India tended to produce and export in the main raw materials and food stuffs, and to import textiles, iron and steel goods, machinery and miscellaneous manufactures of the most varied description'.[32] There can be hardly any doubt that the Industrial Revolution in Britain without a socio-economic revolution, as happened in France and some other parts of Europe, destroyed the previous economic structure without creating any alternative viable economic structure. The impact of the earthquake generated by the Industrial Revolution, with its epicentre in the industrial slums of England, was felt at its severest in the Indian sub-continent. The coincidence of the Industrial Revolution with the rise of the British Indian Empire, clearly indicates the close co-relation between the two. Britain did not conquer India with the altruistic motive of spreading the light of British civilisation. In the history of mankind there has never been any instance of one country conquering another for the latter's interest. The mass-produced standard textiles, without any craftsmanship had to be marketed and the Indian market with its vast population provided a captive market, once India was brought under British domination.

Economy and Social structure are intertwined together and once the economic structure is destroyed, the social structure also crumbles. Economy cannot be made to order, as has been attempted at various time during the British rule and in a more vigorous manner after independence through various five year plans and other projects. These have naturally met with much less success than was expected. Economic development without first developing a viable socio-economic infrastructure is bound to meet with little success. Economy does not work in a social vacuum and divorce of agriculture from industry has proved to be fatal for economic development.

While, Indian industries were decimated, very little importance was given to the development of agriculture. Irrigation, which was a priority item in the development of agriculture and had been the basis of earlier Indian agriculture, did not get the attention it deserved. The Government had been severely criticised for not spending more on the promotion of irrigation, especially in comparison with what had been spent on the railways. Eminent administrators like Sir Charles Trevelyan, Lord Lawrence, besides the father of the present irrigation system in India, Sir Arthur Cotton, highlighted the neglect of irrigation in India. There was no need of Guarantee System, as in the case of railways, as the irrigation works paid for itself, besides yielding a good profit. 'Government irrigation works have yielded a good return on capital invested.'[33] Lord Lawrence developed the Punjab irrigation net-work, whereas Sir Arthur Cotton developed the irrigation system which made the drought prone Tanjore area of erstwhile Madras province, rice-bowl of the South. It was realised that development of irrigation potential in India, with its huge water resources, will make it a powerful agricultural country, which was not to the interest of the colonial rulers.

Huge expenditure was incurred on construction of railways, while expenditure on irrigation was extremely low. Till 1880, only 12 million pound sterling was spent on irrigation, while 170 million pound sterling was spent on railways. Expenditure on railways continued to be more rapid from 1874, due to the fatal facility of borrowing from the English market under an assured return scheme, while the irrigation works languished. Sir Arthur Cotton had visualised a scheme for navigable channels with irrigation facility. Even with the paltry expenditure on irrigation, there was a net gain to the Treasury of half a million a year on irrigation works. Had a balance been struck between expenditure in railways and irrigation, India would not only have been freed from the plague of persistent famines, but would have been a great agricultural country. According to Sir Arthur Cotton, a net-work of canals for steam boat navigation, combined with irrigation facilities, is what India needed. 'Sir Arthur Cotton, the architect of the magnificent Kaveri and Godavari works, was one of the few men of his time who saw the great need of canals in India, both for irrigation and for transit'.[34] Even after a century and a half, Sir Arthur's living monuments of Kaveri and Godavari irrigation system, thrive as the basis of agricultural prosperity of the southern states. Sir Charles Trevelyan, who held high administrative positions in India and was the Finance Minister of India stated, 'Irrigation is everything in India, water is more valuable than land, because when water is applied to land it increases its productiveness atleast six-fold'. 'For twenty years and more, Lord Lawrence had been an advocate of irrigation works in India. He believed irrigation to be infinitely, more important, for the wants of the country than railways'.[35] Inspite of such support from stalwarts, irrigation did not receive the importance it deserved, in the development of the country. Railways, which was a tool of the empire and maltreated the Indians, was the priority. Several high British officials, including the Viceroy, Lord Lawrence had repoted about the ill-treatment of Indian passengers. 'The railroads deliberately lost money on their first-class passengers, who were for the most part British, and made it up by packing their third-class compartments with poor Indians. . . . The railroads were indeed "firm and unaltered memorials of British rule." Was it a coincidence that Indian anti-British nationalism appeared at the same time as the rail-roads?[36] No doubt, railways form the basis of number of books eulogising the British Raj. Irrigation works have always been profitable, but inspite of that, it had been neglected and resources of unprecedented dimension diverted from the country with the purpose of developing a transport system, which did little to benefit India, but helped in ushering in the second phase of Industrial Revolution in England. There can be no doubt, that diversion of such huge resources over a comparatively short period is responsible for pauperisation of the country. The proverbial poverty of India can certainly be traced to diversion of such huge resources from the country. An alternative scenario of development of irrigation-*cum*-navigation canals did not appeal to the colonial rulers. British Government acted in accordance with the interest of British traders and manufacturers, who dominated the British Parliament. 'Indian Economic questions not directly touching the interests of British traders and manufacturers, seldom, receive public attention in England'.[37]

The railways considerably lowered the transportation cost in India, but this only led to British industrial dominance. Karl Marx had said in 1853, 'The devastating effects of English industry, when contemplated with regard to India, a country as vast as Europe, and containing 150 million of acres, are palpable and confounding'.[38] Due to the industrial dominance of India, village industries became non-viable and the indigenous structure was decimated. 'The craftsmen thus deprived of their employment began to flood the cities, where few new industries were growing to give work to the unemployed'. In 1853, Marx had predicted that "England has to fulfil a double mission in India: one destructive, the other, regenerating—the annihilation of old Asiatic society, and the laying (of) the materials foundations of Western Society in Asia." Half the programme—the destructive mission—was accomplished; the other half had to await the end of British rule'.[39] It is of interest to observe that the Britishers had taken upon themselves, the task of destruction of the socio-economic structure of India. This was mainly to dislink production and consumption. Throughout the world, in agrarian societies, socio-economic structures were based on a close linkage between production and consumption. This was the position throughout most of Europe till the end of 19th century and sometimes beyond. The population of the world consisted mostly of peasants.

The economic condition of the French Peasantry was better than that of British Peasantry throughout the 19th century. 'Having been much among the peasantry and labouring class both at home and abroad, I must in truth say that a more civil, cleanly, industrious, frugal, sober or better dressed people than the French peasantry, for persons in their conditions . . . . I have never known. In these respects they furnish a striking contrast with a considerable portion of the Scotch agricultural labourers, who are dirty and squalid to an excess; with many of the English, who are servile, broken spirited and severely straitened in their means of living; with the poor Irish, who are half-clad and a savage condition . . . '.[40] Regarding Indian peasantry, Karl Marx says, 'At all events, we may safely expect to see, at a more or less remote period, the regeneration of that great and interesting country, whose gentle natives are to use the expression of Prince Saltykov (the great Russian Satirist and Novelist), even in the most inferior classes, "more subtle and adroit than the Italians" whose submission even is counter-balanced by a certain calm nobility, who notwithstanding their natural languor, have astonished the British Officers by their bravery, whose country has been the source of our language, our religions'.[41]

It is not that the Indian socio-economic structure was particularly grotesque or despotic. It had similar strength and weakness, as similar peasant societies throughout the world. In the earlier period of colonialism, many of the leading Britishers had high opinion of Indian civilization and its people. Edmund Burke spoke well when he contrasted the Indian and the English: "people for ages civilised and cultivated . . . . while we were yet in woods."[42] This gave way to holding the Indians at a low esteem through arrogance caused by unlimited power over a subject nation. The concept of oriental despotism is more a myth created by conflict of cultures. The abhorrent custom of 'Sati' has an equally close parallel to the custom of burning old and helpless women as Witches, which was prevalent in British Isles and Europe, at least till the end of the eighteenth century or beyond. Britain ruled the non-European world on its supremacy in the sea. One need only read the Captain's report in the real life story of 'Mutiny on Bounty', to find out how dehumanised the conditions were on British merchant and naval ships.[43] Basic recruits were criminals and forced labour, who could be kept under control only through the language of the whip and playing one against the other. The idyllic and romantic picture of life at sea was built-up to lure the gullible youngsters to the Sea. The British Public Schools were models of tyranny, which the future leaders, who were victims, could practice on the colonial subjects and less fortunate of their countrymen. 'Discipline in the public schools was a mixture of flogging and fagging. Major offenders were flogged by masters; fagging was the provision of menial services by boys of the lower "forms" or classes for those of the upper forms: to run errands for them, shine their shoes, prepare their tea, carry their cricket bats and balls and bear their bullying silently; the theory was that one must learn to obey before he is fit to command, (A like theory prevailed in the Army and the Navy, which were also organised on flogging and fagging and silent obedience; in this sense the victories Trafalgar and Waterloo were won not only on "the playing fields of Eton and Harrow" but as well in the halls and rooms of the public schools)'.[44]

Now nobody had suggested dismantling of conditions of semi-slavery in British ships and the tyrannical system of British Public schools, because they were synonymous with British success. Destruction of India's socio-economic structure was not based on any altruistic motive, but on the purely commercial one of making India a consumer society oriented to British merchandise and destroying the production base of the Indian economy. Dislinking of production and consumption, together with drain of the Indian resources, played havoc with the Indian economy. Marx, while condemning England being 'actuated only by the vilest interests, and was stupid in her manner of enforcing them', in her policy towards India, condones the same on the ground 'whatever may have been the crimes of England she was the unconscious tool of history in bringing about that revolution'. Marx believed, Britain caused a social revolution in India by breaking down 'the entire framework of Indian society, without any symptoms of reconstitution yet appearing. This loss of his old world, with no gain of a new one, imparts a particular kind of melancholy to the present misery of the Hindu, and separates Hindustan, ruled by Britain from all its ancient traditions and from the whole of its past history'.[45]

Marx concludes the above-mentioned article by quoting from Goethe, eulogizing the death and destruction meted out by Timur and treating it as historical inevitability. In Marx's own words, 'Then whatever bitterness the spectacle of the crumbling of an ancient world (India) may have for our personal feelings, we have the right, in point of history to exclaim with Goethe:

"Should this torture then torment us
Since it brings us greater pleasure?
Were not through the rule of Timur
Souls devoured without measure?"[46]

Once this type of fatalism and inevitability are introduced, the poorer nations are bound to be ruled by the rich. This is what is happening in the name of globalisation, where economically powerful nations are able to dictate their agenda to the weaker nations through IMF and World Bank. In passing, it may be mentioned that this type of ode to violence, as a historical necessity for cleaning the social system, which is quoted from the German poet and philosopher Goethe's 'Westostlicher Diwan'. An Suleika (1819), forms the philosophical basis of 'Holocaust' in the Second World War. It was not that the final solution of eliminating the European Jews was the act of a paranoid dictator, but had a philosophical base, built-up over centuries through Goethe to Nietzsche and other philosophers. It is another irony of history that Karl Marx of German Jewish ancestry, identifies himself with Goethe's philosophy of historical inevitability of mass destruction for getting rid of evil. Now, what one group of individuals considers as evil, may look different from another stand point. This type of assumed philosophical superiority causes intellectual arrogance, which is the basis of all violence in history.

Marx's justification of the British attempt to break-up

the Indian society, must have been music to the ears of generations of British policy-makers and intellectuals, particularly since the newly educated Indian elite embraced Marxism, as interpreted in British Universities so eagerly and unquestioningly. No doubt, the central theme of Indian Marxism is aimed at destroying the Indian socio-economic structure without having any viable alternative to replace the same. To develop a viable socio-economic structure takes ages and till the advent of such socialist millennium, Indian society should continue in limbo. This is in contrast to the Chinese and Vietnamese communists, who learnt their Marxism in France, rather than Britain. This raises some disturbing questions about the attitude of Marx and his followers, towards British imperialism in India. The basic question is whether one country has the right to destroy the socio-economic structure of another and cut-off its cultural past and treat itself as a tool of history. Once such type of rights are encouraged as a process of historical inevitability, it provides a strong justification of colonialism and imperialism. No doubt, Great Britain was the main hegemonic power throughout the nineteenth century and part of the twentieth century, which role has since been taken over by the U.S.A. The balance of power between Soviet Union and the U.S.A. has since been replaced by a unipolar world, where U.S.A. aided by the U.K. hold the center stage. With the destruction of a bipolar world, a volatile and violent world situation was predicted. This fear was voiced by Huntington in 1993 in his statement that a 'world without U.S. primacy will be, a world with more violence and disorder'.[47] This has come true, with the U.S.A. asserting its right of interference in the internal economy of the countries, through its control over IMF and World Bank. The U.S.A., aided by U.K., the major colonial power of the eighteenth and nineteenth centuries, has also taken upon itself the role of world policeman by sidelining the United Nations Organisation. The world has reverted to the pre-1914 situation with the U.S.A. replacing the U.K., with a much more powerful control over world affairs aided by technology. Economic globalisation is an essential part of political globalisation and once a country has chosen to adopt the former, whether due to volition or necessity, the later cannot be avoided. History is being repeated with a short interregnum.

ECONOMIC NATIONALISM

Gopal Krishna Gokhale, one of the pioneers of nationalist movement in India, said in 1907 in one of his public speeches, 'Gentlemen, as Mr. Ranade once pointed out, the industrial domination of one people by another attracts much less attention than the political domination of a foreign people. The industrial domination is less visible and does its work in a more insidious manner'. Gokhale goes on to say that 'the industrial domination of one people by another may come in an attractive garb. If, as has been the case with India, this foreign domination comes in the shape of more finished articles—especially articles that administer to the daily wants of a community—you unconsciously welcome the domination, you fall a victim to its temptations and its attractiveness. And it is only when the evil grows beyond certain limits, that your attention is drawn to it'.[48] Today, after nearly a century, the western domination of industry and commerce continues and we have ceased to question the same and have accepted it as inevitable. We are inviting the western domination of our commerce and industry and trying to embrace the same more and more closely, so that few of us can enjoy its unlimited benefits, while most of us are reduced to poverty and deprivation. Any debate on this score is stopped as encouraging obscurantism and anti-progress by the new managers of the economy armed with their uni-dimensional Anglo-American economic theories.

A new school of economics which repudiated the nationalist school was being ingeniously developed by bringing the Indian students to a different line of thinking. Professor Gilbert Slater in his Introductory Note to P. Padmanabha Pillai's Economic Conditions in India says, 'It was no doubt inevitable that when, following such leadership as that of Ranade and Naoroji, Indian students and writers began to turn their attention to economic problems, and to realize the intense poverty of India in the commodities that are bought for money, they should aim, with much effort and ingenuity, at fastening the responsibility for that poverty on the alien rule, first of the East India Company, and then of the British Government. Such efforts produced the theory of the Drain, in its various forms'. Slater goes on to say 'In the hands of the older generation of writers and orators who dealt with Indian economics, that study became the handmaid of political agitation, and in proportion as the nationalist movement increased in fervour, the search for economic facts or fancies that could be used against the Government became keener'.[49]

It is clear from the writing and speeches of the statesmen and economists at the beginning of the twentieth century that economic aspects of foreign domination was receiving serious attention from the scholars and public men. In fact, economic nationalism seemed to becoming a major movement, parallel to the movement for political nationalism. Gokhale pointed out that economic nationalism did not receive the importance it deserved during the last fifty years of the nineteenth century, when the movement of political freedom was gaining ground. The situation changed at the beginning of the twentieth century, with 'The industrial problem and its importance are now receiving their due recognition, and today at any rate we appear to have gone so far in this direction that there is now the risk of the industrial problem actually throwing into the shade the political problem which however, to a great extent lies at the root of the industrial problem'.[50] Steps were taken by the Anglo-Saxon school of economists to bring the Indian scholars away from this school of thought. Industrialisation in the national context, relevant to India, was hardly studied and the trend was to superimpose theories developed in a different context, which had already become outdated to Indian conditions. When such theories were applied for development of Indian economy in general and Indian industries in particular, the results were far from satisfactory.

The Keynesian Revolution succeeded the industrial revolution and an *adhoc* theory of countering the industrial depression in Britain during the thirties, just before the Second World War, became the all-encompassing theory of development. I.G. Patel writes about his experience in

Cambridge in the mid-forties, 'It is surprising that 'development', that is the Wealth of Nations, which was the soul and substance of classical economics found little mention in the classroom then. No one read Adam Smith or J.S. Mill or even Marshall Keyneseana conquered all'.[51] Dennis Robertson at the outset of his Cambridge Lectures, delivered between 1945-46 to 1956-57, warns the undergraduate students about the controversial nature of Keynes's General Theory and to supplement its reading by critical writings on the same.[52] Robertson was apprehensive of the sure fire solutions to economic problems offered by Keynes. Keynesian Revolution was not so much the product of General Theory, as the interpretation of the same by his followers. Solution to depression in advanced capitalism was sought to be applied for economic development of newly independent countries. Economic interpretation of history would have been more useful in understanding the causes of Indian poverty and remedies could have been worked out accordingly. The disease should have been diagnosed first and then remedies applied. Instead, the medicines for a different disease was applied, complicating the disease itself.

Notes and References

1. The Blackwell Encyclopaedia of Political Thought (1897) Edited by David Miller, pp. 166-67. Intellectual Revolution preceded the French Revolution, which was not an one-time affair, but released intellectual and social forces, which have permanent ramifications throughout the world, even today. British industrial revolution was not preceded by any intellectual or social revolution, as such the general populace was unprepared for such social upheavals. This created serious discontent, which could be solved only by an agreessive policy of colonisation of settlements.
2. Will and Ariel Durant, The Age of Napoleon (1975), p. 6.
3. Encyclopaedia of Political Thought, p. 166.
4. E.J. Hobsbawm, The Age of Revolution, p. 154.
5. Charles Gide, Political Economy, p. 505.
6. C. Northcote Parkinson, The Rise of Big Business (1977), p. 6, quoted from John Langton Sanford and Meredith Townsend, *The Great Governing Families of England* (1865), pp. 15-16.
7. *Ibid.*, pp. 6-7. Ref. Douglas Sutherland, The Landowners (London, 1968).

8. Francois Crouzet, France, in the Industrial Revolution in National Context (1996), p. 53.
9-10. Sidney Pollard, Peaceful Conquest (1981), p. 137.
11. Herbert Feis, Europe, The World's Banker (1930) p. 34.
12-15. Industrial Revolution in National Context, pp. 47, 51, 381. R. Roehl, 1976, 'French industrialisation a reconsideration', Explorations in Economic History, 13(3), pp. 233-81.
16-17. Peaceful conquest, pp. 174, 186.
18-19. Age of Revolution, pp. 34-35.
20. Industrial Revolution in National Context, pp. 46-47.
21-22. J.C. Jack, the Economic Life of a Bengal District (1916), pp. 6, 92.
23. Age of Revolution, p. 165.
24-25. R.C. Dutt, Economic History of India Under Early British Rule, Preface, pp. VI-VII.
26. Dadabhai Naoroji, Poverty and Un-British Rule in India (1901), Swan Sonnenschein and Co. Ltd., London, Publication Division, Government of India (1969), p. 266.
27. Eduard Marz, Joseph Schumpeter (1991), p. 183. Quoted in 'Notes', quoted from Paul A. Buran and Paul M. Sweezy, 'Notes on the Theory of Imperialism', *Monthly Review*, Vol. 17, 10 March, 1966.
28. Mill's History of India (Vol. VI), p. 671, Quoted in Naoroji, *Poverty and Un-British Rules in India*, p. V in the Introduction, under the sub-heading ' Destructive and Despotic to the Indians'.
29. R.C. Dutt, Economic History of India (Vol. I), pp. VII-VIII.
30. *Ibid.*, pp. XIII-XIV.
31-33. Vera Austery, The Economic Development of India (1957), pp. 5, 163.
34-35. R.C. Dutt, Economic History of India, Victorian Age (1903), pp. 360-61.
36. Daniel Headrick, Tools of Empire (1981), p. 190.
37. R.C. Dutt, p. 362.
38. Karl Marx, The Future Results of the British Rule in India (1853), p. 88, *New York Daily Tribune*, No. 4904, January 7, 1857, from K. Marx and F. Engels, On Colonialism.
39. Daniel Headrick, p. 189.
40. H. Colman, The Agricultural and Rural Economy of France, Belgium, Holland and Switzerland (1848), pp. 25-6, Foot-note in Age of Revolution, p. 167.
41. Karl Marx, p. 88. Marx has quoted from A.D. Saltykov's book *Lettres Sur L' Inde*, Paris, 1848, p. 61.
42. David Landes, The Wealh and Poverty of Nations (1998), p. 19. Edmund Burke's "Speech on Mr. Fox's East India Bill", 1 December, 1783.
43. William Bligh, The Ministry on Board H.M.S. Bounty. Adam Smith in his 'Wealth of Nations' (p. 46) says that the wages of the seamen were lower than the common labourers at the port, although the former faced much greater hardship and risks.

44. Age of Napoleon, p. 362.
45. Karl Marx, The British Rule in India (1853), pp. 34, 39 on Colonisalism.
46. *Ibid.*, p. 39.
47. S.P. Huntington, Why International Primacy Matters (1993), International Security, 17(4).
48. G.K. Gokhale, The Swadeshi Movement (1907), pp. 958-59, in *Speeches of Gopal Krishna Gokhale.*
49. Gilbert Slater's Introductory Note, pp. XI-XII, in P. Padmanabha Pillai, *Economic Conditions in India* (1928).
50. Gokhale, Speeches, pp. 959-60.
51. I.G. Patel, Glimpses of Indian Economic Policy (2002), p. 18.
52. D.H. Robertson, Lectures on Economic Principles, Volume-I, (1957), p. 15.

3

Economics of Colonisation

Adam Smith advocated free trade at a time, when British manufacturing industries, particularly the textile mills had increased their capacity through various practical innovations. When the Britishers had full political and economic domination of India and an indirect control over South America through favourable regimes, free trade with colonies and politically favourable regimes, was certainly to the advantage of Britain. Adam Smith's advocacy of free trade supplied the theoretical framework for the British economic policies of the eighteenth century. A careful reading of the 'Wealth of Nations' clearly indicates that Adam Smith was clearly aware of the pitfalls of the British economic policies regarding the colonies. But the school of thought regarding free trade, which took-off from selective readings of 'Wealth of Nations', clearly overlooked such academic niceties. Economic thoughts were typecasted into particular schools to give theoretical support to government policies of the day, regarding trade and commerce. 'Pitt is reported as saying, "We are all your scholars", when the author (Adam Smith) entered a room in which Pitt was seated with his fellow cabinet members, and the works seems to have had considerable influence on the budget drawn up by Lord North in 1777 and 1778'.[1]

Beyond this immediate impact, Adam Smith influenced generations of economists and policy-makers. Nobody can talk of free trade, without a reverential reference to Adam Smith, who has been made the patron saint of capitalism, as much as Marx was the patron saint of communism. This turning of economists into cult figures, is the greatest disservice to their works, as it prevents the development of a proper intellectual approach to their contributions to knowledge. Smith's approach to economics in his work was historical. This was given a good-bye to, by his followers under the influence of Ricardo and the bits and pieces of his work was developed as various economic laws like the law of free trade or the inexorable law of the 'hidden hand' which controls the entire economy and should not be disturbed. 'It has been a weakness of the science as pursued in England that it has been too much dissociated from History. Adam Smith and Malthus, indeed, had historical minds; but the form of modern text books is due to Ricardo, whose mind was entirely unhistorical'.[2] Laws of economics are relative and valid for particular situations in the economic history of a nation. Elaborating on historical method of economic analysis, Toynbee goes on to say, 'It examines the actual causes of economic development and considers the influence of institutions such as the mediaeval guilds, our present land laws, or the political constitution of any given country, in determining the distribution of wealth. Without the aid of the Historical Method it would be impossible, for instance, to understand why one-half of the land in the United Kingdom is owned by 2512 persons'.[3] This is sacrilege for a British economist, brought up on tradition of unquestioning obedience to economic theories, which were off-shoot of British industrial revolution and applicable to economic conditions as it existed in contemporary United Kingdom. To the British economists, the economic forces generated by the industrial revolution in that country was universal and economic laws were accordingly formulated. What is good for Britain, is good for the entire world, irrespective of differences in socio-economic conditions. 'The Historical Method is also of value because it makes us see where economic laws and precepts are relative'.[4] Toynbee's methodology is summed up by his friend Alfred Milner, 'The facts of economic history and the theories of economists should be studied side by side, and thus studied, they would throw light on each other. Adam Smith, Malthus, Ricardo should be interpreted by a knowledge of the industrial and social conditions of their time. This was an essential feature of Toynbee's projected work on the Industrial Revolution'.[5] This line of analysis posed the danger of opening up a Pandora's box of uncomfortable questions relating to the industrial revolution and was thus never seriously pursued. The projected work of Toynbee never materialised, due to his premature death and nothing much was heard of this method of economic analysis. Trying to universalise economic laws, has been one of the greatest disservice to the science of economics. The attempt by the third world countries to formulate their development plans on the basis of these economic laws, has created serious imbalances in their economy and has kept them perpetually indebted, leading to erosion of their economic independence.

POLICY OF MERCANTILISM

Economics theories are relevant to particular situations and period and have to be viewed in relation to the economic events of the time. Theories of economics cannot be created in vacuum and bear the distinctive stamp of the economic events of the time. In fact, economic theories influence the policies of the time, as well as are influenced by the same. It is no chance coincidence that the greatest authorities on Mercantilism were mostly merchants or men of affairs. Sir Thomas Mun (1571-1641), who is rated very high as a Mercantilist Theorist, was a leading businessman and Director of the East India Company, whose authority and influence reached beyond the business community. Sir Josiah Child (1630-99), a leading authority on Mercantilism, was the Chairman of the East India Company and a prominent businessman. Gerard Malynes (1586-1641), a leading English economist on Mercantilism was a high official of the State and a successful merchant. Edward Misselden (1608-54), another leading mercantilist economist was a leading English merchant of his time. Malynes and Misselden entered into a war of pamphlets, each propagating a theoretical argument for their particular business interests. Mercantilists basic motive for developing an economic framework was to have a theoretical supporting base for their own business interests. Misselden, who was a leading member of the Merchants Adventures, which was a rival of the East India Company, advocated restriction of trade within Christendom, as trade with the Orient was a drain on the country's bullion reserves. He blamed the East India Company for causing trade depression. As with other mercantilist authorities, he was of the view that unregulated trade was harmful for the economic well-being of the nation.

Misselden was the first to use the term 'balance of trade'[6] and use it as an economic barometer to find out whether the trade was in the interest of the nation or otherwise. The State should follow an active policy of ensuring a favourable balance of trade, which ensures that the wealth of the nation increases. Keynes in the notes on 'Mercantilism' in the General Theory, holds that 'For some two hundred years both economic theorists and practical man did not doubt that there is a peculiar advantage to a country in a favourable balance of trade, and grave danger in an unfavourable balance. But for the past one hundred years there has been a remarkable divergence of opinion'.[7] Keynes was of the view that majority of statesmen and practical men in most countries and half of that class in Great Britain remained loyal to the old concept, whereas economists abandoned the old concept and found new light in the theory that the foreign trade mechanism is inexorably self-adjusting and any interference with it will be disastrous for the economy. Any attempt at having a favourable balance of payment will boomerang and will impoverish the nation, as it will deny the benefits of international division of labour. Thus, according to Keynes, for two hundred years, i.e. the seventeenth and eighteenth century, a favourable balance of payment was an essential state policy for countries, which prospered and became powerful nation states. They were also fully supported by the theoreticians. From the second quarter of the nineteenth century, the view gradually became less rigid and the economist discovered the great benefit of the international division of labour. Keynes was speaking from a

British standpoint and his view had far from universal applicability and was relevant to Britain only. Economic experiences of a particular country need not be universalised. Mercantilists wrote for the situation of their time, as much as Keynes did. They did not offer a permanent policy for trade and were well aware of the fact that, their argument did not apply in the long-run, not to speak of a state of long-run equilibrium.[8]

COLONISATION THROUGH TRADE

An aggressive trade policy followed by Britain throughout the seventeenth, eighteenth and till the first few decades of the nineteenth century established the supremacy of British commerce, which made Britain workshop of the world. 'Possessing greater manufacturing ability than any other society at that time and enjoying even higher standards of living, many Britons became proponent of *laissez-faire* economics and of an 'open' trading order in which national boundaries and ownership counted for less and less. Perhaps the great English Economist Jevons best captured this mood when he exulted in 1865.

'The plains of North America and Russia are our cornfields; Chicago and Odessa our granaries, Canada and the Baltic are our timber forests; Australasia contains our sheep farms, and in Argentina and on the western prairies of North America are our herds of oxen; Peru sends her silver and the gold of South Africa and Australia flows to London; the Hindus and the Chinese grow tea for us, and our coffee, sugar and spice plantations are all in the Indies. Spain and France are our vineyards, and the Mediterranean our fruit garden, and our cotton grounds, which for long have occupied the Southern United States, are now being extended every where in the warm regions of the earth'.[9]

This is probably one of the most eloquent statements of British economic colonialism unwittingly made. It is obvious, whether it is a theory of protectionism, as propounded by the mercantilist economists of the seventeenth and eighteenth centuries or the theory of *laissez-faire* as propounded by British Economists in the nineteenth century; the same were the products of their times and circumstances and were designed to serve the interest of the nation, where these theories originated and were expounded. There is certainly no universal applicability of such theories and what is good for one nation, may not be good for the other. The result of the policies of which these theories were the theoretical justification, were highly beneficial for some countries, whereas disastrous for others. In the words of Paul Kennedy, basing on the figures of Paul Bairoch in 'International Industrialisation levels from 1750 to 1980' in the *Journal of European Economic History II* (1982), 'The awful result, according to one calculation, was that whereas the British and Indian peoples had roughly similar per capita levels of industrialisation at the onset of the Industrial Revolution (1750), India's level was only one-hundredth of the United Kingdom's by 1900'. Even nearer home Ireland was on the wrong side of Industrial Revolution. 'Ireland, disadvantaged in many ways (alien political control, lack of infrastructure, lack of coal, low per capita levels of consumption, depressed agriculture) was unable to solve "the central problem of the age . . . how to feed and clothe and employ generations of children out-numbering by far those of any earlier time." By the 1840s, starvation and emigration had reduced population by about one-fifth'.[10]

In the seventeenth and eighteenth centuries, England was openly following a policy of trade restrictions. Adam Smith in his 'Wealth of Nations' has cited number of statutes enacted in England prior to the eighteenth century, which depressed the price of English wool by completely prohibiting the export of the same. By an edict during the time of Elizabeth I (1558-1603), exporter of sheep was 'to have his left hand cut-off in a market town upon a market day, to be there nailed up', besides having all his goods forfeited and suffering a year's imprisonment. Punishment for the second offence was death. An edict in the time of Charles II (1660-1685), imposed the punishment of forfeiture and death as a felon, for export of wool. Woolen manufacturers of England wanted to monopolise almost the entire woolen trade of the world and with that purpose in view prevented the export of any raw wool. Adam Smith, the Scotsman, says that with the union of Scotland with England and the enforcement of English laws in the former State, the price of Scots wool fell to half of its previous price. According to John Smith's 'Memoirs of Wool' quoted in the Wealth of Nations, 'the price of the best English wool in England is generally below what wool of a very inferior quality commonly sells for in the market of Amsterdam'.

Wealth of Nations cites the case of linen industry where the manufacturers 'By extorting from the legislature bounties upon the exportation of their own linen, high duties upon the importation of all foreign linen, and a total prohibition of some sorts of French linen, they endeavour to sell their own goods as dear as possible'. Whereas, 'By encouraging the importation of foreign linen yarn, and thereby bringing it into competition with that which is made by our own people, they endeavour to buy the work of the poor spinners as cheap as possible'. Adam Smith clearly shows duplicity of the policy followed by English traders and merchants to further their own interest and the complete support of the State in their endeavours. In this, they were fully supported by the mercantile economists who were also merchants. Adam Smith castigates the English mercantile system of the eighteenth century as one which is carried on for the benefit of the rich and the powerful and 'That which is carried on for the benefit of the poor and the indigent is too often either neglected or oppressed'. Then again he says about the cruelty and unjustness of the English laws to support the merchants and manufacturers 'Like the laws of Draco, these laws may be said to be all written in blood'.[11] A close reading of 'Wealth of Nations', which has become the Bible of Capitalism and Free Trade, clearly indicates the circumstances under which Smith had recommended an end to Government intervention. It was to get rid of the obnoxious laws enforced by various statutes at the behest of the manufacturers and traders, that Adam Smith advocated minimum of State intervention in commerce and trade. The concept of free trade was a reaction to the extreme State intervention, which was practised throughout the seventeenth and eighteenth centuries in Great Britain at the behest of manufactures and traders.

Mercantilism was an economic philosophy, which catered to the basic political philosophy of the time in the building up of powerful nation States. England, which sought to build up its economic strength on the basis of industrial production, whole-heartedly embraced Mercantilism. According to Marx, 'The first theoretical treatment of the modern mode of production—the mercantile system—proceeded necessarily from the superficial phenomena of the circulation process as individualised in the movements of merchant's capital and therefore grasped only the appearance of matters . . . .' The real science of modern economy only begins when the theoretical analysis passes from the process of circulation to the process of production'.[12] Mercantile system pushes consumption to the background and only considers the interest of the producers. 'In the mercantile system the interest of the consumer is almost constantly sacrificed to that of the producer; and it seems to consider production, and not consumption, as the ultimate end and object of all industry and commerce'.[13] Mercantile system was developed as a theoretical economic framework to support the launching of large-scale industrial production, in which Britain was the pioneer. Limitation of the market was sought to be conquered by military domination and a policy of trade barriers through protective duties, and domination of trade-routes by the British Navy. In the pursuit of industrial domination, the interests of the primary producers, i.e., the producers and manufacturers of raw materials, workers and the consumers are totally subordinated. The system created spectacular economic benefit for a small portion of the population, whereas others were driven to the wilderness of economic marginalisation.

The beginning of this historical imbalance starts from the active policy of colonisation together with factory system of mass production. 'Commercial investments made in the colonies, integrated into the circuit of mercantile capital and tied to the bonds of mercantile policies, substantially and strategically contributed to the economic growth of Western Europe. They opened new areas for investment—areas essential for the growth and mobility and circulation of capital . . . THE COLONIES DID PAY'.[14] Colonies were treated as satellites to sustain the economic prosperity of the colonical country. When Britain was overtly following a policy of *laissez faire* from 1840 onwards, it not only annexed large areas, but was also developing a colonical pattern of economy in the occupied countries to support its economic development. 'In this supposedly *laissez faire* period India, far from being evacuated, was subjected to intensive development as an economic colony along the best mercantilist line. In India, it was possible throughout most of the period of the British Raj, to use the governing power to extort in the form of taxes and monopolies such valuable primary products as opium and salt'.[15] Such acts of deliberate colonisation have destroyed the very fabric of Indian economy as an independent economic entity and has hindered all attempts at development. However, the lie of free-trade, is best summed up in the following statement made towards the end of nineteenth century. 'Col. Torrens well described the situation when he wrote, 'England had acquired a species of property, a vested interest, in the industrial products of all the regions of the earth'. In fact, she had made 'the whole world tributary to herself' through her manufactures'.[16] It was manufactures, backed by military and state power.

Salt and opium were monopolies under the East India Company and then the Government. Salt was manufactured in India under state control and the tax on salt was increased from time to time. Total revenue derived from the manufacture of salt was estimated at sixty million sterling between 1793 to 1844. Even as late as 1937-38, salt yielded a revenue of Rs. 8.25 crores. Under the impact of high tax, the salt manufactured in India became so costly that salt had to be imported from England. This led to a situation, where salt was taxed out of the hands of the common man. 'The selling price of salt is arbitrarily fixed by the Government, and is at all times so high that, though the country has abundant resources for the manufacture of the article, English merchants can afford to import it. . . . The officers employed in the salt department are vested with judicial powers contrary to all principles of justice and policy, and necessarily employ them very irregularly and vexatiously'.[17] Strict control over the manufacture and distribution of an essential item throughout the British rule was certainly according to the mercantilist principles and not *laissez faire*.

Cultivation, processing and trade in opium were company and state monopolies. Opium was a highly profitable item for the East India Company. 'Opium growing made progress, after the occupation of India by the British. . . In 1733, the East India Company gained possession of the monopoly in smuggling opium into China and developed the cultivation of the puppy, first in Bengal, then later in Central India'.[18] Initially import of opium into China was officially banned and the entire trade was through smuggling. The ban was lifted in 1820, and 'For more than sixty years the sale of this drug was to form the principal source of revenue for the British Indian empire in its relations with China. It was thanks to opium that British trade with China avoided falling into deficit during this period'.[19] India did not benefit from the production and trade of opium. The entire opium revenue was appropriated by the Government. 'The value of the opium sold in China amounted to well over two million pounds—getting on for half the amount then annually devoted to paying for the Crown and the Civil Service in Britain. If the Government of India was deprived of the revenue from opium, it would have to be raised from other sources, and the British tax payer might have to be called upon'.[20] India was used as a captive farmland for growing opium and the entire revenue from the trade went to Britain. As regards the method of increasing the cultivable area under opium, 'The company's agents were instructed to put pressure on the Bengal peasants to sow more poppies; as the agents were paid on a commission basis, they needed no inducement, using various forms of blackmail to bring recalcitrant peasants into line'.[21] The opium produced in the native states of Malwa was also under the Company's and State's control. The export of opium was completely under state control, as it had to pass through British India.

Bonded cultivation of opium under state control, did not benefit the farmers and only added to the shortage of foodgrains by reducing the area of cultivation of the same. Subsequent abandonment of opium trade in 1917, put the opium cultivators out of business. India did not derive any benefit from opium trade 'All India's profits of trade, and several millions from her very produce, and with these all the profit of opium, go the same way of drain - to England. Only India shares the curse of the Chinese race. Had this cursed opium trade not existed, India's miseries would have much sooner come to the surface'.[22] Opium contributed to a favourable balance of payments to India. The entire profit was payments to India, but was appropriated by Britain. Opium trade with China clearly brings out that while India was a formal empire, China was an informal empire. 'The real threat that England posed for the China of the first half of the nineteenth century was not nearly so much a military one as an economic one: the imports of opium helped to undermine the economy of an empire whose finances and political system had continuously deteriorated since the end of the eighteenth century'.[23] This led to serious internal crisis in China 'and when the pressure of the industrialised nations grew fiercer at the end of the nineteenth century China had been left so short a breathing-space that she no longer had the time, the means, the peace or the autonomy necessary to recruit her strength and fight effectively against the onrush of imperialism'.[24] China was first economically subjugated through the opium trade. This brought in semi-anarchy in administration, which helped in establishing the hold of western imperialism.

MASS PRODUCTION DESTROYS QUALITY PRODUCTION

In 1832, Charles Babbage, founder of the science of computation, in his book, 'On the Economy of Machinery and Manufactures', mentions, 'The cotton of India is conveyed by British ships round half our planet, to be woven by British skill in the factories of Lancashire, it is again set in motion by British capital, and transported to the very plains wherein it grew; is repurchased by the lords of the soil which gave it birth, at a cheaper price than that at which their coarser machinery enables them to manufacture it themselves. . . . At Calicut (where the cotton cloth called calico derives its name), the price of labour is one-seventh of that in England, yet the market is supplied from Britain'. This is the miracle of British Industrial Revolution, where to quote Babbage again 'machinery supersedes the skill and power of human arm'.[25] The entire operation is put down to the wonders of technology, whereas the things were quite different in economic terms. The fact of the matter was that the India was a colonical captive market for British textiles. This phase of industrialisation was systematic destruction of Indian textile industries, where human skill was an essential ingredient. Standard machine produced goods replaced the qualitative Indian goods. Here, the fatuous argument of the British colonialists, may be that they were clothing the Indian poor. This argument is fallacious in that the Indian manufacturers were much more durable and cost-effective than the British mill products. 'Under the pretence of free trade, England has compelled the Hindus to receive the products of the steam looms of Lancashire, Yorkshire, Glasgow, etc., at mere nominal duties, while the hand-wrought manufactures of Bengal and Behar, beautiful in fabric and durable in wear, have had heavy and almost prohibitive duties imposed on their importation to England'.[26] R.C. Dutt in his Economic History of British India has quoted detailed figures of trade and commerce with Britain to show how the Indian manufacturing industries were systematically destroyed.[27]

Parliamentary Committees were set-up in Britain between 1813 and 1832, to find out ways and means to further expand the market for British manufactures in India. They went into great details and recorded voluminous evidence of high officials, who have worked in India. The reports of the Committees are illuminating in that they highlighted the decline of Indian industries and replacement of Indian manufactured products by British goods. The Committees were far from satisfied and put pressure on the Indian Government to encourage the import of British goods by a differential tariff structure. 'British manufactures were imported into Calcutta on payment of a small duty of 2.5 per cent, while the import of Indian manufactures into England was discouraged by heavy duties ranging upto 400 per cent on their value'.[28] 'The evidence recorded discloses that in purely agricultural pursuits England had little to teach; . . . in all industries which were dependent on machinery, Europe had adopted more perfect methods than India in 1830. It is possible to conceive that a Government, working with an eye to the advancement of the National Industries, might have introduced these superior methods among the industrious and skilful people of India, as they have been introduced among the people of Japan within our generation . . . . A policy the reverse of this was pursued with the object of replacing the manufactures of India, as far as possible, by British manufactures'.[29]

Japan, which was not under a colonial rule, industrialised itself by adopting improved technology to its industries, while India under foreign domination was in no position to do the same. 'In India, the Manufacturing Power of the people was stamped out by protection against her industries, and then free trade was forced on her so as to prevent a revival'. Let us see the reaction to such historical injustice to India in Britain. 'Public men and public writers in England never spoke or wrote of this policy pursued in India. The great political economists of the time, headed by Ricardo, had nothing to say on the subject'.[30] While the English Economists shied away from the problem of colonial trade, continental economists took a more, realistic unbiased view of the situation. Friedrich List termed the British trade policy with India, 'The Theory of the Powers of Production',[31] according to which the country which sold manufactured goods will be supreme while the country selling only agricultural produce will be subservient. This was achieved through prohibition of import of Indian cotton and silk fabrics. Arnold Toynbee in his 'Lectures on the Industrial Revolution in England', (1884) had said, 'the neglect of economic history has been the greatest drawback of the Anglo-Saxon School of Economics'.[32] Whether this was deliberate or accidental? British school of economics was a theoretical support base for the policy of imperialism of free trade. Britain had learnt from the decline and fall of the Roman Empire, that imperialism also carries the seeds of its own destruction. In an article published in 1899 in the Contemporary Review, the fear of the British economy being choked by the continuous drain of resources from the colonies was voiced. According to Ritortus, economy of imperial Rome was choked by the influx of African corn, and by the inroads of Oriental manufacture. People were happy with the easy availability of cheap corn. Manufacturing industries declined in Italy due to the free import of quality manufactured goods from the Orient to cater to the needs of the rich. Pliny, who pointed out the economic ills of this policy was ridiculed as 'little Italian'. British imperialists had studied the economic decline of Rome well. In the words of Ritortus, 'We need not, therefore, fear the fate of Rome. This is in our power to do, for our great English economists have given us the science which was lacking to the Romans. Thanks to our economic thinkers, we are in possession of those principles of trade by which we may be able to restore the equilibrium of trade and of wealth. This equilibrium was disturbed, as we have seen, first by our one-sided Free Trade, and later on by the payments of our incomes from abroad.'[33] Ritortus was well aware of the continuous drain of resources from the colonies, particularly India. He was confident that the English economists will be able to devise economic theories for continuation of the British Empire. His confidence was not misplaced and British economic theories were devised for the continuation of the Empire.

COLONISATION THROUGH TRANSFER OF TECHNOLOGY

India embarked on a rapid phase of industrialisation, after being freed from the shackles of colonialism. Public sector was envisaged to control the commanding heights of the economy, to develop a firm industrial infrastructure. Paradoxically, like the proverbial man in a hurry, it was thought that this could be achieved by obtaining the technology of the erstwhile colonial masters-lock, stock and barrel. Instead of embarking and charting out our own course of industrialisation, we chose to imitate the same colonial technology, which had been a tool of colonialism to keep us in bondage. There was enough technical knowledge available within the country, at the level of technology obtaining at that time in Britain, Germany and U.S.A. The technology available in these countries, was the technology of the depression era, which had proved to be complete failure in ushering a new industrial revolution in Europe and America after the First World War. This out-dated technology would have died a natural death, had the depression run its own course. But the depression was interrupted by the Second World War and this technology gained a new lease of life, by finding a use in armaments production in a war economy.

The technology transferred, was the technology of the pre-war depression period. This technology was not only obsolete, but had little utility for a modernised industrial sector, which India was trying to build. Moreover, importing of technology from Britain, when they were openly hostile to industrialisation of India, was not in the best national interest. I.G. Patel in a Colombo Plan meeting in 1956 at New Zealand, was subjected to the full blast, of British hostility towards industrialisation of India. 'I was to learn within a day or two of my arrival in Wellington—that the British were on the war path against India. They were peeved by Suez; and by our flirting with a bold plan of industrialisation'.[34] This coincided with the time, when we were taking British technical aid for setting up the integrated steel plant at Durgapur. British interest in supplying the machinery for steel plant 'has only been encouraged by steel plant equipment suppliers from developed nations, who are themselves often subsidised with state-provided export credits'.[35] The entire thing exposes the hypocracy of technology transfer. British were afraid that by negotiating with countries like Soviet Union, India may be able to get a better deal in steel technology. However, the machinery supplied to Durgapur Steel Plant was out-dated and the plant suffered losses.

Interestingly, this has also been the history of one of the first attempt of technology transfer in Europe. France, when it felt that it was being overtaken by Britain in industrial development, resorted to import of British technology in areas like steel-making, in the nineteenth century. 'D. Landes has shown that best-practice British equipment (admittedly an ambiguous concept) was expensive and unsuited to narrow markets (actually, French firms were often to install machinery or plant which were obsolete in England)'.[36] As France did not have colonial market, where quantity was the main concern and not quality, the technology proved unsuitable for a narrow qualitative market. France without a colonial market had little use of British technology geared for captive colonial market and had to go in for technology suited to its own needs. Due to high price of coal in France, French went in for water-power and fuel saving devices. 'French-made engines and locomotives surpassed those made in Britain for fuel economy. The same factor was behind the recovery of hot gases from blast furnaces and later improvements in the efficiency of coke ovens'.[37] Britain, having complete control of the abundance of natural resources of the colonies, had no need of efficiency or economy in the utilisation of resources. The market for Britain was not a problem, as it had a huge colonial market at its command. After having achieved the initial break-through in industrial revolution through textiles, Britain tried to cash in on the ambitions of other countries in Europe, who tried to industrialise. British export of machinery to these countries were sporadic and unsatisfactory, as these countries, after initial acceptance of technology, innovated their own technology to suit their own requirements. British attempt at finding a regular market for its industrial equipments, towards industrialisation of Europe, was not much of a success and Britain had to turn to the colonies once again for the second phase of industrialisation. During 1815-17, 'Europe was indeed flooded by what seemed impossibly cheap British manufactures, which killed off many apparently promising continental plants in two or three traumatic seasons'.[38] To cite a French experience, 'Actually, in 1820-21, some newcomers to the industry had established large new works, where the whole set of British technology was applied . . . they had overestimated demand for their production and underestimated costs; most of the new companies failed in the slump of 1828-32'.[39]

British attempt at continuity of its industrial revolution through transfer of technology to western European countries was not a success. Britain's iron and steel industry in the second phase of industrial revolution, consisted mainly of laying down a railway net-work in India, financed by Indian revenue and resources. The Railways did not yield any profit and was consistently working at a loss, but under the guarantee system, the British share-holders of various railway companies, were assured of profit by the Government of India, to be met out of the general revenue. It was decided by British colonial Government to lay down a railway network at a considerable cost to India, without ascertaining, whether the country could bear such a heavy financial burden at that time. This gift of a major railway network immediately after the Mutiny of 1857 was a sound economic proposition for Britain and served as a major tool of the Empire. 'Direct governmental promotion of products required by British industry, government manipulation of tariffs to help British exports, railway construction at high and guaranteed rates of interest to open the continental interior—all of these techniques of direct political control were employed in ways which seem alien to the so-called age of *laissez faire*. Moreover, they had little to do, particularly in railway finance, with the folklore of rugged individualism. 'All the money came from the English capitalist' as a British official wrote, 'and, so long as he was guaranteed five per cent on the revenues of India, it was immaterial to him whether the funds which he lent were thrown into the Hooghly or converted into bricks and mortar'.[40]

The other Western European countries did not have this luxury and had to evolve their own technologies according to available market conditions. Belgium and Germany are two continental countries, which followed the British model of industrialisation. These two countries are held as examples of successful industrialisers compared to France. But in France, during the nineteenth century, 'there were spells of remarkably fast expansion, as fast as any shown by the allegedly 'successful' industrialisers like Britain, Belgium or Germany'.[41] Of the three major Western European countries, France was the only country, which industrialised without going through economic colonisation and displacement of its peasantry. France had the lowest rate of emigration compared to most of the European countries.

France did not have the luxury of development of economic colonies during the nineteenth century, as Britain turned the Indian sub-continent to its economic colony. French colonies acquired during the end of the nineteenth century was more to boost the international status of France, *vis-a-vis* Great Britain. 'France acquired an empire mainly for psychological reasons: wounded pride following the Franco-Prussian War, and the desire to regain status and prestige among the great powers'.[42] As a late entrant in the field of colonialism and due to the non-colonial pattern of its industrialisation, France could not turn its overseas possessions into colonies of exploitation. French economic system also did not encourage large-scale emigration and France did not have any major colony of settlement. Probably, the spirit of the French Revolution was still there amongst the French not to indulge in unabashed economic colonialism and destroy the socio-economic structure of the occupied countries and turn them into economic colonies of France.

Belgium had to acquire a huge colonial empire in Africa, eighty-three times its size, proportionately next only to Britain with a colonial empire of ninety-five times its size, to support its industrialisation drive. Belgium colonialism of Congo was one of exploitation and a cruel one. 'Even today, wherever immense and almost unexplored territories, such as those of the Congo, are to be exploited, governments as a rule, prefer to handover the working of them to private companies, and to invest these with part of their sovereignty. . . . . But as, over immense tracts, the natives may buy and sell only through the Companies, the agents of these exercise a *de-facto* sovereignty'.[43] Congo was colonised in the 1880s as the private holding of a group of European investors headed by Leopold II, King of the Belgians. Berlin Conference of 1885, recognised Leopold, as sovereign of Congo by the European powers. 'The regime, under Leopold's, unrestrained personal control, became notorious for the treatment of the inhabitants. Forced labour was used to gather wild rubber, palm oil and ivory; lashings and the taking of hostages were techniques for encouraging villages to meet their rubber quotas. Belgians introduced multilation as a common punishment even for minor offences. Brutality was widespread in mines and on plantations. The population of the entire state is said to have declined from 20 or 30 million to 8 million'.[44] This, at the end of the nineteenth century and beginning of the twentieth century! Belgians, not only, exploited the natural and mineral resources of Congo, but also forced the local inhabitants to work for them under duress. 'King Leopold was motivated by greed, economic and territorial. . . . He was a patriotic imperialist, his purpose the exploitation of the Congo for the embellishment and glory of Belgium.'[45]

The third 'successful' industrialised country was Germany, next to Britain and Belgium. 'The German process of industrialisation possibly bears next to the Belgian, the closest resemblance to the British, being based on similar resources'.[46] German industrialisation looked for its markets in the industrially under-developed regions of Central and Eastern Europe, including Russia. Germany had historical trade routes to the Central and Eastern Europe and with industrialisation, used the same as captive markets. This stunted the development of an independent industrial structure in these countries and resulted in an incomplete industrialisation. In German industrialisation, 'Eastern trade provided easily available markets, as well as some raw materials'.[47] The industrial revolution passed by Eastern Europe and at best had only a peripheral effect. That part of Europe had to wait till the end of Second World War, when 'The Eastern European an economies were ultimately industrialised on the basis of Marxist-inspired governmental crash programmes'.[48] Control over Central and Eastern Europe, created great tension between Germany and the other major European industrial power, Britain. This resulted in two major world wars in the last century. Economic reasons of conflicts between nations are lost sight of in the search for political and ideological reasons. Industrialisation of Germany coincided with the rise of German imperialism. 'Around 1880, Bismarck discovered the potential of overseas policy. . . . Thus imperialism became an integrative force in a recently founded state which lacked stabilizing historical traditions and which was unable to conceal its sharp class divisions'.[49] Germany, without any major overseas colony in

Asia and Africa, had to follow a colonial policy *vis-a-vis* Central and Eastern Europe. But the underdeveloped portion of Europe was not sufficient to sustain German industrialisation drive and Germany had to go in for annexation of Belgium with its minerally rich African colony-cause of First World War. The same scenario was repeated in the Second World War. There is definitely need to find a less violent method of industrialisation, for survival of mankind. A Third World War can hardly be afforded. There is definitely a need to look at war in a more rational way than treat it in an emotive way, as a mere conflict between good and evil.

CONTINUATION OF COLONIALISM THROUGH TRADE

British colonial economic policy, continued well beyond the period of political colonialism. 'Until the last decade or so, many British firms exported principally to former British colonies, the bulk of them developing countries. Such nations are usually not the most demanding and sophisticated buyers of consumer and industrial goods. British goods were frequently accepted out of tradition if not political and economic necessity. Even today, the British trade balance is much more favourable with developing nations than it is with advanced countries such as Germany, Sweden, and Italy'.[50] The sterling balance in favour of India, due to war time purchases made in India during the Second World War, had to be used for imports from Britain during the first two plans. This launched India in a renewed path of importing from Britain and revert back to the colonial legacy in trade Inspite of Britain's decline in industrial stength, India continues to be an important importer from Britain. Large share of U.K. exports to India, consists of non-metalic minerals. In 1997-98, it was 29% of the total imports from the U.K., as against 36% in 1987-88, reaching a high of 42% in 1988-89 and 1993-94'.[51] 'Non-metalic minerals mostly consist of oil, gas oil, fuel oil, aviation oil and motor oil, where the British share does not place the industry in the top fifty industries'.[52] Power generating equipment, industrial machinery, scientific equipment, transport equipment, iron and steel, electrical machinery, constitute other major items of import from the U.K. None of these industries figure in the top fifty U.K. industries in terms of world export share, according to Porter's analysis. In none of these industries, including non-metalic minerals, Britain enjoys competitive advantage, whereas even in the top fifty industries, listed by Porter, Britain's share of export is extremely low compared to the other European countries, U.S.A. and Japan. India continued to be heavily dependent on Britain, for import of machinery, long after it ceased to be a major industrial power. Now, with further decline in the U.K. manufacturing sector and replacing the same with manufactures from the U.S.A. in our import bill, import of services from the U.K. are continuously increasing, filling the ever rising import bill from that country, maintaining the colonial trade legacy. Britain enjoys advantage in some of the consumer-related industries, compared to other major exporting countries. These consumer-related industries are consumer packaged goods, alcoholic beverages, cosmetics and perfume, household furnishings, including porcelain, ceramic housewares and carpets. British Scotch Whiskey has a huge growing market in India among the upper and upper middle classes. Import of non-essential items from Britain on snob value, poses a serious threat to consumer industries in India. Under the liberalised schemes, import of items of snob value has been going up to cater to the tastes of nouveau riche, who are extremely conscious of foreign brands. This is catering to economic irrationality in the name of free choice and is a perversion of logic. When consumer industries in India can produce the same items there is no point in going for foreign brands, for satisfaction of snob value. 'Possession and consumption are the banner which advertises achievement—which proclaims, by the accepted standards of the community, that the possessor is a success'.[53] Britain has strength in insurance, financial services and consultancy. Although, we have nearly a century's experience in the insurance sector, we have opened up this sector to foreign firms in a haste, quite forgetting that insurance is a need-based sector and foreign firms are not exactly geared to the Indian situation. Invisibles like financial and managerial consultancy are being imported through tied British assistance. The question arises, whether such services are required, when we have huge unutilised technical manpower. Moreover, financial and managerial personnel from a different socio-economic milieu, may not be able to appreciate the Indian situation and provide the correct advice. When we have lost faith in ourselves, others are unlikely to bail us out. These type of panic reactions to get out of the managerial and financial crisis through foreign aid, raises serious questions about our ability to manage our own economic affairs and lowers our esteem in the international community.

In spite of such powerful facts and logic, there is a dominant school of economists, who favour globalisation as a solution to the problems of third world countries. According to them, integration with the advanced economies will bring about a miraculous solution to our problems. Free movement of technology and goods and services, according to the theory of comparative advantages will solve our problems. Vijay Joshi and I.M.D. Little in their book 'India's Economic Reforms, 1991-2001', find fault with the reformist Government of India for not opening the economy completely. They are not happy with the Government's policy of merely allowing import of investment goods, where India has developed technology and has capacity for production of such goods. They want import of all sorts of consumer goods, right from potato chips to candyfloss. They think such items are not being imported due to the legacy of Swadeshi movement. 'The still quite prevalent attitude in India to consumption good imports seems to stem from a more general attitude to foreign goods, going back to the Swadeshi movement'.[54] As if the Swadeshi movement was an irrational political movement, without any economic logic. 'It is quite difficult to get people to understand that it is better to import candyfloss if one is not good at making it, and instead to make and export something one is good at making'.[55] This is probably in a lighter vein, but the message is very clear that free import of all sorts of consumer goods should be allowed, since the India-made consumer goods are of lower quality and Indians should cease to produce them. The learned authors find Indian policy-makers lacking in this basic commonsense. While giving such advice, the authors are forgetting the fact that India is already suffering from serious balance of payments deficit and has a huge foreign debt to service. Once suspects that such facile advice is being given to promote British consumer goods in India. There has been fall in demand in both consumer goods and investment goods in British home market. This has made the British economy to look to its traditional market in the erstwhile British colonies.

Earlier, in his more famous work 'A Critique of Welfare Economics' (1960), I.M.D. Little had strongly criticised the desirability of free trade and the need for its imposition. 'The idea that there exists some *a priori* ground for saying that free trade is desirable is the direct result of having a welfare theory which ignores the distribution of real income. It has also led to the aggressive conclusion that Free Trade must be enforced. There is no good sense in which Free Trade is the best possible state of affairs for the world. The fact that the opposite conclusion is traditional in economics may have arisen as a result of the identification of the interest of all countries with those of the most highly developed countries, where economic theory thrives'.[56] Today, when the disparities of income between individuals and nations are at an all time high, free trade will only consolidate and accentuate the same. According to the UNDP Report, 80% of the world's population lives on about 15% of the world's total gross national product.[57] Free trade is not a solution to the problems of poverty and inequality, either between nations or individuals. 'In fact, the evidence collected in the Reality of Aid shows that the global market is not addressing the problems of poverty and in many cases is a process that leads to increased inequalities and undermines the lives and security of wide sectors of population. . . . We face impoverishment in Africa, South Asia, Latin America, but also in industrialised countries: even where GNP has increased the phenomenon of unemployment has not been halted; even where wealth has been augmented, large parts of society are excluded from its benefits'.[58] There is huge disparity of income between the rich and the poor in the most developed nation of the world, U.S.A. Globalisation has not done much for the poor in America, except that it may create globalisation of the poor and dispossessed at a future date. Free trade is possible only between equals. When there are huge economic disparities between nations and individuals, free trade in its present form is hardly possible and has all the potentiality of leading the world to a catastrophy of unprecedented proportion.

Notes and References

1. Wealth of Nations, p. VI.

2-4. Arnold Toynbee, Lectures on the Industrial Revolution in England (1884), pp. 27-32. Quoted in Introduction by Mikulas Teich and Roy Porter in The Industrial Revolution in National Context, pp. 4-10.

5. Lord Milner, 'Reminiscence' in Toynbee, Lectures (1908), p. XXII. Quoted in *Ibid.*, p. 5.

6. Misselden, not only used the term balance of trade but placed the concept in the center of his argument: The Circle of Commerce; or the Balance of Trade . . . . 1623. J.A. Schumpeter, History of Economic Analysis (1986), p. 355, note.

7. J.M. Keynes, The General Theory (1936), p. 333.

8. Schumpeter, p. 351.

9-10. Paul Kennedy, Preparing for the Twenty-first century (1993), pp. 9-11.

11. Wealth of Nations, pp. 280-83.

12. Karl Marx, Capital, Vol. III (1959), p. 331.

13. Wealth of Nations, p. 287.

14. A.G. Frank, Reorient (1998), p. 295, quoted from Jose Arrua, 1991, Colonies as Mercantile Investments in the Political Economy of Merchant Empires.

15. John Gallaghar and Ronald Robinson, The Imperialism of Free Trade (1953), p. 58

16. Ritortus, The Imperialism of British Trade, Contemporary Review LXXVI (1899) from P.J. Cain and M. Harrison Edited, Imperialism (Vol. I), p. 77.

17. R.C. Dutt, Economic History of British India, Victorian Rule, p. 151.

18-19. Jacques Gernet, A History of Chinese Civilization, p. 536.

20-21. Brian Inglis, The Forbidden Game, p. 77.

22. Dadabhai Naoroji, Poverty and Un-British Rule in India, p. 201.

23-24. Gernet, pp. 545-46.

25. Babbage Charles, On the Economy of Machinery and Manufacture (1835), pp. 1-4.

26. Montgomery Martin, Eastern India (London, 1838), Vol. III, Introduction.

27. R.C. Dutt, Economic History of British India, Early British Rule, pp. 293-98.
28. *Ibid.*, p. 293.
29. *Ibid.*, pp. 288-89.
30. *Ibid.*, pp. 299-302.
31. Friedrich List, The National System of Political Autonomy (1885), p. 42.
32. Toynbee, pp. 6-7.
33. Ritortus, p. 105.
34. I.G. Patel, Glimpses of Indian Economic Policy, p. 53. According to Patel, the Americans supported the British in trying to teach the Indians a lesson. British were still under the impression that they were masters of India.
35. Philip Oppenheim, Trade Wars, p. 100. Oppenheim mocks at countries like India and Brazil, trying to join the steel producers club, which according to him is the monopoly of developed nations.
36. Francois Crouzet, France, p. 46.
37. *Ibid.*, p. 41.
38. Sidney Pollard, Peaceful Conquest, p. 184.
39. Crouzet, p. 49.
40. Gallagher and Robinson, p. 58.
41. Pollard, p. 138.
42. Daniel Headrick, Tools of Empire, p. 6. Ref. Henri Brunschwig, French Colonialism, 1871-1914: Myths and Realities (1966).
43. Charles Gide, Political Economy, p. 93.
44. New Encyclopaedia Britannica, Vol. 3, p. 534.
45. WM. Roger Louis, The Robinson and Gallagher Controversy, p. 34.
46. Sidney Pollard, The Industrial Revolution—an overview, in Mikulas Teich and Roy Porter, p. 382.
47. *Ibid.*, p. 382.
48. *Ibid.*, p. 384.
49. Edward Marz, Joseph Schumpeter, p. 68.
50. Michael E. Porter, The Competitive Advantage of Nations, p. 501.
51. John L. Seitz, Global Issues, Table 1.
52. Porter, p. 484.
53. J.K. Galbraith's Introduction in Thorstein Veblen, The Theory of the Leisure Class, p. XVII.

54-55. Vijay Joshi and I.M.D. Little, India's Economic Reforms, 1991-2001 (1999), pp. 67-70.

56. I.M.D. Little, A Critique of Welfare Economics (1960), p. 257.
57. The Reality of Aid (1997), p. 6, box.
58. *Ibid.*, p. 3, Introduction.

4

Free Trade: No Panacea for Development of Indian Economy

Economic theories are not universal, but product of the social circumstances. Any attempt to universalise the same is to disregard the historical method of analysis and to build up theories by disregarding historical facts. Economic theories have been always worked out to suit national interests and not *vice-versa*. Free-trade argument, as developed in Britain in the nineteenth century is a product of the British Industrial Revolution. The remarkable success of British industrial development, which was unprecedented in economic history and which had broken the shackles on productive forces, had to be given a theoretical basis and what can be better than attribute it to British liberalism, from which flows the argument of free trade. We have already seen the close linkage between British Industrial Revolution and British colonialism. The historical method of economic analysis would have exposed this close linkage and the exploitative nature of this unique phenomenon of economic development, which dazzled the world, particularly the European world, in the second half of the nineteenth century. A theoretical justification will have to be built-up for this unique phenomenon to show the world, how British liberalism could cause economic miracles, while other conservative regimes with their outdated peasantry and production system were lagging behind. 'It was easy to attribute that impressive sequence of undeniable success (Industrial Revolution) to the policy of economic liberalism as its main or even only cause'[1] Free trade was a corollary of British liberalism, which unleashed the productive forces. The concept of British free trade was designed for continuance of British industrial monopoly, particularly when an erstwhile British colony like U.S.A. with its vast resources was in the process of industrial development and other European countries had embarked on industrialisation. According to this theory, France will be reduced to producing frivolous items like wines and silken wires, whereas the monopoly of manufacturing machinery and cotton goods remains with England. 'France will produce only fine wines, ladies hats and silk goods; England, machinery and cotton goods; China, tea; Australia, wool; Russia, wheat; Switzerland, cheeses and clocks; Greece, raisins.'[2]

LIMITATIONS OF FREE TRADE

According to the theory of free trade and globalisation, each country must produce what it is capable of and should not encroach on the others territory. Any country, trying to industrialise will do so, as the subsidiary of the dominant industrial power. If France is reduced to this state of industrialisation during the first decade of the twentieth century, what would be the position of India in this world trade scenario? While, talking of free trade, British free trade economists did not talk of countries like India, which looked to be a perpetual colony of exploitation. Free trade was held up as an ideal, as an abstraction, for the welfare of mankind, which meant in real terms the welfare of the dominant country. Free trade only encourages hegemonism, as Britain was the main hegemonic power in the nineteenth and early twentieth century. This role has been taken up after World War II by the United States of America in a greater way. After the collapse of the colonial system, 'Again the main thrust of economic expansion is directed today towards industrially advanced countries such as Canada, Britain and continental Europe, while investment in the underdeveloped regions is mainly aimed at increasing production of raw material, food and oil'.[3] Free trade is a throw back on Darwinism, the theory of survival of the fittest. If applied to the nations, it has a dangerous connotation, in which only economically powerful nations have a right to survive. This is colonialism at its worst. 'An ideal such as this (free trade), if it could be realised, would mean the demoralisation of all countries, and consequently of the whole human race; for the race has no existence of its own apart from the nations which constitute it'. Then again, 'We can understand a convinced Darwinian sacrificing the individual for the good of the race, but we can hardly expect a country to let itself be sacrificed for the good of humanity. It would be the more absurd, as there is so much more at stake than mere commercial superiority. A nation has another role to play in this world than the simple economic one of producer'.[4] These arguments are as much valid today, as when they were written in the first decade of the twentieth century.

When English economists and government talked of free trade, it was not with reference to the colonies, which were for the economic development of the colonist country. 'Between England and her possessions real Free Trade is impossible. The possessions are built-up by and dependent on English capital. The trade between them, far from being free, is more or less mortgaged or pawned to it. The trade, therefore, is fettered by the necessity of paying profits and interest to English capital'.[5] The colonies were outside the British free trade zone and mortgaged to British capital. With such vast economic empire and the economic power that goes with it, free trade was a sound policy to keep the developing countries in the continent, U.S.A. and Japan at bay.

Britain had built-up her economic supremacy through a policy of protectionism and active state participation. 'In 1815, Britain was still a protectionist power and the state played an important role in directing foreign trade and overseas expansion. Tariff protection was extended not only to agriculture but also to Britain's growing manufacturing industries'. Once Britain became the most advanced industrial nation, a policy of free trade was necessary to maintain her industrial supremacy. 'It was useful for Britain to abandon protection and persuade others to do the same because, given Britain's growing technological lead, free trade would ensure that Britain's rivals did not develop in the same way and would remain dependent primary producers'. After establishing full economic control over the colonies, Britain wanted to outdo its rivals by following a policy of free trade imperialism and both formal and informal empire. 'If we are to make full sense of Britain's emergent policy of free trade imperialism in the 1840s it has to be recognised that it was intended principally as a means to eliminate the burgeoning industrial strength of the U.S.A. and Western Europe and to help maintain Britain's position as the dominant world power'.[6]

Toynbee was one of the first to question the hypocracy of free trade theory, *vis-a-vis* policy.

'Free trade is a sound policy, no doubt, for England, and for all nations at a certain stage of development; but it is open to any one to say that free trade is only good under certain conditions. No English Economists, it is true, has dared to say this'.[7] When Great Britain started a movement for free trade in the mid-nineteenth century to capture the American market, the United States remained firmly outside the free trade movement. England's concept of free trade was a very limited concept, as sarcastically put by Gide in his 'Cours D' Economie Poltique. 'In England, however, the ideas of Adam Smith had borne fruit, England, indeed, had never been very protectionist, except in so far as to secure her maritime trade and the monopoly with her colonies'. The American view on Britain's advocacy of free trade is summed up by General Grant, the hero of American Civil war and the eighteenth President of the United States. 'In 1879 General Grant, Ex-President of the United States, at a reception in Manchester, where it was hoped to convert him to Free Trade, pointed out ironically that England had followed the protectionist policy for two hundred years, but she had pushed it to an extreme and had found advantage in so doing; that it was undoubtedly to that system that she owed her industrial power; that after these two hundred years were over, England had thought fit to adopt Free Trade because she could get nothing more out of protection'.[8]

British concept of free trade was one of maintaining her world-wide monopoly, in trade, based on colonial imperialism. 'Free trade became attractive for Britain when British control over and economic penetration of India was enlarged after 1815 and the evolving ideas of liberality of commerce in Britain did contain a strong imperialist element, though economic hegemony rather than political control became the centre for discussion.'[9] When Britain found that towards the end of the nineteenth century, other European powers are embarking on a colonial policy, they responded by acquiring four million square miles of foreign territory. 'Barrat Brown calls the expansion of the British Empire after 1880 'truly amazing'. In a period of less than 20 years, 4 million square miles were annexed, a territory twice as large as the Indian possession'. 'As Michael Barratt Brown shows, the new imperialist policy was a suitable means of defending Britain's world-wide free trade. 'When Britain's world monopoly was challenged, the actual control of territory became increasingly important, to anticipate the moves of the rivals'.[10] In the race for colonies, to which the other European nations joined belatedly towards the last decades of the nineteenth century, 'Britain forced through this division (of colonies in the agreements concluded in the 1890) so favourable to its capital interests at a time when it had virtually lost the industrial dominance it had held for decades'. According to some German authors like Hilferding, writing before the outbreak of World War-I, this was a situation heading towards a violent solution. (Hilferding, Finanzkapital)'[11]

U.S. POLICY OF FREE INTERNAL TRADE AND REGULATED FOREIGN TRADE

While Britain was propagating a free trade policy in the second half of the nineteenth century, after gaining economic superiority over other countries, the United States remained firmly outside the free trade movement. The country, which was not allowed to "make even a horseshoe" by its colonial master, Britain, revolted against the ex-colonial country by becoming completely protectionist. 'The United

States had always been protectionist in doctrine as well as in fact, one of the principal causes of its revolt against the mother-country being that it was not allowed to make even a "horse-shoe." It was only natural then that its first thought should be to reconquer its industrial autonomy'.[12] Protective duties imposed on the imports to the United States, which were moderate to start-off, gradually became heavier and heavier, and some new reason was cited each time the duties went up. 'First, it was to protect the infant industries this was List's system; after 1866, it was to pay the costs of the Civil War'. When this reason fell through, 'the reason thereafter alleged for maintaining the duties was to defend the high prices and high wages of America against the low prices and low wages of Europe. The duties amounted on an average to 57%, but in case of some goods they were much higher. There was however, perfect free trade between the States within the 'United States'. 'It must however, be remembered that the United States is a Union of forty-eight States some of which are as large as France and between them there is perfect free trade'.[13] Thus, while the United States practiced a protectionist policy as regards foreign countries, free movement of goods and services within the country built-up its manufacturing and agricultural potential. The pre-eminent position of the United States as an agricultural and industrial power in the twentieth century, was built-up on inland trade and commerce. This bears ample testimony to the fact that at the initial stage of development, a country of the size of United States could reach its full economic potential through a policy of protectionism as regards foreign trade. While an island country like Britain could become an economic giant through captive markets and captive sources of supply of raw materials, brought about by a colonial policy, which increased its size hundred-fold.

The 'infant industries' argument was taken up in the United States of America by Alexander Hamilton, Secretary of the Treasury in his Report on Manufacture, submitted to the Congress in 1791. In this report, he outlined a policy of helping the development of infant industries through various protective laws. An elaborate system of incentives subsidies was built-up, under Hamiltonian principles to develop the industrial structure of the country. 'Hamilton attached much greater importance to bounties and premiums to be granted directly to the various branches of industries, and insisted on the adoption of them either exclusively or conjointly with the customs duties'.[14] He advocated the view that a strong manufacturing base is basic to the economic integration of the various States of the Union and the policy of the federal Government should be directed to that purpose. Hamilton's report formed the basis of the protective policies followed by the United States till the First World War, to develop its industrial and agricultural strength. This strong economic bond between the States of the Union, was based on the economic strength of the states, built-up through federal laws against any foreign competition. It was the protective policy pursued by the federal Government of the United States on the Hamiltonian policies which led to the economic and political integration of the states, which constitute the United States of America. 'Hamilton's most enduring monument was the Union, for much of it rested on his ideas'.[15] Thus, we can see that protectionism played a major part in building up the United States as an economic giant. Had the United States followed a free trade policy at that time, her infant industries would not have been able to compete with the well-developed industries of Great Britain. It may be mentioned here that in writing his famous report on manufacture, Hamilton made selective use of Adam Smith's Wealth of Nations, like where Adam Smith has supported the Act of Navigation, enacted by Cromwell as the wisest of all the commercial regulations of England. In fact, it was to Cromwell's Navigation Act, a most protective legislation against imports and foreign shipping, on which the commercial and maritime greatness of England depended. It was only after abolition of corn law in 1846 that this highly protective legislation was abolished. Thus till 1850, Britain followed an active policy of protection in agriculture, manufacturing and shipping.

On the theoretical side greatest influence on the United States policy was of Carey and List, the two greatest theorists on the side of protection. Henry C. Carey (1793-1879), 'the most significant figure in that period's (1790-1870) American economics, conceived of the United States as a world unto itself' in his grand vision, with a balanced and harmonious economy of agricultural, manufacturing and commercial interests, based on protectionism. Carey came in for great deal of criticism from English free traders. Most of Carey's critics were more or less well-trained economists. They had no difficulty in showing that Carey's theory was no good at all. And, on the strength of this, they condemned his message without making it clear and presumably without being aware of the fact—that the essentials of this message were beyond the range of theoretical analysis'.[16] Schumpeter finds that both English free traders and Carey argued from their respective national standpoints and advocated policies that suited some group interests better than others. Carey's prescriptions found little merit with the British School of Economists, because both based their arguments from a comprehensive, social and political vision relevant to their countries. As the national interests differed, so also their vision and prescription for their countries. The main argument of the English free traders was that the theoretical basis for Carey's prescriptions, was inadequate. Schumpeter says, 'Had Carey used the existing analytic tool on the data for the United States, he could have argued that English views on many economic problems did not apply to American conditions and had to be modified by introducing other factual assumption'.[17]

There are no universal laws in economics, as in other social sciences. As Arnold Toynbee says in the context of free trade. 'The Historical method is also of value because it makes us see where economic laws and precepts are relative. The old economists were wont to speak as if these laws and precepts were universal'.[18] 'Comte was one of the first to recognize this truth, and it was from him that Mill learned that 'the deductive science of society will not lay down a theorem ascertaining in a universal manner the effect of any cause, but will rather teach us how to frame the proper theorem for the circumstances of any given case. It will not give the laws of society in general, but the means of determining the phenomena of any given society from the particular elements or data of that society'.[19] Free trade was important for trade and commerce of Britain in the nineteenth century after Britain had developed its manufacturing strength much ahead of other European countries and increased its geographical area hundred-fold. Britain could turn itself into the workshop of the world by a policy of selected protectionism and aggressive colonialism. When Britain was following aggressive free trade policy in the nineteenth century, because it suited the country's stage of development at that period, English Economists built-up a powerful free trade school based on the theory of comparative costs from a selective reading of Adam Smith, who was no free trader in the sense he has been portrayed. For him, free trade was an ideal to be pursued between equals and not between un-equals. Comparative advantage, which Adam Smith talked about, was natural comparative advantage and not advantage built-up through centuries of protection. After building up a powerful theoretical framework in favour of free trade, English Economists tried to universalise it. There was no English Economist who dared to oppose their view. Economists and public men in other countries, who opposed their view, had to face their odium and was portrayed in a manner, which lowered their esteem in academic circles. Even then, such individuals came up with policy prescriptions for their country, based on their vision for their country, built-up on a comprehensive economic, social and political understanding.

Let us contrast the situation in Brazil—geographically the biggest country in South America and the fifth largest country in the world, next to the U.S.A. It had huge natural resources with agricultural as well as industrial potential. It achieved independence from colonial rule of Portugal in 1822, whereas U.S.A. achieved independence in 1789. In spite of this, history of economic development of these two countries has been diametrically opposite. Brazil's economic development has been one of boom—and bust. Mainly due to its dependence on primary products like coffee and rubber, which have been subject to large scale international market fluctuations, both due to economic and political reasons. The different pattern of development in U.S.A. and Brazil can be attributed to the quality of leadership in these two countries.

Whereas, in Brazil the leadership was feudal, in U.S.A. the leadership was progressive. 'This difference is plainly evident in the disparity between the two interpreters of the ideals of the ruling classes in the respective countries, Alexander Hamilton and Viscount of Cairu. But Hamilton became the champion of a process of industrialisation which was not well understood by the American small farmer class, and advocated and promoted a bold and positive governmental policy of direct incentives to industry and not merely passive measures of a protectionist nature, whereas Cairu superstitiously believed in the "invisible hand" and repeated *laissez faire, laisse passer, laissez vendre.*'[20]

The colonial background of both these countries had also much to do with their different pattern of development. Whereas, leadership in Brazil was from the feudal, agrarian, slave owing class; the leadership in U.S.A. was taken by those who had witnessed the industrial revolution in Europe and replicated the same pattern of industrial development in their new country. It is no wonder that Alexander Hamilton, second generation immigrant from Scotland and a later contemporary of Adam Smith, could interpret his 'Wealth of Nations', in the same selective manner for ushering in American industrial development, as the English had done for their country. Cairu in Brazil could only understand the letter of 'Wealth of Nations' and not its spirit. A literal interpretation of Adam Smith, landed Brazil in the boom-bust category of economic development, from which it is yet to recover. 'As producers of colonial articles, despite being faced by a world shut-off on account of 'colonial policies', our country became a champion of economic liberalism on the American continent.'[21] Although both U.S.A. and Brazil were colonies of European countries, there were basic differences in the pattern of their colonisation. While U.S.A. was a colony of emigration; Brazil was basically a colony of exploitation. Colonies of emigration consisted of people of same race and culture as the colonising country and as such used the same method of industrialisation—the mercantilist policy of protection was followed in the U.S.A., as in Britain. To overcome its small size and lack of resources, Britain had resorted to large-scale colonisation. The European immigrants in the U.S.A. colonised over a huge geographical area rich in resources and pushed the natives to the background. The second phase of industrialisation was development of a huge net-work of informal empire in different parts of the world, particularly Central and South America.

GERMAN UNIFICATION

Germany, which consisted of number of States, was economically integrated by Customs Union (Zollverein). Schumpeter calls this customs union the embryo of German national unity. Friedrich List (1789-1846), was one of the pioneers of a free trade movement within the German States, which abolished customs dues for movement of good and services and established a customs union, which reunified Germany. Schumpeter writes, 'what this association means to Germans cannot be understood by members of those fortunate nations for which the right to national existence and national ambitions is a matter of course. It means that List, like all those whose names are associated with that long and painful struggle, is a national hero'. 'List saw a nation that struggled in the fetters imposed by a miserable immediate past, but he also saw all its economic potentialities. The national future, therefore, was the real object of his thought, the present was nothing but a state of transition. He realised that, in an essentially transitional state of this kind, policies lose their meaning when they are geared to the task of administering an existing set of conditions that is visualised as substantially permanent. Furthermore, he realised (like Soden) that emphasis upon the national future modifies welfare considerations of the present. This he expressed by his doctrine of productive forces that in his system hold place of honour as compared with the consumer goods that can be made available at a given level of the productive forces'. 'Finally, as regards his best known contribution to the education of German public opinion on economic policy, the infant industry argument, this is clearly Hamiltonian and part of the economic wisdom that List imbibed during his stay in the United States. He was a great patriot, a brilliant Journalist with definite purpose, and an able Economist who co-ordinated well whatever seemed useful for implementing his vision. Is this not enough?'[22]

Carey and List were two great Economists, who had the greatest influence in their countries during a crucial stage in their development. They went beyond the theoretical framework laid down on the British experience and charted an economic course for their countries, which brought about not only economic integration, but also political and social integration. They could break out of the narrow academic boundaries laid down by the theoreticians, and focus their vision based on a long-term economic and social outlook for their country. It is not that either List or Carey was short on scientific analysis but their prescriptions were based on their national stand points, as those of English free traders. It is not that Carey built-up his economic policy prescriptions on a theoretical vacuum. He drew upon Adam Smith and English and French sources, but he adopted them to the genius of his country. Similarly, List's theory of stages of economic development—hunting, agriculture, agriculture plus manufacture, agriculture and manufacture plus commerce, met with criticism from theoreticians like Karl Knies. Even Schumpeter, in spite of his eulogy to List did not find much merit in it. However, the former admitted that List used this 'as a simple expository device for impressing upon beginners (or the public) the lesson that economic policy has to do with changing economic structures and therefore cannot consist of a set of unchanging recipes'.[23] These thinkers went beyond the class room and could educate the public and policy-makers.

Had Germany followed the economic logic of comparative advantage, as propounded by English economists, Germany would have been a poor agricultural country and not an industrial power threatening to dislodge Britain from its industrial pre-eminence. Citing the case of South America's industrial beginning, Landes says that they followed the rational economic policy of buying their machinery from Europe or the United States. No doubt, industrialisation was a failure, in spite of following the best economic logic. 'It was all very rational: comparative advantage made it easier and cheaper to buy abroad. The trouble with such rationality is that today's good sense may be tomorrow's mistake. Development is long; logic, short. Economic theory is static, based on conditions of the day. The process is dynamic, building on today's abstinence to tomorrow's abundance. Some things will never happen if one does not try to make them happen. If the German's had listen to John Bowring . . . . that British economic traveller extraordinary lamented that the foolish German's wanted to make iron and steel instead of sticking to wheat and rye and buying their manufactures from Britain. Had they heeded him, they would have pleased the economists and replaced Portugal, with its wine, cork, and olive oil, as the very model of a rational economy. They would also have ended up a lot poorer'.[24]

ECONOMIC PURISTS FROWN ON INDIA'S DEVELOPMENT STRATEGY

India's industrialisation, particularly the development of steel industries in the public sector was not favoured by the economic purists. Edward S. Mason writes in 1967, 'The heavy industrial complex which began to take shape some ten years ago provides its own justification for investment funds and grows in an enclave with little connection with the rest of the Indian economy . . . . But to date this industrial complex has affected very little the rest of Indian economic activity'.[25] This is a very superficial view of the situation. A modernised economic structure can only be built on the infrastructural support of core industries like iron and steel. The maintenance and development of the railway system could not have been possible without steel industries. Development activities like road construction, building of bridges and dams, construction of buildings, all require steel. Even the humble bicycle, the universal mode of transport in India, requires steel. Agricultural implements require steel for their manufacture. It is also necessary to build machinery to sustain this development, instead of depending on import of machinery in perpetuity. Mason admits that economics is unable to answer the question, whether such expenditure represents an optimal allocation of resources. 'Whether this has represented an optimal allocation of development expenditures in India, I do not know, and I doubt very much whether any techniques of economic analysis, including linear programming would give us the answer'.[26]

India's earlier economic strength was built-upon a well developed system of inland trade and commerce. 'The great extent of Indostan, too, rendered the home market of that country very great, and sufficient to support a great variety of manufacturers'. According to Adam Smith, in India, 'the confinement of the foreign market was in some measure compensated by the conveniency of many inland naviagations, which opened, in the most advantageous manner, the whole extent of the home market to every part of the produce of every different district'.[27] With the onset of colonial pattern of economy form the later half of the eighteenth century, internal trade within India started getting less and less attention. The decline of river trade and coastal trade, which were important means of commerce within the country, also contributed to this. Internal trade has not been given its due importance during the entire colonial period. This imbalance was hardly corrected after independence and no serious effort was made to systematically develop internal trade, to bring about the economic integration of the country.

The economic strength of a country like India, lies in a well-developed system of internal trade, unlike the island nations and smaller countries, whose examples are being regularly quoted. In fact, economic integration and political integration go hand in hand. We have seen it in the case of U.S.A. and Germany. Even, after independence, little steps were taken to economically integrate different regions of the country through inland trade. Had greater attention been given to the development of internal trade within the country, economy of the country would have been more self-reliant. Economic integration of different regions of the country, would have ensured a stronger economy. The plethora of rules and regulations, which restrict inter-state movement of commodities, should be further simplified. The system of one point taxation needs to be introduced to facilitate inter-state movement of commodities. Areas with good agricultural potential need not be turned into industrial use, with proper development of marketing network.

Rightly G.K. Gokhale held List's economic prescriptions more relevant to India than those of British economists who always looked at this country from the colonial standpoint. 'The German Economist—List whose work on political economy is the best that Indian students can consult, explains how the state can help an old-world agricultural country, suddenly brought within the circle of the world's competition, to build-up a new system of industries'.[28] It is unfortunate that Indian economists chose to follow the Anglo-Saxon school of economics, instead of the continental or even the American school of thought at this juncture. The former was the dominant school of thought in post-independence India, followed by Anglo-American schools of thought. As Britain ceased to be a dominant world power, it followed the American economic thinking, which was closer to its own interests. Britain had started playing a second fiddle to America *vis-a-vis* Europe and U.S.S.R. After Second World War, U.S.A. has become the main hegemonistic power in world affairs, succeeding Britain. Hegemonism, also includes intellectual hegemonism.

Gokhale had this to say about British policy of changing economic prescriptions in his Lecture series in Lucknow on February 1907, 'England's own policy for centuries had been that of protection, and by that policy she had built-up her vast industrial system. But about sixty years ago, after protection had done its work, she decided to give up the old policy and adopt Free Trade, mainly to set right the abuses to which protection had given rise',[29] *vis-a-vis* British economic interests. As the old British colony of the U.S.A., Germany (after unification) and other European countries were becoming protectionist, British interests relating to export of manufactured commodities were affected. But India, which was fully under British rule, had to suffer the full brunt of her policy of free trade, resulting in the destruction of her industrial structure. India was not allowed to adjust her industrial economy to the factory age to which she was exposed by the British practice of turning India into a model of free trade for export of British manufactures and import of Indian raw materials. This turned India into a purely agricultural country. The 'Infant Industry' argument was not applied to India and it had to face competition from a superior manufacturing power. As England had developed her manufacturing power to a much superior level than the other European powers, which were passing through their own version of Industrial Revolution and the U.S.A. was yet to develop her own industrial potential, there was no fear of any competition. England, naturally found free trade beneficial, *vis-a-vis* India under such circumstances.

CHANGE IN POLICY IN INDIA

There was a somersault in Government of India's economic policy in the 1990s. Government of India wet out of its way to admit that the policy of protection followed by it till the 1980s was a wrong one. There was nobody in the Indian situation like Hamilton or General Grant in the U.S.A. or academics like Carey and List in the U.S.A. and Germany to stand up for the policy of protectionism, which had been followed by all the developed countries in the initial stages to build-up their economic strength. Great Britain was the first country to be protectionist, followed by the U.S.A., Germany and other European countries. In recent times, Japan's economic strength was built-up not on free trade, but on a subtle system of protection. The U.S. Government Report of 1989 on Foreign Trade Barriers blacklisted Japan, India and Brazil for restrictive trade practices. Government of India publicly admitted to the wrong policy of protecting new indigenous industries, and to atone for it took hurried steps 'To reduce extra-ordinarily high protection given to indigenous industries, the *ad-valorem* rate of basic plus auxiliary duties of customs were reduced to a maximum of 150 per cent'.[30] This was further reduced to a maximum of 50 per cent by March 1995. Quantitive restrictions on imports have been removed to a level of 95 per cent of tariff lines in pursuance of Article XI of GATT. Tariff lines have been removed on 2714 items, as notified by WTO. Inspite of such liberalisation, India has not been able to win the favour of America or the developed countries. WTO Secretariat initiated large number of anti-dumping investigations against India on the complaints of developed countries. Economic survey of 2000-01 cites without comments. 'The semi-annual reports on anti-dumping put out be the WTO Secretariat reveal that 134 anti-dumping investigations were initiated during the first half of 2001 as against 93 in the corresponding period of last year. A majority of these investigations (88 in all) were initiated by developed countries, with China, Korea, Taiwan and India topping the list of countries subjected to such investigations. Base metals (iron, steel, aluminum), plastics and textiles were the most affected sectors'.[31] There is thus a constant cold war in the trade front with the developed countries using the provisions of WTO agreements against particular developing countries.

This war is further likely to intensify with recession in the American economy, with huge potentiality of global recession. Trade and Development Report, 2001 of the United Nations, Conference on the Trade and Development, Geneva says, 'The United States slow down is likely to have a damaging impact on the developing world, particularly if it is not offset by strong growth in other OECD economies'. According to this report, the economy of the United Kingdom, 'looks set to mirror that in the United States'.[32] As regards, other OECD countries, the report says, 'Economic integration between these two industrial blocs appears to be more significant than a casual discussion of trade ratios might suggest. According to recent estimates, the elasticity of euro-area growth with respect to the United States is as high as 0.4'.[33] The economic recession in the U.S.A. is bound to have its repercussions on the OECD countries. As the dollar weakens, the European currencies will have to be substantially devalued to maintain its export competitiveness. The U.N. report advises the European countries to bolster global demand to maintain its growth, instead of unduly relying on U.S. for export-related growth. This is an unlikely scenario and most of the Asian countries depending on export-led growth to the U.S.A. will suffer from recession and are unlikely to bolster European export.

India's increasing reliance on information and communication technology to cater to foreign demand, makes

India extremely vulnerable to recession in the U.S.A. This sector in the U.S. economy has already reached saturation point and carries considerable excess capacity, according to the UNCTAD report, 2001. The report says, 'The rate of increase in new orders received from the U.S. for electronic goods had already declined by half in October 2000. The outlook is for further decline as inventories in the U.S. continue to increases, and there were clear signs of declining semi-conductor prices in early 2001'.[34] Weakening of dollar, will require further devaluation of the rupee to maintain competitiveness in trade with the U.S.A. and European bloc. Further weakening of the rupee will considerably under value the Indian exports, while increasing the cost of imports. India will have to export much more to remain at the same level. This will certainly be at the cost of Indian consumers, many of whom will be squeezed out of the market. Moreover, export level can be maintained by considerable increase in imports, as number of components in this Industry are imported. With further weakening of the rupee, imports will become costlier and as the trend shows, the U.S. and OECD countries will themselves go in for export-related growth in a big way. U.S.A. and the European Union countries will create greater pressure on the developing countries of Asia, particularly India, to import from the developed West much more than they export. Thus, the balance of payment position of the Asiatic countries, particularly India will further deteriorate. With the concentration of nearly half of Indian exports to the developed countries, of which 20% going to the United States, the export position may suffer further set-back. There will be greater pressure on India and other South Asian countries to increase their imports from the developed world.

IMF FAVOURS THE DEVELOPED COUNTRIES

The world economic scenario is all set for intense trade war, in which WTO, with its disproportionate weightage in favour of developed countries, will pay a crucial role in tilting the economic balance further in favour of the developed world. The adverse balance of payments position, along with huge external debt will push India and most of the South Asian countries to the IMF for bail out packages, as is happening to Brazil and other South American countries. While analyzing the stringent IMF bail out packages for Asian countries, Martin Feldstein, Professor of Economics at Harvad University and President of the U.S. National Bureau of Economic, Research, says, 'The IMF should eschew the temptation to use currency crises as an opportunity to force fundamental structural and institutional reforms on countries . . . . It should strongly resist the pressure from the United States, Japan, and other major countries to make their trade and investment agenda part of the IMF funding conditions'.[35] Dictating legitimate governments how to manage their economic and political affairs, when they are at their weakest, is tantamount to arrogating the sovereignty of independent countries by the IMF and World Bank. The fact that IMF waits till the country's balance of payments and external debt situation reaches crisis situation is a clear indicator that IMF acts as a pressure body to impose conditions favourable to its major creditor countries on the borrowing countries. Feldstein advises, 'The IMF should work with countries that have not yet reached a currency crisis. If the fund is seen more as a client-focused and supportive organisation than as the imposer of painful contractions and radical economic reforms, it is likely to find that countries will be more willing to invite its assistance when it can be most helpful'. While discussing the IMF loan package for Korea, Feldstein points out, 'Several features of the IMF plan are replays of the policies that Japan and the United States have long been trying to get Korea to adopt. These included accelerating the previously agreed upon reductions of trade barriers to specific Japanese products and opening capital markets so that foreign investors can have majority ownership of Korean firms, engage in hostile take overs opposed by local management, and expand direct participation in banking and other financial services'.[36]

George Soros, in his book, 'The Crisis of Global Capitalism,' on the South East Asian crisis had discussed the 'asymmetry in the way the IMF has treated lenders and borrowers . . . . The IMF imposes conditions on a country in trouble. It should also impose conditions on the creditors, particularly when the trouble is caused by the private sector (as in the case of the Asian countries)'.[37] Soros, who has practical knowledge of international financial system and is one of the leaders of the system, says while discussing the failure of the IMF in playing a positive role in a financial crisis. 'Finally the IMF is controlled by the countries at the center of the capitalist system; it would go against the national interests of the controlling shareholders if the IMF penalised the lenders. Yet that is exactly what is needed to make the system stable'.[38] The debtor countries were dealt with more severely by the IMF and the entire burden of mismanaging international financial market by imprudent short-term lending when long-term lending was required, was passed on the debtors, when the burden should have been equally shared by both the parties to the transaction. As Soros says, 'on the other hand, the failure to tackle the debt problem resulted in currency overshoots and punitive interest rates that rendered the borrowers insolvent and plunged the counties concerned into deep depression. Obviously, there is a systemic problem here, and the IMF is part of the problem, not part of the solution'.[39] The IMF should have tackled the problem through conversion of debt-to-equity, which would have led to both lender and debtor sharing the burden of the crisis equitably.

By passing on the burden of the crisis entirely to the debtor countries a dangerous precedent has been created, when the entire burden of stock market collapse, bankruptcies and unemployment has been passed to the debtor countries. The IMF has taken upon itself the task of refereeing both the financial and political system of debtor countries. This is a clear infringement of the sovereignty of individual countries, which is guaranteed by the U.N. charter. The argument that IMF is clearing the financial and political architecture of the debtor countries does not hold good, as the same yard-stick is not applied to the lenders, who have lent irresponsibly in unviable projects or projects requiring long gestation period. In the case of Asian countries, the IMF took no steps to reschedule the loans to longer term, lower yielding instruments. Had this been done 'This would inflict big losses on speculators and imprudent bank lenders',[40] in the loaning countries. IMF's dual standard in dealing with countries, stands out very clearly and countries like India should be very careful in their borrowings not to be drawn to the clutches of the IMF to surrender their independence.

C. Fred Bergsten, Director of the Institute for International Economics and former Assistant Secretary of the Treasury (1977-81) and Assistant for International Economic Affairs to the National Security Council (1969-71) in his article, 'America's two-front Economic Conflict,' says, 'The image of IMF Managing Director Michel Camdessus dictating terms to Indonesian President Suharto is bitterly seared into Asian memories, especially now that prominent Western economists argue that IMF programs actually made the crisis worse and point to how Malaysia has recovered effectively without IMF assistance'.[41] The article fears that East Asian countries may develop their own trade bloc and discriminate against U.S. exports, reducing the same substantially. This is a timely warning, but the U.S. and Western hegemonism over Asia may assert in other ways. As long as the U.S. and the West maintain technological monopoly, there is very little fear of South-East Asian countries, which had attempted to develop their economy on export-led growth, coming out of the economic grip of the West. In another article, titled 'Asia's Bad Old Ways', in the same issue of Foreign Affairs, Hilton L. Root, Director of Global Studies for the Milken Institute, talks of 'crony capitalism'[42] of Japan and other East and Southeast Asian countries. Corruption in high places has struck a responsive chord, both internationally and domestically. This has given IMF and the Western bloc a good opportunity to meddle in the internal affairs of the client countries. It was not that corruption has taken place suddenly. This has been going on for years and has been long tolerated as a part of the so-called booming market economy. Here is what George Soros says, 'I had been fully aware of the corruption of the Suharto regime, and I insisted on selling our share in an Indonesian power plant in which Suharto family members had a financial interest purely because I did not want to be associated with them'.[43]

Economic development without development of

supporting institutional framework, is apt to create aberration in the system. In the absence of formal institutions controlling the system, informal networking develops leading to cronyism. Firms in Japan and South Korea have formed 'internal networks to take direct control over their suppliers and distribution systems. Thus, Japan's keiretsu and South Korea's chaebol (business groupings) have established vertical ties with small-scale domestic producers and horizontal ties with one another'.[44] Whereas Japanese and South Korean business has been working on informal networking, rest of the South. East Asian countries like Thailand, Indonesia and the Philippines have 'gravitated towards a distinctive trading style based on personal relationships—in other words, crony capitalism'.[45] These informal business networks have their strength and weakness. While the business in these countries would not have prospered without these extensive and effective personal networks, the system lacks transparency. According to Root, transparency is dangerous in many of the Southeast Asian nations, where 'firms that disclose profits can still be subject to arbitrary Government audits and expropriation'.[46] He classifies these as predatory or weak states, which discourage industrial development. We have seen this in India too, where profit-making industries have been frequently penalised and loss-making units subsidised through BIFR packages. Development of proper institutional framework and not panic reactions from the Government machinery is essential for healthy industrial development.

Root advocates globalisation as a solution to dismantling the informal networks. This is however wishful thinking, as globalisation is unlikely to be successful, unless there is supporting international legal structure to ensure impartiality in economic interaction between nations. As things stand today, development of an impartial framework of international economic law is a far cry. There is irreconcilable difference of interest amongst nations and between different interest groups within nations. Unless, there is communality of interests between nations, a satisfactory international legal system to regulate the affairs of nations cannot evolve. It is also naïve to assume that developed countries have evolved any reasonably fool-proof legal structure in the matter of trade and commerce. Recent Enron bankruptcy, in which a highly respected audit firm had played a crucial role in manipulating documents, is a case in point. This is not an isolated incident. There are several cases of lack of transparency on the part of multinationals, in which audit firms have played major role in tailoring balance sheets.

MONOPOLISTIC TENDENCIES

Mergers and acquisitions are playing important role in western capitalism and not competitiveness, which is a key factor in capitalism. In India also, with liberalisation, mergers and acquisitions have been a significant feature of the economy. There has been alarming tendency of growth of monopoly in recent years. 'This would simply not be permissible under anti-trust laws in most countries'.[47] While talking of reforms, no steps have been taken to prevent industrial concentration in the hands of a few firms and individuals. With liberealisation in India, monopolistic tendencies through acquisitions and mergers are on the rise and a competitive scenario has become a far cry. This seems to be the age of business magnates and commercial czars. Liberalisation, as practised and industrial-economic democracy have become casualties. Trade Unions, from the repository of all virtues have become the villains of peace. At a particular period in our post-independence development, western-style trade Unionism had become the holy cow and irresponsible trade unionism was tolerated and even encouraged. There were times, a small group, in the name of trade union activities, was holding the entire economy to ransom and all concerned were silent spectator, although the economy was being damaged irreversibly. Today, the entire thing has come a full circle and we have suddenly found our industrialists and businessmen repository of all the virtues. Today's liberalisation, assumes that industrialists and businessmen can do wonders, if they are given a free run of the economy, with plenty of cheap money. These extremes of view are certainly not the product of economic rationality, but have dominant influence on the small power circle both

Governmental and non-Governmental. In the case of India, liberalisation has been an one-way house with the Government of the day pulling out all stops for giving the business magnates—both Indian and foreign, a free run for their money. 'In India, the law on monopolies has been diluted to abolish limits on the growth of firms through mergers to acquisition but laws needed to regulate monopolistic, restrictive or unfair trade practices have not been strengthened. 'In this respect, the present anti-trust legislation is more like a watchdog without teeth. This one-sideness of the industrial policy reform needs to be recognised'.[48] Most of these mergers and acquisitions are backed by foreign multinationals, who have become major players in consumer goods market. Foreign transnationals have already spread their tentacles in the vital sectors of the Indian economy. Apart from well-known transnationals, various fly by night operators, registered in various tax havens, have found their way into the Indian economy, through collaboration and acquisition of Indian firms. Government of India have not developed any legal methodology to prevent such undue incursions. Competition has given place to monopoly and oligopoly in western capitalism. There is no place for small players in the market-place, who will be weeded out in no time. This means that the levers of economic power will be concentrated in the hands of the few. 'Merger and acquisition activity is reaching unprecedented level as industries are consolidating on a global basis . . . . Global monopolies and oligopolies are beginning to emerge. There are only four major auditing firms left in the world, similar but less pronounced concentration is taking place in other financial functions. Microsoft and Intel are on the verge of world-wide monopolies'.[49] In the field of pharmaceutical industry there is enormous concentration with Glaxo, Novartis and Mark, with their enormous research facilities and network throughout the world, being virtual world monopolies. Glaxo has merged with Wellcome and Ciba-Geigy with Sandoz to form Novartis, to eliminate all competitions in the pharmaceutical industry. 'In the seeds sector, Novartis will hold the second position world-wide behind Pioneer Hi Breed, with annual sales world-wide of a bit less then US $ 1 billion'.[50] Novartis, the giant pharmaceutical company with the merger has also become number one in agribusiness. Monsanto is another powerful player in agribusiness. Powerful cartels in pharmaceutical and agro-based industries, backed by patent laws drafted by developed countries to maintain its monopoly over technology are designed to monopolise and control the world production and trade in medicine and agriculture. Development of cinchona as an antidote to malaria in the late nineteenth century provides a case in point, where monopoly over a single drug, proved a powerful tool of colonialism. From the latter portion of the nineteenth century to the Japanese conquest of the Dutch East Indies (Indonesia), world monopoly in cinchona was controlled by a single Dutch marketing cartel, 'the Kina Bureau of Amsterdam, which co-ordinated the purchase of bark, and the price and quantity of quinine sold'.[51] Quoting from authoritative sources, Headrick analyses the role of scientific cinchona production in European colonialism. 'Scientific cinchona production was an imperial technology par excellence. Without it European colonialism would have been almost impossible in Africa, and much costlier elsewhere in the tropics. At the same time, the development of this technology, combining the scientific expertise of several botanical gardens, the encouragement of the British and Dutch colonial government, and the land and labour of the peoples of India and Indonesia, was clearly a consequence as well as a cause of the new imperialism'.[52]

Monopoly and oligopoly are the basis of Western capitalism and not competition. It is not that this is a new trend, it has been always part of this system. The biggest merger of the twentieth century was the formation of U.S. steel in 1901. 'The largest merger or buyout, after adjusting for inflation, was in 1901. U.S. Steel was formed when J.P. Morgan organised a consortium to purchase not only Andrew Carnegie's then huge organisation, but additional steel makers, suppliers, shippers and other peripheral business. Again, it was the largest of the 20th century'.[53] Thus, the 20th century started with a merger in steel industry in the U.S.A., setting the stage for world domination in steel industry by eliminating all competitions. This was not an isolated incident. Mergers and acquisitions were the dominant trend in industrial scenario in the U.S.A., till the stock market crash of the thirties of the last century and subsequent depression. 'Just before and just after the turn of the century in industry after industry, small companies were combined into large ones. The United States Steel Corporation, International Harvester, International Nickel, American Tobacco, and numerous other of the great corporations trace to this period. . . . The primary motivation in all but the rarest cases was to reduce, eliminate, or regularize competition. Each of the new giants dominated an industry, and henceforth exercised measurable control over prices and production, and perhaps also over investment and the rate of technological innovation'.[54] This clearly shows that competition is not the motivating force in Western industrial development, but monopoly and cartel. Industrial democracy in such a situation is a misnomer. The myth that private sector encourages competition and is an antidote to state corruption is exposed by the working of the private sector throughout the world. Private sector thrives on monopoly of control of innovation, production and distribution. Technology control is a key element in the monopolistic situation in industrial development. Through technology, both production and distribution can be controlled. Monopolistic situation did not create a healthy industrial climate and the economy slid into recession in the thirties with large-scale unemployment and distress during the depression years. There is no doubt that similar situation is going to be repeated in an unprecedented scale, in which developing countries will be the worst sufferers.

Control of a single drug through technology developed in the colonies through colonial resources, was a powerful tool in controlling the lives of the colonial subjects and their economy. Malaria proved to be a scourge for the Europeans in their acquisition of colonies. British controlled the production and distribution of cinchona in India, which they used mostly for their military and administrative personnel, leaving the commercial production entirely to the Dutch. There was intensive experimentation in the botanical gardens of India and Indonesia and exchange of seeds and information, to develop a potent antidote for malaria in the second half of nineteenth century, but once the imperial and commercial requirements were met, there was no further experimentation and no attempt was made for increasing the production of cinchona and for lowering the cost to make it available to the common people of India and Indonesia, to save them from the scourge of malaria. 'The annual average number of deaths due directly to malaria in India was estimated in 1909 (at the Imperial Malaria Conference) to be 1.1 million'.[55] After the control of malaria amongst the European population through quinine extracted from cinchona, little was done to increase the cultivation of cinchona or improve its potency through experimentation and research. Java became the source of the bulk of the world's supply of quinine, as it was commercially highly successful in the international market. In India the supply of quinine to the bulk of the population was not commercially viable. Thus, no steps were taken to increase the production of this vital drug and casualty amongst the local population continued to be heavy. 'Malaria is still the outstanding cause of admission to hospital and it cannot yet be said that any real measure of control has been obtained'. (Indian Year Book, 1927)[56]

The world supply of cinchona was inadequate to meet the needs of the local people in the colonies. 'The present world production of quinine would not suffice to permit one-tenth of the total population of India to use quinine as a preventive of malaria. The world supply would suffice for some thirty millions only and the total output of all Indian quinine factories would only suffice to treat some three million'.[57] When there was a major gap between supply and requirement of quinine, economic logic would have dictated the extension of cinchona cultivation and more extensive research to bring down the cost of cultivation, as well as improve its efficiency. Scientific research was limited by the needs of the empire and the production and marketing control of Amsterdam. 'This world monopoly of cinchona resulted not only from scientific methods of cultivation, but also from a marketing cartel, the Kina Bureau of Amsterdam, cordinated the purchase of bark and the price and quantity of quinine sold . . . . which not until the Japanese conquest of Indonesia in World War Two and the development of synthetic malaria suppressants did this Dutch control over one of the world's most vital drugs come to an end.'[58] Thus, the laws of supply and demand in vital commodities do not favour the vast majority of the world's population. Scientific research is limited either by commercial needs or military requirement. Patent laws will put an effective cap on further research on development of cheaper drugs for use of the vast majority of people in the less developed countries and the under-previleged in the developed countries. The less developed countries will be barred from development of cheaper variant of the drugs for use by the majority of population. Commercially-oriented research aided by powerful global patent laws under Intellectual Property Rights regime and the World Trade Organisation will debar commercial access to the world's majority population to vital medicines. This is certainly the use of the same tools of the empire, which enslaved Asia, Africa and South America.

Notes and References

1. J.A. Schumpeter, History of Economic Analysis, p. 396.
2. C.A. Gide, Political Economy, p. 355
3. Edward Marz, Joseph Schumpeter, p. 82
4. Gide, pp. 354-55.
5. Ritortus, The Imperialism of British Trade, p. 111.
6. P.J. Cain, Economic Foundations of British Overseas Expansion, pp. 11-12, 70.
7. Arnold Toynbee, Lectures on Industrial Revolution, pp. 27-32, quoted in the *Industrial Revolution in National Context*, pp. 6-7.
8. Gide, pp. 348, 350.
9. Cain, p. 40.
10. Marz, pp. 68-69.
11. *Ibid.*, pp. 68-69.

12-13. Gide, pp. 348-350.

14. Ugo Rabbeno, The American Commercial Policy (1895), p. 137, Quoted in Celso Furtado, *The Economic Growth of Brazil* (1963), p. 109.
15. Encyclopaedia Britannica, Vol. 5, p. 661.

16-17. Schumpeter, p. 517.

18. Industrial Revolution, p. 6.

19. *Ibid.*, Notes, p. 12. Quotation from J.S. Mill, System of Logic.
20. Celso Furtado, The Economic Growth of Brazil, p. 109.
21. R. Simonsen, Historia Economica de Brazil (1957), p. 406, quoted in Celso Furtado.
22. Schumpeter, pp. 504-5.
23. *Ibid.*, p. 442.
24. D.S. Landes, Wealth and Poverty of Nations, p. 315.
25-26. Edward S. Mason, Comment on Planning in India, from Gerald M. Meier, Leading issues in Economic Development (1975), p. 741.
27. Adam Smith, p. 298.
28-29. G.K. Gokhale, The Swadeshi Movement (1907) from speeches of G.K. Gokhale, pp. 962-63.
30. Economic Survey of Govt. of India, 1991-92, para 2.34.
31. Economic Survey of Govt. of India, 2001-02, pp. 138-39.
32. UNCTAD, Trade and Development Report, 2001, pp. 6-7, 14.
33. *Ibid.*, p. 11.
34. *Ibid.*, pp. 20-21.
35-36. Martin Feldstein, Refocusing The IMF, Foreign Affairs (March/April 1998), pp. 32-33.
37-38. George Soros, The Crisis of Global Capitalism (1998), p. 181.
39. *Ibid.*, p. 148.
40. *Ibid.*, 180.
41. C. Fred Bergsten, America's Two-Front Economic Conflict, Foreign Affairs, March/April 2001, p. 21.
42. Hilton L. Root, Asia's Bad Old Ways, March/April, 2001, pp. 10-11.
43. Soros, p. 147.
44-46. Root, pp. 11-12
47-48. Amit Bhaduri and Deepak Nayyar, The Intelligent Person's Guide to Liberalisation (1996), pp. 35-36.
49. Soros, p. 189.
50. Seedling, March 1996, Vol. 13, No. 1, p. 29, Box.
51-52 Daniel Headrick, Tools of Empire, pp. 72-73.
53. Kirk W.M. Tyson, Competition in the 21st Century (1997), p. 79.
54. J.K. Galbraith, The Great Crash, 1929, p. 70.
55. Vera Anstey, Economic Development of India, p. 75, Note 4.
56. *Ibid.*, p. 76, Note 2.
57. *Ibid.*, pp. 76-77.
58. Daniel Headrick, p. 72.

5

Laissez Faire: Not the Solution

Free trade and private enterprise are today's Mantras for all the ills besetting the World's economy, particularly the third world countries. Third-world countries, which have been experimenting with economic development and met with initial success, were being touted as models of free trade and private enterprise leading to their becoming economic tigers. That all is not well with the economies of these countries, viz. South Korea, Thailand, Malaysia, Indonesia, Singapore and Hong Kong, became apparent when the tremors of shock waive in the Stock Exchanges of these countries gave way to a crash in the major stocks in 1997. Stock Exchange crisis is the typical signal in the American pattern of capitalism of a prelude to a long period of economic depression, leading to recession and unemployment, weakening of the currency and the financial institution and severe debt burden.

SOUTH-EAST ASIAN EXPERIENCE

Free trade suits countries, whose geographical area is too small to make them self-sufficient. In Europe, when the debate in favour of free trade started towards the middle of the nineteenth century, spearheaded by Britain and continued till the beginning of the First World War, most of the countries were not persuaded by the free trade argument and followed a policy of trade in national interest, with limited protectionism. Gide, writing before the First World War says 'with the exception of England, then, there are in Europe, at the present time, only a few small countries, Belgium, Holland, Norway and Denmark, which have remained faithful to Free Trade, their areas being too small to allow of their being self-sufficient. Smaller a country is, the more important, relatively, is its foreign trade. And this stands to reason'.[1] In recent times, economic growth of Singapore and Taiwan, both island nations, could not have been possible without foreign trade. Similarly, Japan, an island nation like Great Britain, but without its huge colonial hinterland, could not have achieved its economic status without foreign trade. Pre-merger Hong Kong was basically a trading outpost, where the Chinese communist regime could take advantage through informal channels of capitalist trade, particularly through its huge expatriate community living overseas. Indonesia and South Korea, which were Asian growth models, are in different category. All these countries have considerable external debt and as such vulnerable to external pressure. Indonesia, inspite of its considerable oil wealth and being a member of OPEC since 1962, slipped into serious economic decline, from which it has not yet recovered. It had an external debt to GNP ratio of 113 per cent. South Korea is perhaps the only country, which has recovered to some extent from the economic depression of 1997, but continues to be carrying a high external debt which is 32% of its GNP. South Korea's external debt is offset to some extent by its favourable balance of payments position. But with the market in computer components like semi-conductors shrinking and U.S. market restricting imports of Korean electronic goods, besides high import duties on Korean steel, the balance of payments advantage may not last long. Korea still carries a very high level of non-performing assets to the extent of 45% of its total loaning, in its banking structure, which had started the financial crisis of 1997. Korea with high external debt and non-performing bank loans, is highly vulnerable to foreign pressure, once it is unable to maintain a favourable balance of payments, particularly *vis-a-vis* U.S.A.

According to the World Development Report, (World

Bank, 1982), during the period of 1960-80, Singapore, South Korea and Hong Kong registered growth of 7.5 per cent, 7 per cent and 6.8 per cent respectively and were called 'baby tigers' by I.M.D. Little in his book 'Economic Development: Theory, Policy and International Relation'. 'These are, of course, all economies with private ownership and markets . . . . Hong Kong and Singapore are essentially city economies . . . . There are no great rural masses to drag them down'.[2] As regards, South Korea, 'The Government played a major part in fostering economic growth in South Korea, and as has been argued, 'no State outside the socialist bloc ever came anywhere near this measure, of, control over the economy's investible recouces'.[3] Moreover, 'South Korea had a military dictatorship during much of its post-war history. The consensus-building tradition of Japan and the checks and balances that charaterize a democracy were missing'.[4] The economies of these countries are too closely linked with Japan and the U.S.A., that economic recession in the latter country will be passed on to these countries, particularly South Korea, Thailand, Philippines and Taiwan. The brunt of the shock of economic recession can be transmitted to countries depending on dominant economies of the West, for their export-led growth. The lever of technology control is a powerful economic weapon for controlling subsidiary economies, which are technological dependencies of the West. Technology of the West creates Technological Colonialism, where a subsidiary technology is created for the high technology country. Computer Chip-oriented development is one such example, where labour-intensive work is firmed out to less developed countries. This is, however, a short-term arrangement, as when the technology develops further and gets more and more automated, the production process changes and the export-market comes crashing down. We have seen this in the case of Korean economy. Such quick change in production process lead to serious unemployment and causes economic distortion. Labour force can not be changed from one activity to another like an economic weather-cock. Export-led growth with dominant economies, has serious economic drawbacks and countries should be careful before hitching their economic bandwagon to dominant western economies.

George Soros traces the origin of South East Asian crisis of the nineties of the last century to the Wall Street crash of 1987. The crisis was transmitted through Japan to Thailand, Indonesia and Korea, 'The recession in Japan, the second-largest economy of the world and an important trading partner of the other Asian countries, aggravated the severity of the economic down-turn in the rest of Asia . . . . The financial collapse was followed by economic decline. Domestic demand came to a standstill and imports shrank, but exports did not expand, because a high proportion of the exports were directed towards countries that were also affected. In addition, exports were concentrated in a limited number of commodities where the increased selling pressure drove down prices. Semi-conductors, in which Korea; Taiwan; and, to a lesser extent, Japan vied for the world market, were particularly hard hit'.[5]

The Korean economic boom created a huge industrial work force, drawn from the countryside, who basked in the economic sunshine. Once, the economic down-turn started, due to the drying up of exports, there was huge retrenchment, closure of industries and unemployment. This class of workers, who have been drawn away from their traditional employment, for a short-lived industrial boom will find it difficult to readjust to their traditional employment. Presence of huge unemployed work force in the wake of a short-lived artificial industrial boom, created by export-led growth has the potentiality of serious socio-economic tension and unrest. Work-force transplanted from their traditional habitat and employment, without any hope of future employment, due to shrinking of the economy, will be a burden on the economy and besides being a source of social and economic tension, will be a drag on the economy. Speaking about the economic decline in the wake of the economic crisis of Korea, Soros says, while the external crisis abated. 'The internal situation, by contrast, continues to deteriorate. Most Companies operate at a loss and their balance sheets go from bad to worse. . . . In spite of a reduction in interest rates the economy continues to languish. Unemployment and labour tensions are on the rise'.[6]

Industrial revolution in these countries has been too short. There are no colonies and virgin lands to export the surplus labour, as in the case of British industrial revolution.

Asian financial crisis originated in the private sector and IMF, which had no experience in dealing with private sector imbalances and lacked proper understanding of financial markets, failed to address itself to the problem and made the situation worse. 'What made the Asian crisis different from any the IMF had faced before was that it originated in the private sector; the public sector was in relatively good shape'. Soros analyses that IMF, which 'had developed its methodology for dealing with imbalances in the public sector',[7] applied the same remedies for financial market imbalances. IMF remedies like curbing public spending and sudden closure of financial institutions, without making adequate provisions for the protection of depositors' interest, created a financial panic. It ruined the small and medium depositors, who are the backbone of any economy. The big business houses who are mostly borrowers from the financial institutions, escaped any penal action, although they were the people, who were basically responsible for mismanagement of the economy. The IMF policies in South-East Asian countries and Korea penalised the small depositors, whereas the loanees, who were mostly the rich businessmen, kept their assets intact.

Malayasia avoided the crisis by strict control on flow of foreign fund. Although this policy was not popular in the West, Malayasian economy escaped unscathed from the crisis. Bigger Asian economies like India and China were not much affected due to their lesser exposure to the international financial markets, 'The countries that kept their financial markets closed weathered the storm better than those that were open. India was less affected than the South East Asian countries; China was better insulated than Korea'. This should hold some lesson for those, who want to open up Indian capital market to international financial vagaries. Foreign banks are likely to prove much more fickle than domestic banks. 'There is much to be said for developing a domestic source of capital as Chile has done by establishing private pension funds'.[8]

World Bank and I.M.F. went out of the way to champion the East Asian miracle, as a model for developing countries. This was mainly to demonstrate the futility of Government sponsored development programmes and to change the economic policies of these countries to market friendly strategy. 'The World Bank's (1993) study, the East Asian Miracle is a highly visible and controversial effort to explain the success of eight high performing Asian economies. It also takes pains to denounce the usefulness of government intervention and industrial policies'.[9] In this, the World Bank faithfully followed the American line laid down by Reagan in his address before the annual meetings of the World Bank IMF, 1981. 'The societies which have achieved the most spectacular, broad-based economic progress . . . . (are those that) believe in the magic of the market place'.[10] This marked the great watershed of change in economic thinking, when the state was prime-mover of development and actively involved in the development process to the situation where the State plays a secondary role, as an adjunct of the private sector, which knows best what is good for the country's economy. The dominant academic circle immediately embraced this view with enthusiasm, as the collapse of the Soviet Union shattered their faith in socialism. The swing in view from socialistic economy to market economy was without any apology or murmur. Overnight, governments of developing countries were pilloried for their industrial policies, with the public sector holding the primary position; for their policies of subsidies to cushion the inequalities and the entire gamut of policies being followed by them. The governments of many of the developing countries meekly accepted that they had been following the wrong policies, as the ideological backing for the earlier policies were withdrawn by the dominant economic thinking. This new found wisdom dawned more on governments, which were heavily indebted to the World Bank and IMF and continued to depend on them for being further loan-worthy to keep their foreign sponsored programmes running. Indian government switched over to a policy of dismantling the economic structure, built-up since independence in the name of liberalisation, under pressure from World Bank, IMF and the western lobby. The industrial policy was changed, withdrawing the various measures to safeguard the Indian industries. This led to large-scale industrial sickness and unemployment. Politically also, the change was convenient, as the year 1990 marked the end of Nehru-Gandhian era in India politics. Politically, it was convenient to make a clear break from the past.

DEPRESSION OF THE THIRTIES IN THE U.S.A.

History in the affairs of men, is a great pointer to the maladies, which troubled a past generation. Crisis of capitalism in America and Western Europe during the thirties of the twentieth century should hold some lesson for those who want to embrace the American brand of capitalism for reaching economic heaven. The situation in the thirties of the last century was similar to the World economic scenario of the present days and should be a fair indicator of the working of unbridled capitalism. Immediately after the First World War, the U.S.A., which remained least scathed by the War, went into huge expansion of capacity both in the agricultural and industrial sectors, without taking into account the market for such products. U.S.A. was caught in an over production trap, without the simultaneous increase in market for the same. The severe depression which the American economy suffered in the thirties, was preceded by the stock market crash of 1929. Immediately, prior to this major economic debacle, the American capitalism was complacent and looking forward to an economic boom in the coming years. Prior to the onset of the Great Depression, which took the American Economy to the brink of economic collapse, even the President of the U.S.A. in his state of the Union message predicted a bright picture of the American economy. President Calvin Coolidge's last state of the Union message to the Congress on December 1928 reads 'No Congress of the United States ever assembled on surveying the state of the Union, has met with a more pleasing prospect than that which appears at the present time. In the domestic field there is tranquility and contentment and the highest record of years of prosperity'.[11] He went on to say that the

American nation can regard the present with satisfaction and anticipate the future with optimism.

The motive force of capitalism is the desire of people to get rich quickly. According to the theoreticians of capitalism, this is a harmless pastime and can divert the aggressive tendencies to constructive channels, which apart from enriching the individual, will, increase wealth of nations and create employment. 'Dangerous human proclivities can be canalised into comparatively harmless channels by the existence of opportunities for money-making and private wealth, which, if they cannot be satisfied in this way, may find their outlet in cruelty, the reckless pursuit of personal power and authority, and other form of self-aggrandisement'.[12] In America, during the decade prior to the depression, people were displaying an inordinate desire to get rich quickly with a minimum of physical effort. This was only possible through speculation in real estate and stock market. Real estate boom in Florida, which was mostly swampy scrublands, was pictured as the Riviera of America, primarily because of its temperate climate, collapsed in the hurricanes of 1926. The area was and continues to be highly cyclone-prone, which aspect did not seem to have entered the calculation of the real estate speculators, who seemed to be interested in only quick profits. The collapse of the Florida real estate boom preceded the collapse of the stock market. 'Even as the Florida boom collapsed, the faith of Americans in quick, effortless enrichment in the stock market was becoming every day more evident'.[13]

It is not that the stock-market boom was authored by mindless speculators who followed the herd instinct and jumped into the bullish bandwagon. Economists from the Universities were keen observers of the market and taking a keen interest in the stock-market. They lauded the role of leaders of the automobile industry, the steel industry, the radio industry and other such industrial leaders in moving the stock prices at a galloping speed. Such dynamic movement in the stock-market took the ordinary traders by surprise and they had no other alternative than follow the market leaders. 'Observing this group as a whole Professor Dice was especially struck by their 'vision for the future and boundless hope and optimism'. . . . 'Led by these mighty knights of the automobile industry, the steel industry, the radio industry.....' he said, 'and finally joined in despair, by many professional traders who, after much sack-cloth and ashes, had caught the vision of progress, the Coolidge market had gone forward like the phalanxes of Cyrus, parasang upon parasang and again parasang upon parasang . . .'.[14] The fact that the captains of industry deserted their fields of specialization in producing different commodities and started dabbling in stock market, is a clear indication of the depressionary conditions in the American economy.

A period of Golden Age of capitalism was sought to be ushered in through a number of investment trusts, a new innovation in the capital market, which sought to project a practical Utopia before the small investors to make them a partner in the largesse of capitalism. Investment trusts had top financial professionals and economists from the Universities. Galbraith has called it 'a golden age for professors'.[15] Trusts had well known professors from almost all the American Universities. With such a plethora of talent, there was no reason for the investment trusts to come to grief. But the investment trusts, which were themselves not financially viable could not protect the interest of small holders in the stock market crash. The fact that personal misfortune of small investors, who put their entire earnings to the tender mercy of stock market, is not publicised by the media, which suffers from selective amnesia, does not make it less awesome. This was also the fate of small and medium investors in India, who had enthusiastically participated in the short-lived stock market boom of the nineties, which collapsed in the Securities Scam. The same story was repeated in U.T.I. Scam. While the big operators had hedged their bets carefully enough and protected their interests, it was the small and medium investors, who lost heavily and were wiped out from the securities market. This has been the story of the stock exchange meltdown of Asian Tigers. The stock market bust and the subsequent collapse of the economy, has cost Indonesia dear in continuous rioting by disgruntled and disappointed people, who were hoping for a capitalist utopia. The fall-out apart from disgracing the leader of the country, who led the country from the brink of Communism and Chinese hegemony to an independent self-reliant country, threatened to disintegrate the country. As long as Indonesia pursued an independent economic policy, the economy was under control. Once, it opened up its economy completely to foreign economic forces, the problem started in investments through heavy borrowings from foreign and domestic institutional investors. Foreign investment was heavily underwritten by the Indonesian Government. In Indonesia, non-performing loans were assessed at 85% of the total loans, valued at 34.1 billion U.S. dollars.[16] The immediate cause of the crisis was the recession in Japan, which had been in the cards for quite sometime and reached serious proportions in 1997, with sharp fall in the value of Japanese Yen *vis-a-vis* the American dollar.

The entire story of South-East Asian collapse started from the Wall Street crash of 1987, which was not simply a financial phenomenon due to currency imbalance, but was triggered by the recessionary forces, which were gaining momentum within the American economy from the eighties and reached alarming proportions by that time. This was reflected in the continuous balance of payments deficit *vis-a-vis* Japan. American federal budgetary deficit was continuously high throughout the eighties and industrial unemployment was on the increase. To sum up, the economic situation in the U.S.A. in the eighties, it can be categorically stated that the American economy was far from healthy during the entire period. All the basic economic indicators pointed to this conclusion. Unemployment was exceedingly high, coupled with high federal budgetary deficit and balance of payment deficit. Wall Street crash of 1987 heralded a major depressionary situation in the U.S. economy. This could be averted by manipulating the world financial market. Japan tried to bail out the American economy out of the crisis by pumping in money. 'Their decision helped the World to overcome the effects of the crash but it left Japanese financial institutions with many losses abroad and engendered a financial bubble at home that reached its climax in 1991'. Decision to bail out the American economy was taken by the Japanese Ministry of Finance, which had a tight control over the financial institutions. This was the point from which trouble in the Japanese economy started. 'Japan's troubles go back to the Wall Street crash of 1987'.[17]

The economic catastrophy of the Great Depression developed from a tranquil and prosperous economic scenario, while the forces of depression were gradually but surely gathering momentum to suck the American economy through a vortex of economic decline. Galbraith rightly points out, 'The farmers were unhappy and had been ever since the depression of 1920-21 had cut farm prices sharply but left costs high'. While analyzing the causes of the depression, Prof. Galbraith points out 'perhaps, although less probably, trouble was transmitted to the economy as a whole from some weak sector like agriculture'.[18] After mentioning the role of agriculture in weakening the economy, Galbraith points out that agriculture was the weak link in the American economy, which could have contributed to the American economic depression. He goes on to point out the highly unequal income distribution leading to a high level of luxury consumer spending, which are of highly fluctuating nature. There was an adverse balance of trade between agriculture and industry, because of depression in the agricultural economy, coupled with high cost of inputs, since the 1920s. As such agricultural depression preceded industrial depression by about a decade.

Galbraith in his 'The Great Crash 1929' has made a detailed analysis of the causes of industrial recession; there is however no analysis of the linkage of the agricultural sector to the all round economic recession, although his background in practical and theoretical agriculture, made him suspect that the weak agricultural sector has contributed in pulling down the economic edifice. In fact, it is no coincidence that there was a serious 'wheat problem' during the years of depression. This was due to a serious problem of world wheat surplus, in which the U.S.A. was saddled with maximum marketable surplus. It surfaced in 1928-29, after a record world crop of 4,794 millions of bushels, compared to 3,731 millions of bushels in 1925 and 3,798 millions of bushels in 1913. The U.S. share of world production of wheat had increased from 690 millions of bushels in 1913 to 915 millions of bushels in 1928. 'National Polices of wheat-exporting nations have restricted their markets for imported goods to such an extent that wheat-importing nations encounter grave difficulties in finding export markets for the goods with which they could pay for wheat and other imports. The United States has given potent examples of such broad tendencies, notably through tariff policy and shipping subsidies, and thus made substantial indirect contribution to the creation of world wheat-surplus problem'.[19] The main reason for shrinking of wheat exports, was the United States policy of squeezing of the export markets of wheat importing countries. Wheat farmers had got accustomed to higher production and higher prices during the first fifteen years before the First World War due to improved methods of production'. The experience of the fifteen years before the war, of rapid expansion of wheat production with no persisting surplus, probably cannot be duplicated now, for the growth of population in general outside of Russia and India is proceeding much more slowly, and displacement of other cereals by wheat for food has not so far to go'.[20] There was as such problem of plenty, due to increased method of production brought about by new technologies both in the field of agriculture and industry. Dilemma of the times was 'over expansion of agriculture and to extensive overbuilding of the world's physical plant in all sorts of factories, in land transportation, and in shipping. Huge savings have thus been invested in enterprises that could not be profitable. The outcome has been disastrous to producers and investors, and in turn to consumers through the decline in the income they have to spend'.[21] There was increase in the production of capital goods and durable consumer goods, whereas production of mass consumer goods lagged behind. Increased production of capital goods led to an inventory glut and falling demand. There is a limit beyond which production of capital goods become counter productive, as other branches of industry and agriculture catering to mass consumer markets do not increase proportionately. This gap between production of capital goods and consumer goods is one of the main reasons for demand recession of the former.

Raw cotton, which was the most important single

export item, constituting nearly 14% in 1931 of the total value of all merchandise exported from the United States, suffered a set back. 'After 1929, stocks of American cotton accumulated as a result of continued heavy production, particularly in 1931-32, and a substantial decline in consumption'. The prospect of American cotton also appeared bleak during the depression years, due to growing competition from man-made fibers, particularly rayon. 'World production of rayon grew phenomenally after the war.'[22] In fact, the United States was the principal contributor to the world's supply of rayon. The depressionary situation in the agriculture sector of the American economy was quite apparent immediately after the First World War and was continuing throughout the 1920s, although superficially there was a boom in the industrial and the real estate sectors. Inspite of clear signals of depression from the agricultural sector, a booming economy was predicted. President Calvin Coolidge and his successor, President Herbert Hoover, captains of industry and commerce, financial and business experts and leading economists did not find any signal of the forthcoming stock market crash and subsequent depression. Prof. Galbraith in his book, 'The Great Crash 1929' has quoted extensively from various statements of these leaders from both the practical field and the intellectual field to show that they were not aware of any sign of the forthcoming stock market crash and subsequent economic depression.[23]

Between 1930 and 1940, unemployment was very high and on an average one person in every four in the labour force was out of work and even in the best of years during that period one person in five in the labour force was out of work. While most of the reasons for the great Depression lay in the inherent defects in these economies and the depression in the Agriculture sector and over-expansion of the economy, another important cause lay in the war-debt payments, which the allied powers imposed upon Germany. The treaty of Versaillas (1920) provided for war reparation of an unprecedented magnitude, which amounted to not less than $ 750 million yearly. Such huge payments could not continue for any length of period and had to be revised in 1924 to an yearly $ 595 million.[24] When Germany failed to pay these huge amounts, reparation loans were given to her by floating bonds in the United States and Europe. This type of artificial indebtedness had far reaching consequences, not only on the economy of Germany, but also on the economies of the U.S.A., U.K., and France, the principal allied powers, which sought to benefit from huge war reparations. The consequences were quite remarkable and contributed to an artificial economic situation, leading to an economic depression which nobody knew what to do about. In the management of economic affairs, whether of an individual or a nation, greed and cunning, do not always pay. This is perhaps one lesson, which everyone should have learnt from this economic tragedy of the thirties. But as in the case of mice and men, one refused to learn from experience. As President Woodrow Wilson once said, 'Experience is the name, we give to our own mistakes, as also of our previous generations.' The mistake of huge indebtedness *vis-a-vis* one country to another is sought to be repeated. This will damage the economies of debtor countries, as well as creditor countries.

FOREIGN DEBT COMPROMISES NATIONAL SOVEREIGNTY

One can draw a parallel today, in the indebtedness of developing countries to the Western World, particularly to the U.S.A. Is free trade possible under such circumstances? Today's world economic scenario resembles the situation of the twenties and thirties of the last century. India's foreign debt repayment obligations have placed India in a very piquant situation by creating an unfavourable terms of trade against India. Continuous decline in the value of Rupee *vis-a-vis* Dollar has turned the terms of trade against India in its economic relations with the U.S.A. and other borrowing countries. We have to export several times the amount of what we were exporting, before the major devaluation of the Indian rupee, under IMF World Bank dictat in early 1990s. Thus, we are losers in real terms. India will have to shift resources from domestic capital investment to the production of exports. Indian unit costs of manufacture will have to be reduced substantially, since the volume of manufactured exports will have to rise substantially to cope with the adverse balance of payments, on the brink of foreign exchange crisis. Downward journey of the Indian economy started in 1966 with the devaluation of the Rupee in response to pressure from the export lobby, particularly manufactures and exporters of Engineering goods. Indian engineering goods hardly had any market in countries like the U.S.A., the U.K., West Germany, the Netherland and Japan, which had their own advantages in manufacturing industries. India was competing with these countries for marketing in Middle East and South-Eastern Asia, where there was marginal increase in exports. Since then, devaluation of the Indian Rupee *vis-a-vis* dollar and pound have been tried as a short-cut to boost Indian export, but without much success.

India's constant dependence on foreign debt created a serious foreign exchange crisis and servicing of foreign debt became a burden on the economy from the late 1980s, creating a serious foreign exchange crisis in the early 1990s, leading the Indian economy beign opened up to foreign multinationals. India's abject surrender to the Western economic powers, is due to India's increasing foreign exchange crisis created by burgeoning foreign debt. India was forced into the IMF sponsored reform in 1991, through a huge loan package of $ 3 billion or Rs. 65 hundred crores. This was to avoid an imminent balance of payments crisis, brought about by an aggregate external debt of Rs. 1307 hundred crores or $ 66.5 billion as on March 31, 1991 which was around 25 per cent of the country's GDP'.[25] Without this IMF debt, India would have failed to service its external debt and severely restrict its imports. This would have damaged the western economies which were on the way to recession. In excharge of IMF assistance, India had to give a number of concessions in the shape of allowing foreign investment and commodities. Privatisation of state owned units, was also one of the concessions extracted by the IMF. Subsidies in the agriculture sector had to be withdrawn, without consideration of the fact that balance of trade is heavily tilted against the agricultural sector. This is the typical IMF method of enforcing economic surrender by leading a country into the garden path of debt and more debt.

India's capitulation started from the Cancun summit in Mexico in October 1981. 'Whether Cancun represents the end of an era or merely an interlude between periods of north-south dislogue and debate remains to be seen. In the short-run, however, it was a tactical success for the Reagan administration. At Cancun, the United States deflected pressures for International economic reform, without having to grant any substanative concessions. Moreover, the Reagan administration used Cancun to broadcast its own alternative economic message'.[26] Cancun was obviously end of an era of third world hard line in economic matters against the U.S.A. and its allies. In the earlier stages the north-south dialogue had effectively focused on the economic problems of the Developing countries. 'The south argued that the essential roadblock to international reform was the lack of "political will" in the north. The statesmen in the industrial West were either too preoccupied with other issues, too subservient to immediate, *status-quo* interests; or too intellectually narrow to enter into serious negotiations. This analysis was reflected in the report of the Brandt Commission, released at the end of 1979'.[27] Economic interest of the 120 members of the third world countries, known as Group of 77 were contradictory, and they could not present a common front at the Cancun summit. In Cancun the Western block led by the United States, was able to confront the Developing countries about the vagueness and contradiction of their stand on various issues, while at the same time taking an ambiguous attitude and giving away nothing substantial. The final Cancun document noted only that consensus had been reached 'to launch Global negotiations on a basis to be mutually agreed and in circumstances offering the prospects of meaningful progress'. Inspite of lack of substantial progress, the participants declared the meeting a land mark in international economic co-operation. The irony of the situation has been clearly brought out by Richard Feinberg in his Reaganomics and the Third World. 'The explanation lies partly in adroit administration tactics and partly in the structural weakness of the southern position. . . . The Reagan administration's success was thus a product of its ability to project a generally positive if ambiguous attitude toward the summit and global negotiations while maintaining a firm position on the less visible substantive issues. Ronald Reagan was the perfect showman to implement a policy of public smiles coupled with private evasion and toughness'. Reasons varied for individual countries from not confronting the United States. 'Venezuela was seeking a preferred relationship with Washington. India and Guyana were hoping to convince the United States to take a less hostile attitude toward loans pending in the international financial institutions.'[28]

The U.S. Government report on Foreign Trade Barriers of 1989, blacklisted India, alongwith Brazil and Japan, for possible retaliatory 100 per cent duties on selected exports to the United States if they failed to remove specified trade barriers within eighteen months. Under the 1988 Trade Act, Super 301 clause empowers the U.S. trade representative to identify trading practices pursued by countries, which are inimical to American business interests and take unilateral retaliatory action, if no agreement can be reached with the offending country. Super 301 is illegal because it violated the GATT principles of adjudication in trade disputes by a member country. The U.S. government Report on Foreign Trade Barriers (1989), was discriminatory, in the sense that although Australia was imposing a high duty on manufactured goods, it was not blacklisted. Similarly, European community practice of grants and subsidies for agricultural products and tariffs on a wide variety of products which severely disadvantaged American exports, did not attract any penal action, particularly since the U.S.A. was running a trade deficit of $ 12.8 billion in 1988 with the E.C. countries. How the pressure of Super 301 clause is used, in trade war, is best illustrated by the following example. 'Air India decided to switch an order for Rolls-Royce's large Trent turbofan engines for its Boeing 747 air craft in favour of American Pratt and Whiteney powerplants in suspicious circumstances after U.S. pressure was brought to bear on India to buy more American goods-pressure which included a Super 301 action against India.'[29] The author, a British member of Parliament, has highlighted this, as he felt the decline of Rolls-Royce was due to such meddling in trade affairs by America. It is not a question, whether the American product was better than the British product, but a sovereign country could not exercise her free choice in the international market and had to bow to foreign dictation. In this case, since the other party was a powerful British Company, a British author has mentioned it. There are numerous such cases in international trade, where there have been arm twisting by powerful players. So much for free international trade and freedom of the market.

India was led to this sorry state of affairs in the international market, because she allowed herself to walk into an external debt trap, created by institutions like World Bank and IMF. It is perhaps no coincidence that the voices of Developed countries became shrill against Indian protectionism, as soon as India fell into the debt trap, led by external lending agencies. I.M.F. and World Bank did not bother to inform India of the impending debt trap throughout the eighties. During 1986, gross disbursement of foreign loans, equalled Total Debt Services. This position continued for the next two years and from 1990 to 1992 total debt services continued to be higher.[30] A country, which has walked into a debt trap can hardly be expected to be in a level playing field in international trade with its creditor countries. Frequent devaluation of the Rupee since 1991 has reduced the value of Indian exports in real terms. Reduction in price of exports, lowers its value in real terms and the steep devaluation of Rupee, has made it necessary for the exporters to increase the quantity of exports manifold. While devaluing the Rupee for export stimulation, one should take note of the observation of Keynes in 1929 to the German debt problem 'if a reduction in price of 10% stimulates the volume of trade by 20%, this does not increase the volume of the exports by 20% but only by 8%'. The devaluation entails greater export effort and the monetary or foreign exchange value will continue to be low. Moreover, by diverting scarce resources from domestic market, the Indian consumers are denied the benefits, particularly when demand in the Indian market needs stimulation. Indians will have to pay more for imports and sell cheaply abroad. Such a situation, certainly cannot be beneficial for the country. No economic logic, except a perverse one, can be used to justify such a situation.

The international economic scenario of the present time, is reminiscent of the post First World War situation, when Germany was saddled with heavy war reparations. This created an economic paradox, when vanquished Germany had to stimulate exports and check imports. The devaluation of the German Mark, under such circumstances created disastrous consequences for the German economy, leading to the Great Economic Depression of the thirties in the U.S.A. and U.K.; the France, which had an agricultural base could avoid the more disastrous consequences of the Depression. There are definite parallels of this situation with the Indian situation today. The main reasons, why the situation has not become as disastrous in India, is that foreign trade constitutes a small part of India's Gross National Product and cushioning of the economy by the agricultural base of the country. To the market economists Indian agriculture continues to be inefficient and economically non-viable. But in the ultimate analysis, it is the agrarian economy of the country, which is the insurance against economic disaster and poverty. Indian agriculture, however, maligned by the market savvy, has been able to sustain a huge population. There has been no need of large scale migration from agriculture, as has happened in the wake of Industrial Revolution in Great Britain and other European Countries. Had an active colonisation not accompanied industrial revolution, the British peasantry would have been in a sorry state indeed. We have already discussed it earlier. The solution to the economic problem in India lies in strengthening the agriculture base and not in dismantling it. France and some of the continental European countries have held on to their traditional agricultural base and have not allowed the same to be dismantled in the wake of industrial revolution. European agriculturists in the continent, have not allowed the WTO to meddle in their agricultural production policies in the name of economic optimisation and marketisation. The French and Dutch farmers have proved to be the stumbling block to WTOs move for commercialisation of world agriculture, which would have ruined traditional farming communities. Commercialisation of agriculture in a densely populated country like India, would render bulk of the population jobless and rootless. Perverted market logic, which plays havoc with the lives of millions cannot be accepted. It is perhaps in the fitness of things that the banner of revolt against WTO policy of commercialisation of agriculture, has been raised by the French peasantry, who raised the slogan of Liberty, Equality and Fraternity at the end of the eighteenth century, to make the world safe for the common man.

Let us see the frightening economic scenario created by the war-debt imposed on Germany after the First World War. 'The results of large reparation payments upon international trade and upon the economic life of Germany and other countries were discussed by Professor F.W. Taussig in an article in the Atlantic Monthly soon after the signing of the peace treaty.'[31] Reparations which were imposed on Germany by the Allied powers, were unprecedented in international accounts. The reparation payment is limited by the availability of exportable goods. 'Somehow a huge "favourable" balance of trade—never has the phrase had greater irony—must be rapidly developed. Exports must expand, imports must shrink'. (Taussig, "Germany's Reparation Payments", *Atlantic Monthly*, March 1920). Germany must promote exports to the maximum to meet the international reparation payment imposed on it. 'Among available devices are export bounties, special rates of transportation for exported goods, and specially reduced prices of export commodities. Remission of taxes or reduction of taxes, on export industries might also be on the list. Under ordinary circumstances practices of this sort are to be condemned in the interest of the very country that applies them. Though they may promote export trade they do so to the disadvantage of the exporting country itself'. He analyses that this exercise puts Germany in a no-win situation, with serious damage to the economy. In addition, Germany will be accused of starting an export war on other countries, who will be dislodged from their traditional exports. The countries like Great Britain and France, victors of the First World War, who sought to benefit from this arrangement, will be big losers in the battle for markets. Taussig concludes his article, with this note of caution 'And so, like all the international arrangements that the war has led to, this one faces a problematic future. Who can say what sort of a world we shall find ourselves in ten years hence?'[32]

The article was published in 1920. After ten years, there was a catastrophic depression in the western world, leading to the Second World War in another eight years. This story should have a moral for the Indian planners and the World Bank and IMF bureaucracy. Under the influence of World Bank and IMF, India has been borrowing more than its capacity and has been led into a debt trap. According to the World Development Report of 1993, 'India's debt servicing as a percentage of exports of goods and services was as high as 30.7%, with Indonesia at 32.7%, whereas China had the figure of 12.1% and Pakistan 21%'.[33] India was singled out for special treatment by the IMF with a low foreign exchange reserve in 1991. A propaganda was mounted through Western credit rating agencies like Standard and Poor and Moody that investors 'lost their confidence in India'. India was not given the opportunity of rescheduling its debt, as was done on earlier occasions relating to countries that had experienced debt-servicing difficulties. During the international financial crisis of 1982, Latin American countries like Mexico and Brazil were allowed to reschedule their debts, because United States had greater economic and security stakes in these countries than in India. IMF's failure to caution India when it was walking into an external debt trap and stepping in only when debt-servicing reached critical proportions, is a clear indicator of its failure to manage international credit. IMF is sympathetic to the lenders and not to the creditors and by its policies have encouraged the lenders to act irresponsibly. 'IMF programs have served to bail out the lenders and thereby encouraged them to act irresponsibly; this is a major source of instability in the international financial system'.[34] 'Mounting a propaganda drive that there is no alternative to a massive IMF loan of 5-7 million dollars and the standardised reform package of IMF and World Bank, India launched the reform in full swing in July, 1991. The Prime Minister prefaced it in Lok Sabha with a cooked up aphorism. "Desperate maladies call for drastic remedies."[35]

How did this sorry state of affairs arise and why no steps had been taken to remedy the same, before it reached crisis proportion? Government of India's Economic Survey of 1990-91, as well as of 1991-92, pointed out 'the hardening of terms of India's external assistance in the 1980s arising from the falling share of IDA (International Development Association) assistance in the World Bank's lending profile as well as the shortening of the maturity period of IDA lending since 1987'.[36] International Development Association was set-up in September, 1960 for loaning on more flexible terms than those of World Bank. IDA contributions have come mainly from the U.S.A. and other developed countries. India fell for the World Bank bait in a big way in the seventies. Gross foreign aid received in 1972-73 was only Rs. 626 crores.[37] This more than doubled in 1974-75 to Rs. 1314 crores and became Rs. 1841 crores in 1975-76. In that year (1975-76) debt service payments on foreign assistance was Rs. 626 crores, which was equal to the gross aid received in 1972-73.[38] During this period, balance of payments gap had been widening. The balance of payments gap, which was Rs. 432 crores during 1973-74, rose to Rs. 1190 crores, the very first year of the Fifth Five Year Plan.[39] The disastrous drive of the economy into foreign exchange crisis started from the very inception of the over ambitious fifth plan. The consequences of unrealistic planning was already on the cards, when the draft fifth year plan was being formulated.

According to Economic Survey of the Government of India, 2002-03, India's external debt stood at U.S. $ 101.97 billion at the end of September, 2002. In the Economic Survey of 2001-02, Government of India congratulated itself for 'improvement of its position from close to severely indebted category in 1991 to less indebted benchmark in 1999', by quoting from World Bank report on Global Development Finance, 2001. World Bank report had assessed India's external debt at US $ 94 billion in 1999, whereas according to the Government of India's Economic Survey of 1999-2000, external debt at end-September 1999 stood at U.S. $ 98.87 billion. 'India's position improved from the third largest debtor after Brazil and Mexico in 1991 to tenth in 1999 after

Brazil, Russian Federation, Mexico, China, Indonesia, Argentina, Korea, Turkey and Thailand'.[40] According to the World Bank Global Finance Report of 2002, India slipped to ninth position in 2000, being overtaken by Thailand. This is hardly a satisfactory state of affairs, where India is competing for improving its position towards the bottom of the economic ladder of indebtedness. It is one step forward and two steps backward. The outstanding external debt increased from Rs. 359.77 billions in 1987-88 to Rs. 1215.43 billions in 1991-92.[41] Throughout the nineties, external debt has been continuously rising, reaching a figure of Rs. 3696.82 billions in 1998. The foreign indebtedness position stands at Rs. 4935.02 billions in end-September, 2002.[42]

The steep rise in external debt has been continuing over the years. With the free fall of the rupee since the beginning of the nineties and the prospect of full convertibility of the rupee, external debt will be going up steeply and will go out of control, if not checked. That this has not rung an alarm bell with the authorities, is surprising. None of the governments, since the debt crisis surfaced in the beginning of the last decade, has addressed this problem seriously, as the present debt position indicates. There has been no major effort to bring down the level of external indebtedness. The international humilation, which India faced in 1991, should not be forgotten in a hurry. The World Bank's report 'India: Sustaining Reform, Reducing Poverty 2003', warns India of a financial crisis worse than in 1991. The report is a prelude to the second generation of IMF-World Bank sponsored reforms. The sharp increase in the flow of foreign exchange over a relatively short period, cannot be taken as a vote of confidence when other economic parameters are far from satisfactory. Employment situation continues to be grim and the sudden inflow of foreign funds, coupled with easy money policy have not been able to increase employment opportunities. In fact, foreign exchange from sources like foreign institutional investors, non-resident Indians are highly volatile. Bulk of the funds from these sources are in the bourses. Once the alarm bell, which has been already rung by the World Bank goes into a higher pitch, coupled with that from the IMF, a reverse drain of foreign exchange as happened before the 1991 crisis, cannot be ruled out. The first sound of alarm bell rung by the World Bank, is a clear indication of the IMF-World Bank agenda of second generation of reforms in India. With the second generation of reforms, India will be firmly in the Western economic net with increase in unemployment. Poverty alleviation will have to depend on Western doles and charities.

Notes and References

1. Charles Gide, Political Economy, p. 352.
2-3. Amartya Sen, Resources, Values and Development, pp. 102-3.
4. George Sores, The Crisis of Global Capitalism, p. 139.
5. *Ibid.*, pp. 140-49.
6. *Ibid.*, p. 150.
7. *Ibid.*, pp. 146-47.
8. *Ibid.*, pp. 192-93.
9. Edward J. Malecki, Technology & Economic Development, p. 277.
10. Kenneth A. Oye, *et al.*, Eagle Defiant, p. 141.
11. J.K. Galbraith, Great Crash, p. 30.
12. J.M. Keynes, General Theory, p. 374.
13. Galbraith, p. 35.
14. *Ibid.*, pp. 42-43.
15. *Ibid.*, p. 80.
16. George Soros, p. 144.
17. *Ibid.*, p. 139.
18. Galbraith, pp. 31, 194.
19-20. Roorbach, Problems in Foreign Trade, pp. 46-47.
21. *Ibid.*, p. 44.
22. *Ibid.*, p. 71.
23. Galbraith, pp. 30, 42-43, 77-81, 95-99.
24. Roorbach, p. 18.
25. Government of India, Economic Survey, 1991-92, para 5.61, 5.62.
26. Eagle Defiant, p. 136.
27. *Ibid.*, p. 133.
28. *Ibid.*, p. 135.
29. Philip Oppenheim, Trade Wars, pp. 27-28.
30. Alternative Economic Survey, 1993-94, p. 24.
31. Roorbach, p. 18.
32. F.W. Tausig, 'Germany's Reparation Payments', *Atlantic Monthly*, March, 1920, Reproduced in F.W. Roorbach, pp. 19-20, 23.

33. World Development Report, 1993, World Bank, p. 284.
34. Soros, p. 180.
35. Alternative Economic Survey, 1993-94, p. 28.
36. Government of India, Economic Survey, 1991-92, para 5.45.
37. B.S. Minhas, Planning and the Poor, p. 132.
38. Draft Five Year Plan, 1978-83, Planning Commission, Government of India, p. 77. (*Source*: Economic Survey, 1977-78)
39. *Ibid.*, pp. 75-76.
40. Economic Survey, 2001-02, Government of India, p. 159.
41. India Reducing Poverty, Accelerating Development, The World Bank, Oxford University Press, 2000, Table A 4.14, p. 238.
42. Economic Survey, 2002-03, Government of India, Table 6.14, p. 125.

There is considerable difference between World Bank figures and the Government of India figures. For example, outstanding external debt is shown as Rs. 2245.32 billions for 1997-98 (provisional) at current prices in the World Bank Report (p. 238) mentioned at note 41, whereas Government of India figures are Rs. 3696.82 billions. The World Bank Report at box 8.1, p. 109, points out several discrepancies in data furnished by Reserve Bank of India and Government of India and asks for improving its quality and consistency. It may be that the accounting methods followed by the World Bank and Government of India vary. However, such variation of figures, points to a serious discrepancy in the accounting practices of World Bank and Government of India.

World Bank and IMF practice has been to soft-pedal the external debt problem of the debtor countries and blow the whistle suddenly when the country is in a political transition phase and at its weakest. According to Government of India estimates, which can be taken to be more reliable, as being based on primary sources, India's external debt position is far worse than that being shown by the World Bank.

6

What is our Priority: Luxury or Necessity

The present world economic structure is being built-up on consumerism, the need for which is being created by mass motivational campaign, subtle or otherwise. During the last three hundred years, demand pattern and how the same can be manipulated, has been the subject of discussion and concern not only for traders and manufacturers but also for statesmen. It had long been realised that consumption or demand aspect of the economy is a powerful economic tool but had been neglected because of its vexatious nature. Propensity to consume is not uniform and varies from masses to the classes. 'Supply creates its own demand' seems to be the basic postulate on which economic theories were based. Societal consumption function is too complex a phenomenon on which to base economic theories. Keynes calls this aggregate effective demand, but he has dealt with it in monetary terms by relating to money-wages and interest rate. This is only one aspect of the problem. In his 'Note on Mercantilism'[1] in the 'General Theory', Keynes has made extensive use of Heckscher's book on Mercantilism, to highlight the major theme of Mercantilists' 'fear of goods', which is the basis of under consumption, which weakness the economy, as it discourages employment. Fear of over-production is basically limitation of the market, which is the basis of economic nationalism and trade war. It was also the basis of British Colonialism and Capitalism in search of new markets.

'Minutes of Evidence, etc. on the Affairs of the East India Company (1813),'[2] clearly indicate the keen awareness of the British Parliament of the potential of the Indian market for factory produced goods. Great Britain was on the threshold of the Industrial Revolution and the necessity of a vast market to consume factory produced goods was felt. It is of significance that the enquiries were primarily about the demand pattern of the Indian peasantry and not about the demand pattern of the higher classes. This shows the keen awareness of the British Parliamentarians that Industrial Revolution could only be achieved on the demand-base of mass consumer goods. Demand for consumer goods of mass consumption is likely to be constant and not subject to vagaries of taste and fortune like luxuries. Demand for luxuries by the Indians in higher income groups, did not offer any immediate scope for large scale factory production of goods. British parliamentary committee was keenly aware of the need for finding new markets for the products of their factories to achieve the Industrial Revolution. They were sufficiently aware that unless constant long-range demand could be ensured, proper production-planning, to ensure the organisation of the factory system on a long-term basis with definite production pattern was not possible. Prior to the factory system, items of commerce were mostly luxury goods and Europe was a net importer of the same from the East. Demand for items of luxury goods is guided by several factors like changes in taste, quality and the surplus income available for being spent on luxuries. Tastes of people in demand of luxury goods fluctuate, as such it is not possible to have a long range production plan for luxury goods.

While, demand for luxury goods is subject to fluctuations, demand for necessities is more steady. Necessities and luxuries vary from one economic situation to another, but in a static economy the demand for necessities is unlikely to fluctuate. With such assured demand, it is possible to have long-range production planning. For organised industrial activity, it is necessary to ensure adequate demand for matching the increased supply. Thus, while the academic economists neglected the concept of aggregate effective demand, as too complex a phenomenon to fit in with the existing economic logic, the British Parliamentarians and men of affairs were fully aware of the role of aggregate effective demand in supporting organised industrial activities. The awareness of the role of aggregate effective demand is clear from the searching questions put to different witnesses regarding the potential of Indian market. It is also significant that emphasis was given on ascertaining the demand-pattern of the Indian peasantry. This shows clearly that the British men of affairs of the day, who influenced the course of economic history, were clearly aware that number of consumers is an important determinant of the demand pattern. Export of manufactured goods became for the first time quantity-oriented with the coming of factory system. The employees and agents of the Company and the British Government were expected to promote consumption of British manufactures. The Parliamentary Committee was aimed at a market survey of the potentiality of the Indian market. Persons who had served in the highest offices in India were expected to provide information to the committee on the prospective demand for British goods by the Indian consumers.

During the period of mass production of goods, which characterised the first phase of industrial revolution, when the mercantilist theory had intellectual authority, the concern for finding markets was quite rational. This was not solved by increasing the wages of the workers and raising their standard of living, along with an increase in demand. A picture of happy co-relation between industrialists and workers has been projected from time to time. This rosy picture was believed by some, under consistent English propaganda. France, nearest to England was made to believe, 'Thus, by the working of a system that seems paradoxical, the English have grown rich by consuming'.[3] This statement dates to 1792 in France and might have been one of the causes of the French Revolution, when French wrongly believed that the condition of the working class was much better in England. French merchants were unhappy with their government for not pursuing a pro-active policy of industrialisation. This picture was completely wrong, as we have seen industrial revolution depended on cheap raw materials, low cost of production and finding an assured market. The first and third were assured by colonisation. It is naive to assume that the profits of higher production were ploughed back to the workers. In case this was done the living standard of the English workers would have gone up spectacularly, which was not the case. This utopia of increased production creating its own demand, was subtly built-up to cover another facet of industrialisation, viz. colonisation. Moreover, increased production requires increased capital, which is only possible through increased savings and not increased consumption of the gains from industry. Charles Babbage, who was acquainted with the mechanics of industrialisation, along with an understanding of the forces of industrialisation, observed, 'The division of labour cannot be successfully practised unless there exists a great demand for its produce; and it requires larger capital to be employed in those arts in which it is used'.[4] No doubt, the production side was taken care of by thrift and increased investment. Protestant ethics of saving had a lot to do with British Capitalism. The economists of the industrial revolution, from Adam Smith onwards to Pigou, who have been charcterised as classical school of economists, were right in holding that capital is increased through parsimony; and frugal man is benefactor of the society and spend thrift the opposite. Frugality is a virtue, as excess income over consumption, increases wealth through increased investment. Keynes's lampooning of the classical school, including his own teachers like Marshall and Pigou, is based on wrong premises. Had Britain of industrial revolution indulged in lavish spending, instead of practising parsimony; the ever increasing investment in keeping the wheels of industry moving, would not have been possible. The profits from industries were ploughed back for increased production. The consumers were basically colonial people, where quantitative cheap mass produced goods displaced quality goods. This was done in a variety of ways, which we have discussed. As has been put by German mercantilist Becher, 'that it is always better to sell goods to others than to buy goods from others, for the former brings a certain advantage and the latter inevitable damage'.[5] The profits were obtained from captive consumers in India and in formal and informal empire.

After the Indian peasants and artisans were deprived of their means of livelihood, due to the onslaught of industrial revolution and became net consumers instead of producers, they could hardly be depended on as purchasers. As we have seen industrial revolution destroyed the production base and impoverished the countryside. As such, their priority as consumers became low. The second phase of industrial revolution tried to explore the possibility of introducing luxury goods produced in England, amongst the Indian rich and the nouveau rich. British administrators and commercial interests were quick enough to see the tendency towards emulating the consumption pattern of the rulers among this class of Indians. The rulers were looked upon as ideals and their consumption pattern provided so desirable a commodity that there was competition among this class of Indians to emulate the same. However, even this class of Indians through their luxury consumption, could provide a limited incentive to further the steam of industrial revolution. The second phase of industrial revolution was not based on consumption, but on investments at guaranteed rates of interest, as was done in the case of construction of railways in India. There was also the desire to industrialise on the part of other countries and this also provided boost to the capital goods sector. The machinery exported were second generation machines and did not help to generate any major industrial development in the importing countries. The machinery based on earlier technology soon became out-dated and obsolete. The investment on these machines hardly repaid themselves in most cases. But it immensely helped in continuing the second phase of industrialisation in Britain, which was based on coal and iron.

It was left to heretics like Mandeville to praise conspicuous consumption. There was however, no dearth of conspicuous consumption as the drain of wealth from the colonies were enormous. Fox-hunting, country houses, theatres and opera came up to cater to the needs of the British rich. However, this did not generate any wealth and only helped in embellishing a feudal, coupled with colonial life-style. The employment generated was only marginal and that too of a slavish class of servile retainers and not independent industrial workers. Bernard Mandeville in his book, 'The Fable of the Bees: or Private Vices, Public Benefits' (first published in 1705), which was probably a satire on the prevailing morality of colonial England, mentions that 'I have laid down as Maxims never to be departed from, that the poor should be kept strictly to work, and that it was prudence to relieve their wants, but Folly to cure them; . . . It is in the Interest of rich Nations, that the greatest part of the poor should almost never be Idle, and yet continually spend what they get'.[6] Meszaros comments, 'Undoubtedly, the unfolding productive and distributive practices of the capital system bring major changes in this respect, at least for the 'large stirring Nations'. Since there can be no production without consumption of some kind, the expansion of capitalist production necessitates the broader distribution of the produced good'.[7] Historical coincidence of industrial revolution and colonisation was not an accident but a deliberate design. Without heavily populated colonies like India, mass-production of textile was not possible. According to Meszaros, Mandeville, writing in the initial stage of industrial revolution, could see through the cause and effect of the same. Individual greed, which can only be satisfied by luxury spending and accumulation, was the dominant spirit of industrial revolution and the *raison d' etre* of the capitalist social structures, which it created. The benefits of the few can be continued through constant accumulation of wealth and luxury spending, without which the steam of industrial revolution will run out.

Mandeville had been criticised severely by his contemporaries. This was primarily because he exposed the prevailing hypocracy of colonial Great Britain. Meszaros, while discussing about Mandeville's thesis, writes, 'These are major insights into the real motivating spirit and objective structural imperatives of the capitalist system from its origin to the present, arrived at notwithstanding the limitation of

Mandeville's social standpoint. The conclusions he draws about the nature of 'luxury' are particularly important. Being a truly radical thinker within the boundaries of his class horizon, he seizes the issue at its roots by bringing into focus its vital practical implications'.[8] Mandeville's basic preoccupation with the poor, as the sources of wealth for the rich, both as producers and consumers of goods, is the basic philosophy of colonialism and eighteenth century British capitalism. Production of wealth is directly proportionate to the number of poor, with some degree of purchasing power. The poor need not be limited by the geographical area of the country, but can be found throughout the empire and beyond. While writing about luxury, Mandeville states, 'Many things, which were once looked upon as the invention of Luxury, are now allowed even to those that are so miserably poor as to become the Objects of Public charity, nay counted so necessary, that we think no Human Creature ought to want them'.[9] Thus even the poor are sought to be tempted with worthless commodities at the cost of their necessities. 'The Hidden Persuaders' of consumerism can be also let loose among the poorer sections. This has been also the history of colonialism, where the colonial people were tempted with small trinkets to part with their land. Use of the hidden persuaders of consumerism, has also been one of the means of colonialism in addition to guns. Manipulating the tastes of the consumers to suit the production pattern, is one of the subtle tools, cleverly used.

Keynes thought that what Mandeville had said about consumption as a prime mover of development in the beginning of industrial revolution and colonial pattern of development, may be possibly a remedy for depression ridden Britain. Mandeville finds favour with Keynes for advocating 'Lavishness' instead of 'Frugality' for development of the country's economy. Keynes quotes from Leslie Stephen's summary of Mandeville's Fable of bees from the Dictionary of National Biography (1873) and History of English Thought in the Eighteenth Century (1876): 'Mandeville gave great offence by this book, in which cynical system of morality was made attractive by ingenious paradoxes. His doctrine that prosperity was increased by expenditure rather than by saving fell in with many current economic fallacies not yet extinct'.[10] In support of his doctrine of conspicuous consumption, Keynes has quoted a number of less known authors. 'In 1662 Petty justified "entertainments, magnificent shows, triumphal arches, etc.", on the ground that their costs flowed back into the pockets of brewers, bakers, tailors, shoemakers and so forth'. Keynes has also quoted Von Schortter (1686), Barbon (1690) and Cary (1695), as protagonists of prodigality. According to Barbon (1690), 'Prodigality is a vice, that is prejudicial to the Man, but not trade'.[11] Pyramid building by the Ancient Egyptians and search for precious metals, created the fabled wealth of Ancient Egypt, according to Keynes in the General Theory.[12] Building of cathedral in Europe in the Middle Ages, created employment and enriched the society. Keynes was not probably aware that these monuments were built on slave labour or indentured labour. From the pictorial depiction and other available records of the construction of these monuments, it is clear that the casualty amongst the work-force was exceedingly high due to accidents, caused because of lack of minimum safety considerations for the workers. There was also pestilence and other diseases caused due to unhygienic conditions of living. In fact, such type of construction activities have been responsible for creations of slums from ancient times to modern times. J.D. Bernal in 'Science in History', in which he deals with the interaction of science and society, has this to say, 'We may rightly admire the Pyramids as a feat of architecture and engineering, but what they do represent is a waste of labour of tens of thousands for the hypothetical benefit of the soul of the Pharaoh, and for the real prestige and rake-off of the priestly contractors'.[13]

It is probably no coincidence that Italy, which has the largest number of magnificent Cathedrals in Europe, was also affected by plague and other pestilences in the Middle Ages, when Cathedral building was an industry in Europe. The classics of Boccacio-'Decameron', Dante-'Divine Comedy' in the fourteenth century Italy are full of tragedies created by such pestilences and the author's attempt to find a religious meaning of the same. It is obvious that the slum like conditions created in the cities and the pestilential diseases, breeding in the same did not spare the rich and the powerful. Beautiful and artistic cities of Europe, were the breeding grounds of pestilence and disease. People were drawn away from the countryside, either forcibly or through religious fervour to live a sub-human existence in cramped work-places under unhygienic conditions in the cities and build magnificent monuments. Magnificent cities of Europe, were also the breeding ground of Plague and other diseases, which were unknown in the countryside till they were transmitted from the cities. Will Durant in his 'The story of Civilisation (Vol. 4)—The Age of Faith', while dealing with pestilences has referred to Garrison's History of Medicine, 'The harassed population ascribed these epidemics to famines, droughts, swarms of insects, astral influences, poisoning of wells by Jews, or the wrath of God; the likelier causes were the crowded condition of the small walled towns, poor sanitation and hygiene, and consequent lack of defense against infections carried by returning soldiers, pilgrims, or students'. To add to the woes of common people, public baths, which was an institution of Roman Civilisation, was abolished as offensive to Christian morality. 'Cleanliness, in the middle Ages, was not next to godliness. Early Christianity had denounced the Roman baths as wells of perversion and promiscuity, and its general disapproval of the body had put no premium on hygiene'. Then again 'Cleanliness was next to money, and varied with income: the feudal lord and the rich bourgeois bathed with reasonable frequency, in large wooden tubs'.[14]

An analysis of the labour dynamics in building these magnificent monuments in the ancient and medieval times would show that the peasantry was drawn from the country-side either forcibly or through allurement to spend their life miserably in the ghettos of towns to build magnificent monuments, palaces, cathedrals and tombs for their temporal and spiritual masters. Times of crop-failure, famine and other distress conditions in the country-side were found most suitable to draw away small peasantry from their agricultural holdings and use them for construction of monuments and magnificent palaces in the cities. This exercise will also help the richer peasantry in the country-side from appropriating the holdings of small farmers, who had to leave their holdings for the cities due to bad harvest. Middle ages was the time when rich peasantry was turning themselves into landlords by expropriating the smaller farmers, who were driven to the cities to eke out a living by working as construction workers for magnificent palaces and monuments built out of the agriculture surplus generated in the countryside. To call these people, who spend their resources in building unproductive assets, benefactors of society in creating employment, as, has been made out by Keynes in 'General Theory' is travesty of truth. Keynes is, however, honest enough to admit, 'It is not reasonable, however, that a sensible community should be content to remain dependent on such fortuitous and often wasteful mitigations when once we understand the influences upon which effective demand depends'.[15] There is, however, no prescription in the General Theory besides 'building houses for the posterity' and 'digging holes in the ground for precious metals'.[16]

'General Theory' of Keynes goes on to say that Mandeville's 'Fable of the Bees' stands out in the history of the moral sciences for its scandalous reputation'.[17] Adam Smith, the founder of English classical School of Economics, was highly critical of Mandeville's work 'Compare Adam Smith, the forerunner of the classical school, who wrote, "What is prudence in the conduct of every private family can scarce be folly in that of a great Kingdom."[18] Schumpeter in his "History of Economic Analysis" suspects that there is more to Adam Smith's hostility to Mandeville than the latter's advocating spending against thrift. 'Smith cannot have failed to perceive that Mandeville's argument was an argument for Smith's own pure Natural Liberty couched in a particular form. The reader will have no difficulty in realizing how this fact must have shocked the respectable professor—particularly if it should be the case that he learned something from the offending pamphlet'.[19] Keynes mentions that 'Only one man is recorded as having spoken a good word for it, namely, Dr. Johnson, who declared that it did not puzzle him, but "opened his eyes into real life very much."[20] Samuel Johnson (1709-1784) was critical of the hypocrisy of his time.

Johnson was a harsh critic of England's policy towards India and the colonies. 'His bitingly sardonic dissection of a dilettantish and complacent study of the nature of evil and of human suffering, A free Enquiry into the Nature an Origin of Evil, by the theological writer Soame Jenyns, may well be the best review in English during the "18th century: This author and Pope perhaps never saw the miseries which they imagine thus easy to be borne."' Johnson's sarcasm to the Americans, who opposed England's right of taxation, '"How is it that we hear the loudest yelps for liberty from the drivers of Negroes?" can be traced in large part to a principled and consistent stance against colonial oppression'.[21] Samuel Johnosn could see in the work of Mandeville, a theoretical justification of the rapacious economic policy being followed by Great Britain towards its colonies and its own poorer people (as has been vividly depicted by Charles Dickens in his novels), in the name of industrial revolution. Mandeville's great crime was that he chose to speak the truth blatantly, while other scholars and theologians indulged in polemics or tried to give a moral authority to the theory of Exploitation. 'This relativisation of luxury and necessity, destruction and production, vice and virtue—together with the underlying interests and contradictions—is spelled out, with a clear and unashamed admission of the exploitative character of the system, in Bernard Mandeville's Fable of the Bees'.[22] Hayek, the high priest of market capitalism found Mandeville's role pioneering in the development of individualism and self-regulating market mechanism.[23] Keynes, not a believer in the self-regulating market-mechanism at least in the twenties and thirties, when his most important works were written, found much to bolster his theory of under-consumption in Mandeville's hypothesis of unbridled consumerism.

Schumpeter in his 'History of Economic Analysis' has mentioned about Becher's principle. Becher's Politischere Discurs (1668), 'contains the rudiments of an analytic schema that turns upon people's expenditure on consumption the prime mover or, as Becher said, the "soul" of economic life. In itself the observation that one man's expenditure is another man's income—or that consumer's expenditure generates income—is as old as it is trivial. We shall call it

Becher's Principle, because he seems to have been the first to realize its theoretical possibilities. He did little to develop any system of Monetary Analysis and, of course, left plenty for Lord Keynes to do'. Schumpeter wryly comments that Keynes makes no mention of Becher, although the latter was the pioneer of the theory of under-consumption, albeit in a rudimentary form. 'Becher he does not mention. Instead he mentions W. Von Schroder (1640-88); main work: Furstliche Schatz-und Rentkammer, (1686), a less important especially less original, contemporary of Becher, who seems to have been influenced both by the latter and by Thomas Mun'.[24] Keynes in the General Theory, while mentioning about earlier economists advocating greater spending on luxury items, writes, 'Von Schortter (1686) deprecated sumptuary regulations and declared that he would wish that display in clothing and the like were even greater'.[25] The reason for Von Schrotter (or von Schroder, as Schumpeter writes), instead of Becher, finding favour with Keynes, is not far to seek. Becher's principle fostered a school of thinkers and administrators in Germany. 'It is not surprising that Becher found successors in Germany. The German Consultant Administrators were far indeed from understanding the analytic importance of his principle. But Monetary Analysis, in the sense defined, works with concepts which, though actually very abstract and indeed unrealistic, carry a surface meaning that is perfectly familiar to everyone. . . . Thus, many of them believed in the pivotal importance of high-level mass consumption or, to put the same thing into their normative way of expressing themselves, in measures that would stimulate mass consumption'.[26] The school of thinking developed by Becher in Germany favoured mass consumption to stimulate the economy, whereas Keynes was trying to develop a school of thought which favoured luxury spending and magnificence.

This falls in line with the prevailing English attitude towards economic inequality. Five years before, the publication of 'General Theory', the English Economic Historian, R.H. Tawney, a contemporary of Keynes had brought out his book 'Equality' (1931) Tawney found England to be one of the most non-egalitarian countries. 'While in

France and Scandinavia, and even in parts of the United States, there is, at least, an initial sympathy for the conception, and disposition to be proud of such economic equality as exists, in England the instinctive feeling is one, not of sympathy, but of apprehension and repulsion, as though economic equality were a matter upon which it were not in good taste to touch? . . . they are determined to reject the idea (of equality).[27] Any talk of equality became further unfashionable. 'By 1960 England had become a more muffled society. The condition of its people, rich, middling and poor, was concealed by a combination of myth and computer incompetence. Inequality, as a subject of political discourse, was less in evidence every where. . . . The Common man, his rulers assured him in common language, 'had never had it so good'. It was high time he was led into the larger market place of choice where he could purchase for himself and his family whatever he preferred in the way of education, medical care and social security. Was this the end of equalitarian ideology?'[28]

Keynes lent his considerable academic weight in favour or conspicuous consumption. In that, he was making a complete break from the past traditions of economics. Adam Smith's Wealth of Nations had a strong moral streak in it and the classical school could not get away from it. 'We must not forget that the author of the Theory of the Wealth of Nations was also the author of the Theory of Moral Sentiments; and we cannot understand the economic ideas of the one without some, knowledge of the philosophy of the other'.[29] It was natural that under the weight of such moral ethics, thrift was a virtue and profiligacy a vice. Keynes of the Bloomsbury set could break out of such moral shackles and openly espouse conspicuous consumption, so far reserved for heretics of economic science. The cult of thrift, however did not prevent accumulation of Wealth. Britain, particularly London, has all the 'manifestations of long-accumulated wealth'.[30] In Britain, during the nineteenth century, 'what previously had been courtly preferences in music and art trickled down to the nouveaux riches. . . . As capitalism expanded across the globe these cultural institutions were carried by its dominant class'.[31] Britain had specialised in wealth and Luxury-related industries and services due to huge flow of colonial funds through trade and taxation, 'Many of the industries in which Britain still has competitive advantage today are related to luxury, leisure, entertainment, and wealth. Early and advanced demand often provided the initial seed'.[32] While, Britain specializes in luxury goods, the average consumer is left high and dry. 'The average British consumer today has become a less demanding buyer than consumers in many other nations, and more resign to poor service or sub-standard quality. . . . A foreigner notices immediately how loath British people are to complain openly. Unfortunately, a staff upper lip is not good for upgrading an economy'.[33]

Literature on the subject of expenditure on consumption, of the pre-revolutionary France, is of interest to us, as focusing on the economic causes of French Revolution. According to Schumpeter, Boisguillebert's contribution in the matter, was the most noteworthy on the subject. 'Boisguillebert (1646-1714) was a public spirited member of semi-hereditary civil service gentry of pre-revolutionary France'. A cult had developed round him and he was considered by some authors like Eugene Daire to be the forerunner of the Physiocratic school of thought, particularly Quesnay and the Columbus of economics. The cult was subsequently revived by some of the authors like Bordewijk in Theoretisch-historische Inleidingtot de Economie (1931) and Roberts, Boisguillebert: Economist of the Reign of Louis XIV (1935). Boisguillebert's theory is of interest to us in the sense that he considered landowners, to be the most dependable spenders, as against the wage earners. 'While we look upon the wage earners as the most dependable spenders, Boisguillebert, in the social pattern of his time, assigned this role to the landowners. But these differences serve only to emphasize the fundamental similarity both of his theory and his outlook upon practical problems with those of our own time'.[34] Schumpeter's grounding in the Austro-German school of thought favoured the mass-consumption theory developed by Becher and his intellectual successors. Schumpeter goes on to say that Boisguilleberts's 'horror never surpassed by anyone's outside the United State Senate, of that worst of all disasters—cheap bread. With delightful naivete he warned lawyers, physicians, actors, and so forth not to clamour for low prices of agricultural products: in doing so they were 'digging their own graves'; for the landowners, who are nothing but intermediate spenders, would then find their incomes reduced and have to reduce their expenditure, and where would those lawyers, et cetera, be?'[35] Boisguillebert's conception of a prosperous society was Dearness and Plenty, not Cheapness and Plenty. Schumpeter says, 'Quesnay was of the same opinion in regards to prices (see, especially, his Maximes generales, 1758).[36] The argument was that cheapness of agricultural commodities, is not of advantage for the poor, as it makes their wages fall. The fallacy of their argument is that such a situation is possible, only if there is full-employment. Full employment is a hypothesis, which has not been achieved anywhere at any time. There is always underemployment and unemployment. Even if there is some marginal increase in wages in the agricultural sector, all the wage-earners will not benefit equally, whereas the high price will be the same for all. Labour force which is unemployed or under-employed will be worse hit by rising prices. Workers in other trade and profession, where the prices have not increased proportionately, will also be hit by rising prices in other sectors, particularly agriculture.

Will and Ariel Durant in their 'The Story of Civilization (Vol. XI)', while analyzing the economic causes of the French Revolution mentions that at that time, French upper middle class controlled half the money of Europe, according to the estimate of Necker, Finance Minister of Louis XVI. They utilised their money in speculation on the stock exchanges of Paris, London and Amsterdam. They controlled the industries of France. 'They managed the capitalist industry that was replacing the craft shops and guilds of the past; they welcomed the doctrine of the physiocrats that free enterprise would be more stimulating and productive than the traditional regulation of industry and trade by the state'.[37] The advice of the economists like Boisguillebert, Quesnay and the Physiocrats contributed significantly to the causes of French Revolution. Policy against cheap bread and lower prices was the principle reason for alienating the urban and rural poor against the State. Marie Antoinette's aphorism, 'Let them eat cake, if they don't have bread' directed against the poor, was in tune with Boisguillebert and the Physiocrats policy of high prices and openly advocating a policy against cheap bread. It is perhaps the advice of such prophets given under false assumptions, which create great damage to the society and country. At the outset of the French Revolution, France was not a poor country and there was sizable population of rich people, but majority of the French people were poor, due to the economic policies followed under the advice of Boisguillebert and the Physiocrats, which the King and his advisors had taken too seriously. In case Statesmen are guided by theoreticians, instead of harsh realities learnt from their experience as public men and their own vision, this type of catastrophy may repeat itself. It should be remembered that economic laws are not inexorable. They are based on certain hypothetical conditions which change. Man should not be slave to certain so called laws which exist in the realm of theory. Economic forces can be controlled by man and for that vision is required.

The temporary eclipse of socialism should not blind us to the vision of an egalitarian society, which emerged through the ages and promised a great future for mankind. Similarly, the second generation problems of the gigantic public sector projects, which was to control the commanding heights of the economy, should not lead us to dismantling this mighty industrial structure, which was the pride of the country and product of a vision of awakening a sleeping giant, i.e. India. We should not fall into any shortsighted trap to dismantle this mighty structure in the name of privatisation. What belongs to the nation and built-up on the blood and toil of millions and on the vision of great Indians should not be handed over to a few money-bags, either Indian or Foreign. The slogan of defeatism will make us a nation of losers. We have sufficient technical manpower in India to save these public sector units, within the resources available in the country. India's basic economic strength is based on the public sector projects and dismantling the infrastructural projects would put the economic clock back. Basic industries may not be in fashion today in the international economic scenario dominated by the West.

World markets have been tailored to the consumer-oriented industries. But such industries sustain the world economy, as they have low-employment potential, with bulk of the economic activities being concentrated in the developed western countries. To cite the example of automobile industry, which is a high valued consumer goods industry, manufacturing passenger cars targeted at the nouveau rich of the developing countries; the multinationals saw a great opportunity in this industry of exporting out-dated foreign technology at an exorbitant cost. This experiment proved to be economically non-viable, as the market was limited and there were too many competitors in the field. This did not prevent the multinationals from repatriating their profits and leaving the smaller Indian shareholders, who have been trapped in the bourses with promises of a profitable investment, with the entire loss. Automobile industry throughout the world is going through a crisis and they are trying to avoid the collapse through mergers and remergers. These automobile companies saw in the Indian market an opportunity to revive their sagging fortunes by trying to sell their out-dated models. This met with a limited success as far as the multinationals are concerned. But it completely ruined the indigenous automobile industry and a large network of ancillary industries, which had been built round it. The small-scale sector, which was providing components for the passenger cars, was destroyed, as components manufactured by Indian small-scale industries, were not favoured. Indigenous component manufacturing was not encouraged in the name of quality control. Servicing sector of these automobiles was closely guarded, so that no servicing sector develops indigenously. The foreign manufacturers ensured that there is no spread-effect of industrial development and the manufacturing facilities limited to the parent country, with minimum assembling work being done in India.

IMPORTS OF LUXURY

Colonisation of India led to the Indian rich taking to the English consumption pattern, towards the last quarter of the nineteenth century. This was a new trend in Indian commerce, because since times immemorial, India was a net exporter of luxury goods and not importer. It was no accident of history, but a deliberate policy to create a market for British goods amongst the Indian rich, who were so far dependant on Indian products, which were much superior to foreign products, due to superior workmanship. Over the past several centuries, luxury items had always travelled from India to the West. Even, 'In 1857, a writer could remark, "the native land-holder, and banker, and merchant, and judicial officer, in his articles of luxury, in his ornaments, and in his dress, to a large extent, uses still the products of his country." But the growing figures of import during the period under consideration (1870-1930) . . . . leave no room for doubt as to the sources on which the rich and the comfortable were increasingly depending for the supply of their domestic needs. . . . It is in this widening of the range of imports, as marking a departure from the old immemorial habits of the native population, that the new era stands out in sharp relief against any preceding period of Indian commercial history'.[38] From the beginning of the nineteenth century, British colonialism was able to introduce the western culture in India, amongst the rich. Being the culture of the rulers, this was considered superior to the culture of the ruled and the Indian rich took to it in a big way. Since that time there has been no let up in this and after liberalisation under the guise of globalisation, consumption of foreign goods has gone up by leaps and bounds. Now the rich can go on shopping junkets to London and other exotic places. 'Britain also retains a domestic consumer base for luxury and wealth-related goods, especially around London. . . . Wealthy foreigners buy products in London and also, provide a base of foreign demand'.[39] This, while, the average British consumer has to put up with poor service and substandard quality of goods in his home market. The rights of the rich and the nouveau rich to foreign goods have been asserted, whereas the rights of the majority to have a decent existence is a far cry. Wonderful is the achievement of globalisation and liberalisation.

The colonial government in London was keenly aware of the need for creating a market in India for English luxuries, amongst the richer classes of the population, in addition of pushing up the mass-produced goods throughout the length and breadth of India, through deliberate state policies. The former was in the guise of export of British culture. House of Commons' Committee of British Parliament of 1832, enquired, 'Has there been any increase among the natives in the indulgence of English tastes, fashions, and habits'? To which the reply was, 'Judging from Calcutta, there has been, I think, a marked tendency among the natives to indulge in English luxuries.'[40] The export of British culture to India, created a stable market in India for a variety of English consumer goods, including artistic products, where the Britishers were newcomers, as France and other continental countries were far superior in this sphere. 'British tastes and culture were exported throughout the Empire. The Empire reinforced the tendency toward high-end or luxury demand. Expatriates served as the elite administrators of British colonies and defined the tastes of those abroad with the wealth to buy imported goods.'[41] British administrators, in addition to their administrative duties, had the unwritten job of spreading British culture with a view to create markets for British products. Britain continued to depend on former British colonies for export to support its industries. Britain has slipped down the economic ladder, because 'Not only is demand quality low in Britain's traditional markets but their potential to buy British goods has lagged behind as well'.[42] Even after two centuries, British colonisation of Indian economy continues. Large-scale import of British machinery for industrialisation of India has not led to any satisfactory result for India. It has only increased our economic imbalance with Britain. The first public sector steel plant at Durgapur, built with British technology has been a non-starter, mainly due to defective technology, although cunningly the blame has been passed on to labour.

As regards luxury consumption, the craze to copy the Western culture, particularly British and now American, has occurred due to the cultural onslaught. Britishers in India deliberately created a taste for British culture, mainly enjoyment of British luxury goods amongst the Indian rich. The explanation lies in consumer culture controlling the individual, rather than the other way round. 'Possession and consumption are the banner which advertises achievement—which proclaims, by the accepted standards of the community, that the possessor is a success'.[43] In Velben's own words, 'The motive that lies at the root of ownership is emulation. . . . The possession of wealth confers honour; it is an invidious distinction'.[44] This is not the behaviour of a rational economic man and goes more in the realm of anthropology than economics. The motivations of the rich are no different from the festivities of primitive tribals. 'The effort to establish precedence for one's self and the yearning for the resulting esteem and applause are the most universal of human tendencies. Nothing in this respect differentiates a Whitney, Vanderbilt or Astor from a Papuan chieftain or what one encounters in for instance, the tribes of the Andamans'.[45] The base conspicuous consumption of today, made possible by bending technology to the needs of the rich, is a throw-back on barbarism and cannot be treated as an advancement of civilization. When technology becomes a tool in the hands of the rich and powerful, the frivolities of the latter reach unprecedented dimensions. Barbarism of this type, while pandering to a society of conspicuous consumers, will continuously widen the gap between the rich and poor. To Veblen, 'The rich are merely anthropological specimens',[46] whose behaviour makes them more ridiculous and the study of the same more interesting. But the connotations of unlimited enjoyment are more serious than this. Society's resources being limited, diverting a greater share of the same for unlimited luxury, is at the cost of necessities. Increase in luxury spending is proportionate to the increase of deprivation. Technology in the hands of the rich and powerful poses a serious threat to mankind. A thickly populated country like India is the most vulnerable in this matter. It goes beyond the question of morality and is a problem of basic economics, with constant resources. The luxury items are not created simply by value additions, but by diversion of community's resources. Luxury cars consume huge amount of fossil oil, besides minerals like iron and bauxite, which are in limited supply, as also creating enormous amount of pollution for others, who are less fortunate. Luxury villas and estates, occupy large portion of land, which is a scarce commodity; at the same time creating slums for the huge work-force required to serve them.

Malcolm Waters in his book 'Globalisation', writes, 'Consumption-based cultural globalisation actually began in the nineteenth century but in the arena of elite or bourgeois culture'.[47] Globalised consumer culture is an extension of colonialism. As we have seen, the colonial rulers had the task of cultural colonialism, which provided a growing market for luxury goods and services. This assured a regular market for export of such goods and services from England to India. The rich Indians emulated the life-style of the British lords. 'Individual identity is conflated to culture. Capitalism transforms people into consumers by altering their structure of wants, in directions that serve capitalist accumulation'.[48] Individual and national identity is lost in this cultural colonisation, which is now known as globalisation. This universal culture, will be available only to a select few. A small portion of the population in developed countries will be part of this cultural globalisation and a much smaller portion in developing countries. In the case of a country like India with a vast population, such cultural globalisation will cover a minuscule portion of the population. Such cultural globalisation creates an universal club of the rich, which transcends national barrier. Under the scheme of globalisation, this club is expected to rule the world economically and politically. This has various implications for the vast majority of world's population, who are stuck within national boundaries and have no hope of joining this exclusive club. The unification of the world's rich and powerful under the guise of globalisation, is a trend, which needs to be watched. It may create a world Government of the rich and powerful, in which the majority of the population, will have, less and less the benefit of their national and local Governments, to look to their survival.

SOCIAL OBLIGATION OF GOVERNMENT

Bread, one of the cheapest items in the diet of the rich and the upper middle-classes, but one of the key items in the food of the urban poor and children can play a major role in bringing about a major event in world history, is probably incomprehensible to a majority of policy-makers and their economic advisers. Probably, they can say with Marie Antoinette 'Let them eat Mc. Donalds' pizza and burger, if they do not have bread'.[49] This absence of any cogent economic thinking in any attempt to address itself to the needs of the poor, constitutes a disturbing trend in today's dominant economic prescriptions. Poor do not create wealth or improve the international growth statistics as the rich do and are gradually becoming non-economic persons, who live in the periphery of the economic world. The majority of world's population, who have been deprived and are being gradually deprived of their means of production are becoming non-persons in the economic sense and will have to increasingly live on charities and doles.

The system of charities and doles for the poor, which is being envisaged by the rich, will certainly assuage the conscience of the rich nations and the rich people, but will only marginally be of any use otherwise. Charities and doles, while good for the conscience of the rich nations and rich individuals is an attempt to address an economic problem through non-economic method. Are we to understand that economic science has reached a point of no return in addressing itself to the problems of the majority of the population? Talks of scientific socialism and communism have become meaningless today for the world's poor, after these failed to address themselves to their problems. Economic science has made an about turn under the auspices of IMF, World Bank and their cohorts, to make the rich richer and poor poorer. It is technology, which creates wealth and technology is the monopoly of the rich. The present brand of technology creates islands of prosperity, surrounded by oceans of poverty. These oceans are meant for poorer countries, while developed countries will have their seas. Even in the paradise of prosperity, the U.S.A., 'In the mid-1990s, thirty-six million American lived below income levels officially designated as poverty'.[50]

In the zeal for privatisation, which has seised the present a day policy-makers in India, Modern Bakery was one of the first public sector units to be on the chopping block. It went into oblivion unsung and unwept and as a good riddance. The new private owners of this enterprise did nothing to revive the units and sold away the assets, besides profiting from ownership of prime properties located in metropolitan cities. In fact, one of the main reasons for purchase of public sector units by private parties is their locational advantage, as prime real estates, which can be used for speculative purposes. Modern Bakery had become a laughing stock and all concerned ridiculed the very idea that government had thought it fit to set-up a public sector unit for manufacturing a simple and non-essential item as bread. Government itself felt embarrassed that they were manufacturing a non-essential item like bread. Had they read the history of French Revolution, they might have thought otherwise. It is unlikely that none of these worthies knew about the French Revolution. It is more likely that they had no sympathy for the basic economic needs of the urban poor. All concerned agreed that government should not be in non-strategic business and it was common sense that the humble bread is the most non-strategic item and the government should have nothing to do with it, least of all manufacture it. Now, whether, bread, which constitutes the basic item of food of the common people, is a strategic or non-strategic item, is a matter of economic judgment. If the government has the welfare of the greatest number in mind, it is certainly a strategic commodity. If the government has the welfare of the upper classes in mind, then certainly it is not a strategic commodity. It is only on such matters that the credibility of the government can be judged and not on the rhetorics, which are dished out from time to time for public consumption.

Modern Bakeries (India) Ltd. was started on Octobter 1, 1965 to manufacture bread fortified with protein, vitamins and minerals to improve the dietary standard of the masses and improve their nutritional standards. The Company was also manufacturing special variety of bread for feeding of school children. It had succeeded in its effort to a great extent, in holding the price line of bread through constant inflationary situation. This obviously did not suit the private sector and their camp followers, because they could not profiteer on this item of mass consumption. Government's efforts were richly rewarded, as bread, which was mostly an item of middle class consumption, became available to the poorer section of the populace. These positive aspects of this public sector undertaking, did not appeal to government, while selling it off unceremoniously.

It is true that this was a loss-making government Company, but they could have gone in to the reasons for the losses and try to remedy the situation. This option did not appeal to government. There are various other loss-making undertakings like Indian Airlines and Air India, which are running up enormous losses, compared to which losses of Modern Bakeries are peanuts. Government is in no hurry to sell-off these undertakings, as they cater to the rich and powerful. It is clear, where the government's sympathy lies. It is a disturbing trend that these are happening without any popular protest from the press and public. In fact, a section of the press has hailed the sale of Modern Bakeries and even of profitable undertakings, as a step in the right direction. This has created a situation, where even profit-making public sector undertakings are being offered for sale to private bidders, irrespective of whether they are Indian or foreign. The votaries of dismantling public sector think they have economic logic on their side, quite forgetting that development of private sector in India, has been an off-shoot of a strong public sector. The economic base of the country since independence had been created by the public sector. A close look at industrialisation of different countries shows that private sector has always developed with active government assistance. I have discussed it, while analyzing the history of industrial development in different countries.

Private sector has no social obligation and is motivated by maximization of profit. If production of necessities like bread is left entirely to the private sector, without checks and balances, this vital item will be priced out of the reaches of the majority of the consumers. Profiteering in necessities cannot be allowed in a welfare State. No democratically elected government can abdicate its responsibility in this respect. The price-control of necessities can better be done through market intervention, instead through regulations. Counter-productiveness of regulatory methods, forms a crucial part of the ammunition of the globalisation brigade. It is argued that government regulations give rise to corruption, which can be weeded out by dismantling all regulatory bodies. This has obviously not happened and with privatisation there has been creation of plethora of regulatory bodies. This has been a paradoxical situation, with the creation of number of apex regulatory bodies, without any enforcing agencies. It is probably expected that dictum from apex regulatory bodies will be enough to control the evils of privatisation. This has also not happened, as regulatory, agencies must have also inspecting agencies. 'This argument is supported by evidence showing that more open economies tend to have relatively, larger government than do less open countries'.[51] Globalisation and privatisation do not mean less of government, but more of it. We have seen multiplication of regulatory bodies in the wake of privatisation drive. In the Energy sector, which was one of the first to be privatised. regulatory authorities have come up in the center and states. Similarly in the telecom sector, regulatory authority has come up.

Flourishing stock market of the early nineties was one of the major achievements of private sector where small investors could multiply their money. Growth of the stock market was miraculous and prosperity seems to be growing in the air, since the industries were in a downward phase. All concerned were happy with this miracle of the private sector and the unhappy memories of the financial crisis of 1990 was quickly forgotten. This was, however, a false dawn and once somebody blew the whistle out of turn, the government agencies moved into action, the entire thing crumbled down together with the reputation and credibility of a number of financial wizards, who were the prime-movers of this buoyancy in securities market. The major architect of the bull run in the stock market, Harshad Mehta went on record, saying that had the whistle not be blown at an inconvenient time and everybody moved into action, he could have set the matter right. However, it is more likely that had this situation been allowed to continue indefinitely, serious damage would have been done to Indian financial institutions and banking machinery, from which it would have been difficult to recover. The stock market buoyancy was ideal for fuelling demand for consumer goods. It is no coincidence that number of foreign multinationals in the consumer goods sector made their inroads in the Indian economy during this honeymoon period of privatisation and globalisation. Money earned through speculations by the middle classes, would have fuelled unprecedented consumerism. However, before this could have happened, stock market bubble burst.

The authorities do not seem to be unaware of the going-ons in the capital market. The Government and the Reserve Bank of India issued number of guidelines to the stock exchanges. 'In August 1991, Government issued a directive to the stock exchanges to ensure greater transparency in transactions in securities for the benefit of the investing public and stricter regulation of trading in 'specified' shares, timely settlement of transactions and broad-basing the governing bodies of stock exchanges'.[52] The guidelines did not have any effect on the operations of the stock market and the stock exchanges did not make any attempt to follow these. On the other hand, computerization helped the main share broker, Harshad Mehta, to operate within a veil of secrecy, as the Government agencies were unable to crack the secret code, under which he had stored his information in the computer. Since, little or no physical accounts had been kept, a greater part of the stock exchange transactions could operate in secret codes which cannot be deciphered easily. So much for transparency under E-Business. This was our first brush with E-Business in a major financial scam.

The Securities and Exchange Board of India (SEBI) was made a statutory body by a Presidential Ordinance on 31st January, 1992. Making SEBI a statutory body in a hurry, without consulting the Parliament, clearly shows that the authorities were aware of the going-ons in the capital market. SEBI, armed with statutory powers could do little to control the capital market. Vesting of SEBI with statutory powers, has not prevented a number of scams in the stock market.

Interestingly, these scams have not been detected by SEBI, but through extraneous sources like the press or the failure of a non-nationalised bank. The main lacuna is that there is no systemic control and when the lid is blown off, the blame is squarely put on a few individuals heading the organisations. There is a period of intense witch-hunting, after which the entire thing is forgotten. Joint Parliamentary Committee was set-up in August 1992 to enquire into the securities scam. The Joint Parliamentary Committee submitted its report to Parliament on December, 1993. The pre-budget Economic Survey of 1993-94 merely says 'the report is under examination',[53] and the action taken or proposed to be taken on various recommendations will be reported to Parliament. Even important recommendations of the Joint Parliamentary Committee have not been mentioned in the report. This is in striking contrast to the report of the Committee on Insurance Reforms set-up by the Ministry of Finance in April 1993, submitting its report on January 7, 1994. Recommendations of this Committee, which consist mainly of privatisation and globalisation of insurance business and setting up of number of regulatory bodies, have been highlighted in the same Government of India report.[54] This clearly shows privatisation and globalisation are more important in the government's agenda than reforming the system. No doubt, securities scams have been occurring with regular frequency. The latest major one being the UTI scam, which completely shook the faith of investing public in a major mutual fund, controlled by the Government of India. It is also of interest to note that greater importance is given to committees set-up by the Ministry than to Parliamentary Committees.

Setting up of various regulatory bodies, following privatisation, clearly shows lack of faith in any self-regulatory methodology in the working of the private sector. There is no in-built checks and balances in the mechanism of the market economy. The record of the working of the private sector throughout the world, is no better than the public sector. The major difference between these two sectors is one of accountability. Although both these sectors function with public money, there is no social accountability with the former. When a private sector unit collapses, all concerned, except the promoters are left high and dry. There is no dearth of failed private sector units, but the entire price of failure has been passed on to the community, in the shape of shrinking labour market and the loss to public sector banks in the form of huge non-performing assets. There has been no loss to the promoter or private industrialist, who has on the other hand gained by the various systems of subsidies and incentives introduced by the Government. Privatisation has not led to self-controlling market mechanism. It has only punished the economically weak for failures, while rewarding the rich. There has been also tremendous increase in bureaucratisation with multiplication of regulatory bodies, which have not been able to regulate. Privatisation drive has led to more of government, together with abdication of social responsibility of government in the economic sphere.

Globalisation creates more government rather than less. In the case of India, globalisation and privatisation have not reduced Government expenditure. On the contrary, this has been constantly going up. This is not peculiar to India, but has been happening throughout the world. Dani Rodrick finds 'Contrary to what most economists would predict, more open (globalised) economies have had bigger governments. This correlation turns out to be statistically very strong and quite robust'.[55] Rodrick gives detailed empirical support for his theory, ranging from a study conducted on OECD countries to World Bank figures of government expenditure in different countries. In India, also, our experience has been more of government through creation of various regulatory bodies. government expenditure both at the Centre and the States has been going up by leaps and bounds and to support themselves the governments have been resorting to borrowing. Globalisation has only led to expansion of government machinery in different form and has added to the burgeoning cost on the public exchequer. Governments have abdicated its responsibility in various spheres and have passed on these responsibilities to bodies created at greater public cost. These bodies having been given quasi-judicial status, and to that extent, have been kept out of parliamentary control. Creation of quasi-judicial bodies, with powers of government transferred to them has been a major development of the liberalisation regime. This is certainly not reduction of government, but multiplication of government agencies, which have little parliamentary control. Reduction of the role of legislature in the functioning of government, through creation of quasi-judicial bodies, is also an important scheme of the liberalisation process, which has both an economic and a political agenda. Liberalisation from parliamentary control is one of the main aims of this process. It aims at structural change in the parliamentary system of government, with primacy of the legislature in financial matters, being seriously diluted.

Notes and References

1. J.M. Keyns, General Theory, pp. 333-51, Keynes subtly revived the Mercantilist theory of state intervention. This, in fact formed the theoretical background to his theory propounded in the General Theory. No doubt, Keynes's sympathy lay more with the Mercantilists than with the classicists, as the former advocated an active state policy in economic matters. Keynesian theory in fact acted as the bridge between Mercantilists and English classicists.
2. Minutes of evidence, etc. on the Affairs of the East India Company, (1813), quoted in R.C. Dutt, *Economic History of British India*, Early British Rule, pp. 258-62.
3. David Landes, Wealth and Poverty of Nations, p. 222.
4. Charles Babbage, on the Economy of Machinery and Manufacture, p. 1.
5. Eric Roll, A History of Economic Thought, p. 66.
6. Bernard Mandeville, The Fable of the Bees: or Private Vices, Public Benefits (1705), quoted in Meszaros, Beyond Capital Vol. 2, pp. 558-59.
7. Meszaros, Beyond Capital, Vol. 2, p. 56.
8. *Ibid.*, p. 559.
9. Mandeville, quoted in Meszaros, p. 559.
10. Leslie Stephen, Dictionary of National Biography, quoted in General Theory, p. 359.
11. J.M. Keynes Theory, p. 359.
12. *Ibid.*, p. 131.
13. J.D. Bernal, Science in History, p. 885.
14. Will Durant, The Story of Civilisation (Vol. 4) The Age of Faith, pp. 1003, 835.
15. Keynes, General Theory, p. 220.
16. *Ibid.*, pp. 100-101, 106, 129-31.
17. *Ibid.*, p. 359.

18. *Ibid.*, p. 361 note.
19. J.A. Schumpeter, History of Economic Analysis, p. 184 note.
20. General Theory, p. 359.
21. Encyclopaedia Britannica (Vol. 22), pp. 366-67.
22. Meszaros, p. 554.
23. Mark Parlman's Introduction to Schumpeter's History of Economic Analysis, pp. XXV.
24. Schumpeter, p. 283 (foot note 11).
25. Keynes, p. 359.
26. Schumpeter, p. 284.
27. R.H. Tawney, Equality, p. 44.
28. *Ibid.*, Introduction by Richard M. Titmus, p. 11.
29. Eric Roll, p. 146.
30. Michael E. Porter, The Competitive Advantage of Nations, p. 499.
31. Malcolm Waters, Globalisation, p. 142.
32. Porter, p. 499.
33. Porter, pp. 500-01.

34-35. Schumpeter, pp. 215, 285.

36. *Ibid.*, p. 287.
37. Will and Ariel Durant, The Story of Civilization, Part XI, The Age of Napoleon, p. 5.
38. P. Ray, India's Foreign Trade, pp. 9-10.
39. Porter, p. 500.
40. Evidence before the Commons' Committee, 1832, quoted in R.C. Dutt, Economic History of British India, Under Early British Rule, p. 290.
41. Porter, p. 499.
42. *Ibid.*, p. 501.
43. J.K. Galbraith, Introduction to Thorstein Veblen's The Theory of the Leisure Class, p. 35.
44. Veblen, The Theory of the Leisure Class, p. 35.
45. Galbraith's Introduction to The Theory of the Leisure Class, p. XVI.
46. *Ibid.*, p. XVI.
47. Malcolm Waters, Globalisation, p. 142.
48. *Ibid.*, p. 143.
49. Marie Antoinette, the queen of French during the time of French Revolution, was attributed to have made the callous remark 'Let them eat cake', on being told that the people had no bread. (Encyclopaedia Britannica, Vol. 7, p. 844).
50. Robert Heilbromer and Lester Thurow, Economics Explained, p. 50, box.
51. Richard E. Baldwin *et. el.*, edited, Market Integration, Regionalism and the Global Economy, p. 2.
52. Economic Survey, 1991-92, Government of India, para 6.31 (IV).
53. Economic Survey 1993-94, Government of India, para 108, p. 56.

54. *Ibid.*, para 109 and box 3.4, pp. 56-57.
55. Dani Rodrik, Globalisation and labour, or: if globalisation is a bowl of cherries, why are there so many glum faces around the table? In Richard E. Baldwin, *et. al.*, edited Market Integration, Regionalism and The Global Economy, p. 142.

7

Fickle Fashions in Economic Policies

For today's economists (both left and right), the market is becoming synonymous with democracy for the political scientists. Once, we have accepted the western concept of democracy in our political life, we should also accept the concept of market economy in our economic management. Now that the genie of the market has been freed from the bottle of communism and socialism, it should be given a free-run of our economy. It is quite another thing that almost all the economists worth their salt, were swearing by socialism—varying from British Labour Party's mild socialism to Mao's extreme communism, including cultural communism. The fashion in today's economic world is very fickle. The theories which were touted from roof tops, as solution for the economic malaise of the third world countries, no longer seems to be in fashion. Days of public ownership of means of production, shadow pricing and social costs are gone and in its place, we have the unbridled capitalism of the market place, which favours the cunning and greedy. Rules of the market place change according to the requirement of the dominant players. Perfect competition exists only in theory and is at best a concept, based on unrealistic assumptions.

Market has become a cult invocation and anybody with any economic pretension must swear by the market god. This great belief in market forces, is not based on rationality, but a blind belief that what is good for the developed West, is also good for us. Economics is becoming more and more a discipline, where belief is more important than rationalism. Why this great belief in the absolute goodness of the market forces? We are cited the example of nineteenth century Britain, which could become a super-power through market forces. Thatcherite dogma would make us believe that democracy and a free market are the bulwark of the Western civilization. Before the advent of Thatcher and Reagan, the British and American school of economics, in spite of Friedrich Von Hayek and Milton Friedman,[1] would have us believe that path of socialism is the only path to economic development. Government spending was the cornerstone of economic development. Of course, pioneer of advocating government spending was none other than John Maynard Keynes, whose ideas originated from depression ridden Great Britain of the thirties of the last century.

KEYNESEAN PANACEA

Keynes's 'General Theory' was one of the first books on economics addressed to the general public. Keynes in his preface to General Theory laments the 'deep divergence of opinion between fellow economists which have for the time being almost destroyed the practical influence of economic theory, and will, until they are resolved, continue to do so'.[2] Until the publication of 'General Theory', economists were generally content with their discipline within the four corners of the academic world. Keynes was one of the first economists, who foresaw a glorious future for Economics as a practical discipline, to educate the politicians and the general public, about the role Economics can play towards the prosperity of a country's and even world economy. Economists had earlier shied away from offering advice to businessmen and statesmen on the basis of their economic studies. This is primarily because economic analysis is based on the general assumption that number of factors remain constant. Keynes was one of the first economists to visualize the role economics and its practitioners can play in the management of statecraft.

Keynes's ideas, as expounded in his 'General Theory of Employment, Interest and Money', had a far reaching sway on the economic thinking of the post-Second World War period. Keynes was the guiding deity of the post-war economic scenario. The origin of Marshall plan for development of post-Second World War Europe was based on the Keynesian concept of 'pump priming' or increased public expenditure to create employment. Since he was writing his *magnum opus* 'General Theory' at the time of the Great Depression, naturally creation of employment was foremost in his mind. Keynes's prescription of increased public investment for creating assets, which cannot be immediately utilised (consumed), proved attractive to economists and politicians alike. The 'General Theory' advocated increased activity on the part of the state through large scale pump priming of the economy at low interest rates. Of all the possibilities of investment, the best course was thought to be to build houses for posterity. This type of activity can only be undertaken by the state, as no private investor would invest in a line of activity, for which there is no demand in foreseeable future. Moreover, it is not possible to forecast market demand for a future generation, besides assets are likely to deteriorate with the passage of time.

Period of depression is marked by huge inventory, as the production process has come to a standstill due to a lack of effective demand, caused by increased unemployment, reduction of wages and a lack of demand for machinery and plants. In such a situation, private investment is not possible and government investment in projects with a long time lag is the only easy way out. Keynes had earlier said about the future in his 'A Tract on Monetary Reforms', 'But this long-run is a misleading guide to current affairs. In the long-run we are all dead. Economists set themselves too easy, too useless a task if in tempestuous season they can only tell us that when the storm is long past the ocean is flat again'.[3] This is not a light hearted sentence made in jest, but Keynes's belief that 'in economics there is no scientific basis on which a mathematical probability could be established'.[4] This absolves the economists of any long-range damage to the economy and encourages demagogues and publicists.

Economics deals with the future on the basis of present and immediate past and once applied to policy-making, which is basically an exercise in futurology, it can prove to be disastrous. Keynes has lent himself on this score to strong criticism from the leader of anti-Keynesianism like Hayek. He has read into it the basic fallacy of Keynesian prescriptions and come up with his own prescription, which denies any role to Economics in policy-making. Keynesian prescriptions led to the macro-economics of development through his followers, who advocated a policy of investment and more investment to the third world countries to get out of the poverty, to which they have been reduced by two centuries of colonial policy. A rosy picture of development was presented to the economists, politicians and people of the developing countries. Money was posed as the panacea of development, as investment has to be only in monetary terms. Money, which is a barometer of the economy was taken off its base and was allowed a free-run of the economy. Instead of Economy controlling the flow of money, it went the other way, with the economy on a free drive on the roller coaster of money supply. 'The General Theory' is basically 'monetary theory of production'. According to this thesis money is a bridge between past and future. This bridge constructed for moving the economy to the land of prosperity, proved to be extremely shaky and caught the real economy in the snares of an unrealistic monetary economy. Investment for distant future carries no accountability for the politicians and their advisers. The future generation may not need the assets, which are being created for them. In fact, these assets may become liabilities for them. As we are witnessing the huge edifice of public sector, built-up at an enormous public cost, putting future generation in a debt-trap, being dismantled in a hurry, even without an apology of an eulogy. In fact, not too long back, Jawaharlal Nehru, the main architect of the public sector had visualised them as 'temples of modern India'. Ironically, this dismantling of the edifice built-up by Nehru, is being done by the very same people, who swear by him.

'General Theory' states that gold-mining is an activity of greatest value and importance to civilization, because increased production of gold does not suffer from the disadvantage of diminishing utility, which house-building activity suffers. Any commodity of utility suffers from the disadvantage of diminishing utility, with increased production, whereas the activity of gold-mining, which Keynes quaintly calls 'digging holes in the ground'[5], suffers from no such disutility. It is not known why Keynes thought that increased production of gold will not suffer from increasing disutility as other commodities. We all know that gold is subject to the law of diminishing marginal utility, as other commodities. Fluctuating price of gold in the world bullion market bears enough testimony of this. Obviously, Keynes had not come out of the legacy of the mental shackles of gold standard, which ruled the British financial system till 1931, although Keynes himself was an ardent critic of the gold standard. During the period from 1925 to 1931, when Britain was in the gold-standard, the Bank of England suffered from an inadequacy of stock of gold and of the cash reserves of the other banks, as alleged by some of the critics of gold-standard, including Keynes. The contemporary state of affairs of this period is best described by a famous work on money by Hartley Withers titled, 'The Meaning of Money'. Hartley Withers, who was the Editor of 'The Economist' of London, had written a number of scholarly and popular works on financial matters.

Hartley Withers in his famous work, 'The Meaning of Money' (sixth edition), published in 1937 noted that Keynes was a great critic of the tight money policy of Bank of England, due to the conservative credit policy brought about by the gold-standard. Withers had this to say, 'It (the task of Bank of England in protecting the country's gold reserve) had also been complicated by the appearance of a host of critics, ranging from Mr. J.M. Keynes, an economist of outstanding ability and world-wide fame, to amateurs who believe that the way to make humanity happy is to provide it with heaps of money, forgetting that what we consume is not money but goods and services'.[6] Keynes was a great advocate of easy money policy and abundance of credit for economic prosperity. In advocating this, he was obviously playing to the gallery and catering to the interest of a powerful business and political lobby. At that time there was a clamour amongst some businessmen for more credit and access to an easy credit market. Political Circles were also interested in having their say in the credit policy of the banks. They 'go on to urge that the governing body of the Bank of England should be made responsible to the community and not merely to individuals, and for this purpose should include representatives of the Treasury, the Board of Trade, Industry, Labour and the Co-operative movement'.[7] Do we hear in this, the rumblings of the clamour, which eventually became a trumpet call for eventual nationalization of the Banks and money market? The echo of this was heard in the nationalization of the Imperial Bank and creation of State Bank of India in July 1955 by taking over the assets and liabilities of the Imperial Bank. This echo further became a trumpet call for complete community (government) control of almost the entire Banking system by Nationalization of almost all the major private Banks working in India in July, 1969. This gave the government enormous clout in controlling the entire credit system of the country.

Withers tried to make monetary theory understandable to general readers, whereas, Keynes wanted to reduce them to mere 'eavesdroppers', so that they are not confused by contradictory prescriptions of economists. In the preface to the first edition of his 'The Meaning of Money', Withers wrote in January, 1909, 'This book is designed to meet the difficulty experienced by the average reader in understanding the money market. It chiefly expresses views and facts gathered from practical men at work in the great machine which it describes'.[8] His purpose of popularizing monetary theory was not in vain. In the preface to the sixth edition, he wrote in August, 1937, 'The book has made me many friends'.[9] Keynes's purpose was different. The preface to the 'General Theory', opens with the line 'This book is chiefly addressed to my follow economists'.[10] He regarded the general public as 'only eavesdroppers', in his attempt to bring unanimity amongst economists to restore 'the practical influence of economic theory'.[11] His attempt to bring unanimity amongst the economists was not successful. But his ideas on easy money policy proved to be very popular in

India, a country looking for an easy way to development. A generation of economists, trained in the Keynesian school of economics provided the necessary grist to the mill of economic development.

It is obvious that the great genius of Keynes had sensed the mood of the times and saw in it an opportunity to give it his powerful backing. He lamented the role of economists in being mere academicians, instead of taking up the much more lucrative and challenging role of economic wizards. He denigrated the English classical economists, right from Ricardo, Marshall, Edgeworth and Pigou as being impractical and not having any practical prescriptions for the politicians and the general public. He remarked on 'the celebrated optimism of traditional economic theory, which had led to economists being looked upon as Candides, who, having left this world for the cultivation of their gardens, teach that, all is for the best in the best of all possible worlds'.[12] Keynes brought out his classic, "The General Theory of Employment, Interest and Money" in 1936 to give his powerful intellectual and theoretical backing to the prevalent clamour for easy money in a depression ridden economy. After the publication of 'General Theory' the fraternity of economists never looked back and had greater and greater sway over the politicians and economic affairs of the nation.

According to classical economists, as enunciated by Keynes, any productive economic activity will create employment, as the cost of production must be spent on purchasing the product. In J.S. Mill's 'Principle of Political Economy', quoted by Keynes in his 'General Theory'[13], if the productive powers of the country could be suddenly doubled, not only the supply of commodities in every market be doubled, but also the purchasing powers will also be doubled. Demand will automatically be doubled, as everybody would be able to buy twice as much'. The classical economists firmly held the view that supply creates its own demand. From this postulate, Keynes draws the corollary that according to the classical school of thought, savings will release labour and commodities from consumption channel to production of capital wealth. Keynes supports this by quoting from Marshall's 'Pure Theory of Domestic Values', according to which it is a familiar economic axiom that a man purchases labour and commodities with that portion of his income which he saves just as much as he does with that he is said to spend. This is the basic doctrine of the classical economists and according to Keynes, classical theory would collapse without it. Earlier Economists held that money plays only a marginal role in the theory of production and employment, which can be better analysed based on actual exchange of commodities. Classical economics is based on commodity exchanges playing a vital role on economic activities of production, marketing and employment, money playing only a secondary role. Bringing money in the forefront as a major tool of economic control, oblivious of the functioning of commodity markets, is a major development in economic thinking brought about by Keynes. No economist before Keynes had dared to give such exalted role to money, as Keynes did. This created a serious misconception in equating money with prosperity and economic development. As we shall see, Keynes's prescriptions of easy money policy had disastrous effect on the economy of the newly independent countries taking the path of development through an easy money policy. This was particularly so as there were substantial non-monetised sectors in these economies. Agricultural sector in these economies was to a great extent non-monetised.

Schumpeter in his 'History of Economic Analysis' (1950), says 'General Theory of Employment, Interest and Money (1936) was the outstanding success of the 1930's and it dominated analytic work for, a decade after its publication, to say the least'.[14] The dominance of General Theory continued well beyond a decade after publication and economics of depression very well became economics of development. Development economics, which dominated economic thinking from the fifties and held out hopes for economic miracles, took off from the General Theory. The concept of 'vicious circle of poverty', made famous by Ragnar Nurkse in his 'Problems of capital formation in under-developed countries' (1951) and the solution thereof, are based on Keynesian analytic framework of General Theory. In the words of Nurkse, 'We recognize, in one of its aspects, the vicious circle of poverty. We perceive a constellation of circumstances tending to preserve any backward economy in a stationary condition, in a state of 'under-development equilibrium' somewhat analogous, perhaps, to the 'under-employment equilibrium', the possibility of which, in advanced industrial countries, was impressed on us by Keynes'.[15] Development economics, which dominated the economic scenario of the newly independent countries, particularly India, was an extension of the Keynesian economics. Basic analytical framework of the 'General Theory' was based on the 'characteristics of England's aging capitalism as seen from the stand point of an English intellectual'.[16] According to Keynes these characteristics are 'plausibly ascribed to our (the English) world on our general knowledge of contemporary human nature'.[17] Even Adam Smith and earlier economists, who had profound influence on British economic thinking made no attempt to propagate their ideas. Keynes on the other hand vigorously pushed forward his views and he had the advantage of not only being an academic economist but also 'by the 1920s he was already the great man and the confidante of senior statesmen'.[18] Keynes seems to be having a messianic view of economics and never shied away from offering advice to statesmen and financiers, through numerous committees in which he was member. The financial situation between the two world wars, was ideal for an economist who could see straight without being bothered by the lanes, bye-lanes, not to speak of the dark alleys, which inhabit the financial world. Keynes had no time for disbelievers or madmen, as he calls them. Biography of Keynes by D.E. Moggridge gives detailed account of the discussions and comments of economists like R.G. Hawtrey, Roy Harrod and D.H. Robertson, whom Keynes had shown the draft of General Theory and discussed its structure. Robertson responded to Keynes 'a large part of your theoretical structure is still to me almost complete mumbo-jumbo'![19] Keynes reacted that all economists, except R.H. Kahn, his protege and collaborator in General Theory, were mad. Keynes seems to be quite intolerant of criticism and does not seem to be in the best of mental health, while writing the General Theory, due to his various physical ailments and heavy commitment of work both at the national and international levels. Statement like 'Hawtrey has gone quite mad and arguing with him one finds oneself in a mad house', shows extreme intolerance, to say the least. Then about Robertson 'His mind, though frightfully ingenious, seems to me to be maliciously perverse. Again it is like arguing with a mad man. But when I talk with Alexander (R.F. Kahn), it is all so different'. Then 'Are all the economists mad except Alexander (R.F. Kahn) and me? It seems to me so, yet it can't be true'.[20]

The fundamental difference between Keynes and D.H. Robertson, who was never convinced of Keynes's arguments in the 'General Theory' and was aware of its mischievous potentiality to the economy in the long-term, was the difference between money economy and real economy. 'Keynes concentrated on monetary aspects and monetary policy from the first, whereas Robertson emphasised 'real factors'—as against both monetary and psychological ones—from the first. There were thus wide stretches of ground that were Robertson's own and into which Keynes's analysis never penetrated. Within this wider frame, monetary propositions acquire a meaning—and one that is very relevant for practical applications—that is wholly different from the meaning and implications which the same monetary propositions convey if taken by themselves'.[21] Robertson, quite early in his career, as an economist, had grasped the idea that economic cycles of prosperity and depression were related to the effect of development of new industries. 'These swings in the value of money are bound up with roughly similar swings in output, employment and consumption (not to mention such thing as births and bankruptcies), and if we try to analyse them we very soon get heavily involved in our old troubles about what is cause and what is effect'.[22] Robertson analyses the effect of increased industrial activity of greater rate of growth of output, through new invention, or a new method of industrial organisation or the openings for development in a new country. This will require an increase in requirement of circulating capital. According to Robertson, if the industry will depend on the banking system for additional funds and 'Thus a pressure is set-up on the banks; and the banks, so far as they allow themselves to submit to it, pass it on to the public in the form of rising prices and enforced saving. And once the rise in prices sets in, there are all sorts of reasons why it should tend to continue and to grow in strength'.[23] Robertson analyses at length that this type of artificial expansion of loans by the banks, is a cause of continuous rise in prices and forced saving in the society. We have practical experience in India of continuously rising prices due to high bank loaning and unusually high savings, 'And the way this forced saving is imposed on the public is through a fall in the value of money'.[24] Prof. Robertson warns about the evils of a trade boom (not an economic boom) and recommends that the monetary system should restrain the same and not promote them. 'The dissipation of savings which have been embodied in monetary form, the artificial lengthening of the period of production by what our ancestors called the forestalling and engrossing of goods, the numerous errors of judgement and forecast which mark the course of a trade boom—these things are evils in themselves and bring evils more spectacular in their train. We have a right to ask that our monetary system should be so managed as to restrain and not to promote them'.[25]

No doubt, Keynes found Robertson's ideas inconvenient and chose to ignore it. Keynes was all along keen on unanimity among economists and was not interested in any doubts or debates about the certainty of his theory. An academically and theoretically sound thesis will not shy away from an academic debate. Keynes wants the general reader to be faced with academic certainty and not dare to question them. He laments 'Even on matters of principle there is not yet a complete unanimity of opinion, amongst professional students of the subject'.[26] Keynes was striving for unanimity of view on a subject, where no such unanimity of view is possible. He berates the writers of the series for their failure to present an uniform and straightforward view to the readers. 'The writers of this series must apologise to the general reader and to the beginner if many parts of their subject have not yet reached to a degree of certainty and lucidity which would make them easy and straightforward reading'.[27] Not the best way of introducing an academic discussion. There is no doubt that the General Theory had inherent theoretical defects and most of the economists had great doubt about its basic assumptions, structure and prescriptions. The co-relation between agriculture and industry does not form a part of the theoretical framework of the General Theory. Role of agriculture which is a dominant sector in most of the economies, has not been considered at all. According to Keynes, agricultural causes of economic fluctuations are of much less importance, mainly because agricultural output is a much smaller proportion of total output and secondly because good and bad harvests in different parts of the world balance themselves globally. Whereas the Keynesian economic structure is based on a closed national economy, agriculture has been omitted on the ground that it balances itself internationally. There is no doubt that an economic system which does not take into account agriculture, will not be relevant for a country, where agriculture constitutes the dominant sector. This is typical of the Anglo-Saxon schools of economics which conveniently did away with agriculture. This school of economics was basically product of the Industrial Revolution and as the latter developed by completely decimating the agricultural structure, economic theories developed by this school, either ignored the agriculture sector completely or treated it as of little consequence in the general economic dispensation.

Industrial Revolution made Economics basically an Anglo-Saxon subject and the basic economic structure on which various economic theories were formulated, was the British colonial economic structure. As Hobbsbawm has said, 'the Industrial Revolution put the Britishers into unquestioned first place in the field of economics'.[28] Now let us see the views of Keynes in this matter. 'Before Adam Smith this apparatus of thought (Theory of Economics) scarcely existed. Between his time and this it has been steadily enlarged and improved. Nor is there any branch of knowledge in the formation of which Englishmen can claim a more predominant part'.[29] This makes Economics, specially Keynesian Economics, a purely English discipline, without any linkage with various continental schools of thought. After the physiocrats in the eighteenth century, the field of Economics was completely dominated by the Anglo-Saxon school of thought. The so-called miracle of the Industrial Revolution, gave them the *raison d'etre* to offer economic panacea to anybody in search of such miracles. In fact, the Industrial Revolution and its experience, were the practical basis on which the British economic theories were developed in the nineteenth and even early twentieth centuries. As the British Industrial Revolution was considered a miracle by all concerned, nobody questioned the wisdom of the Anglo-Saxon School of Economic thought. It was touted as a model for industrial development and modernisation, which could be replicated in other countries. India, which had been under colonial rule too long, saw in these theories a possibility of an industrial revolution of its own, by faithfully following these theories. It is, however, another matter that there were lot of non-economic factors in British Industrial Revolution. We have discussed these at length in other chapters in this book. Keynes came to the economic scene at a time, when the Industrial Revolution had run its full circle; world monetary situation was in doldrums, on the brink of abandoning time tested gold-standard for the rough sea of unlimited paper currency. In such an uncertain economic climate, most of the economists were chary of offering any economic panacea. Keynes, however had no such inhibitions and in the 'General Theory' gave a clarion call to the believers to abandon old ideas in economics, built-up by generations of economists. 'The difficulty lies, not in the new ideas, but in escaping from the old ones, which ramify, for those brought up as most of us have been, into every corner of our minds'.[30] With the publication of 'General Theory', Keynes 'felt himself to have led Economics out of 150 years of error into the land of definitive truth'.[31] All did not share Keynes's enthusiasm. Robertson found the work highly controversial and in his Cambridge Lectures advised the students to supplement the reading of General Theory with one or two critical studies that have been made of it. J.R. Hicks did not believe in the universality of the ideas of the General Theory, which were directed towards the monetary disturbances of the 1930s. 'Monetary theories arise out of monetary disturbances. This is obviously true of the General Theory, which is the book of the Great Depression'.[32] Keynes' message in the General Theory gave a novel view of the capitalist process, particularly relating to saving, interest and underemployment. It is perhaps for this reason 'Keynesianism appealed primarily to young theorists whereas a majority of the old stagers were more or less strongly, anti-Keynesian'.[33] Schumpeter goes on to elaborate that this is not so much due to resistance to new ideas by the older economists but mainly due to the lack of adequate analytic experience of the younger economists. In the words of Schumpeter, 'In a field like economics, where training is often defective and where the young scholar very often simply does not know enough, this element (analytic experience) counts heavily'.[34] Be that as it may be, in the 'General Theory', the economists found new hope for capitalism, which was in crisis during the thirties, without going the Marxist way. Keynes provided 'An alternative theory to the bankrupt, free market economies'.[35] 'General Theory' provided sufficient amount of hope for the masses in the shape of full employment equilibrium and egalitarianism in the concept of effective demand to boost the purchasing power of the people, to be the Bible of neo-capitalism. It effectively ensured that the Economists of the non-communist world do not jump into the Marxist band-wagon. 'General Theory' or the Keynesian Revolution, as the faithful would like to call it, established intellectual-political hegemony on the economic thinking of the so-called free world, particularly Britain and its colonies and the U.S.A. and its sphere of influence. State intervention became an integral part of the economic world and the role of the State in striving for full employment and general economic welfare, was clearly visualised. Public investment became more and more important for overcoming persistent tendencies towards under employment equilibrium and striving towards full employment. 'The fundamental aim of Keynes was precisely how to save the system through the injection of massive state funds for the benefit of private capitalist enterprise, so as to regulate the overall reproduction process on a permanent basis within the framework of undisturbed capital accumulation'.[36]

Keynes was trying for certainly on a subject, where no such possibility exists. Divergence of views would have led to a healthy public debate, from which the best possible solution would have emerged. However, Keynes was keen on confining the debate to academic circle and presenting the general public with a *fait accompli*. Lord Keynes realised that British industrial revolution had run its full circle and a new set of economic theories had to be presented to maintain the Anglo-Saxon dominance of thought on this vital subject. Genius of Keynes lies in the fact that he realised that the discipline of economics would dominate the world scenario for the rest of the twentieth century. Maintaining British monopoly over this subject, which would dominate international political scenario, would compensate for Britain's disappearing empire and maintain Anglo-Saxon hegemony in world affairs. No doubt, the American academic circles became a powerful votary of Keynesian economics in the post-war years. Keynes was not looking for an academic discipline, but for a tool for continuance of a vanishing empire. Keynesian economics became a tool of empire in the hands of the followers of Keynes.

EXPERIMENT IN DEVELOPING COUNTRIES WITH KEYNESIAN MONETARISM

Indian planning was over influenced by Keynesian school, because of dominance of Keynesian thinking in the economic field at that time and the planners, theoreticians and bureaucrats trained in either the British Universities or the Anglo-Saxon school of thought, carried too much of Keynesianism in their economic baggage. Talking about Cambridge University, I.G. Patel in his recent book, 'Glimpses of Indian Economic Policy', says, 'It is surprising that 'development', that is, the Wealth of Nations, which was the soul and substance of classical economics found little mention in the class room then. No one read Adam Smith or J.S. Mill or even Marshall—Keynesiana conquered all'.[37] Keynes was obviously the counterpart of Marx in post-war capitalism and Keynesian theories of depression were being prepared for development of newly independent countries, particularly India. 'Ideas which arose in the thirties, and which were appropriate in the thirties, have been carried over, through Keynes' influence, into a world where they do not at all so obviously belong'.[38] Keynes' idea of easy money policy was particularly attractive to politicians and planners alike.

Deficit financing or raising resources through inflationary means, is one of the most inequitable means of raising resources. We have on the authority of Hugh Dalton, British Chancellor of Exchequer in the post-war Labour Government, 'Inflation, therefore, causes a redistribution of income in favour of business men, who secure large wind fall profits, at the expense of wage earners and, still more, at the expense of the recipients of fixed money incomes. On balance, inflation is likely to increase the inequality of incomes and to operate, on the whole, not as proportional, but as a regressive tax, supplemented by a subsidy to business men, ordinary shareholders and many classes of speculators'.[39] He goes on to say, 'That budgets should be balanced is often regarded, not only as an unquestioned precept of finance, but as a moral precept as well . . . But in 1933 this sentiment had so far weakened that in influential campaign was set on foot to persuade the Chancellor of the Exchequer deliberately to unbalance the budget in order to increase employment. He was not persuaded. But the campaign rallied much support'.[40] The underdeveloped countries were chosen as fertile ground for easy money policy, which completely distorted their economies and once this was started, there was no holding it back. The 1970s was the era of high Government spending in India ushered in by the fifth plan and various other over ambitious programmes. A vivid picture of unrealistic financial planning is given in 'Planning and the Poor' by B.S. Minhas, who resigned from the Planning Commission in December 1973, after two and a half years of turbulent tenure. In the words of Minhas, 'In fact in the latter part of 1972, disturbing trends had already made their nasty appearance in the economy. Political and financial discipline had started to sag. Deficit financing was running at a fairly high level. Any talk of sound fiscal management and the threat of inflation was at best suspect.

At worst it was dismissed as reactionary nonsense'.[41] Once the financial discipline had been given a good-bye to, there was no question of going back to it. The fiscal gap had been constantly widening, leading to the need of high dose of deficit financing. The appeal of Dr. Minhas was a cry in the wilderness and he took the honourable course of resigning his Membership of Planning Commission in December, 1973, after trying to bring the dangerous situation to the notice of the Prime Minister. The Note on the Draft Fifth Plan, in which he pointed out the glib assumptions on which the resources of the plan were projected and the dangerous reliance on foreign and to bridge the resources gap, which was already becoming alarming, was laid on 27 February, 1974 in the Lok Sabha, which according to the constitution, is the supreme financial authority in the country. But the entire exercise was in vain and the bureaucratic and academic martyrdom of Dr. Minhas achieved little. Parliament chose to ignore it and nobody in the academic world or Planning Commission came out in-his-support. Planning Commission was preparing the plan not on any realistic basis, but on unrealistic assumptions. A populist plan, with a rosy picture for the future, was sought to be presented. The exercise was not a harmless one, confined to the four corners of Yojana Bhawan, but set the Indian Economy in a downward spiral, from which it never recovered.

The words of Dr. Minhas were prophetic and the fiscal situation started deteriorating immediately. The fiscal deficit of the Central Government, which was maintained at 1.8 per cent through a difficult period of three major wars (Chinese Aggression, 1962, Indo-Pak conflicts, 1965 and 1971), serious drought situations and the Oil Crises of 1973, rose to 4.1 per cent in 1975-76 and never went below that level, rising to 8.3 per cent, 9 per cent and 8.1 per cent respectively in 1986-87, 1987-88 and 1988-89, according to the pre-budget Economic Survey of 1991-92 of the Ministry of Finance, Government of India. It was during 1990-91, when the fiscal deficit was 9.4 per cent of G.D.P. and the balance of payments position became alarming with the possibility of default in international repayment obligations in July 1991, that the I.M.F. warned the Indian Government of continuing with such huge fiscal deficit. The I.M.F. medicine of deficit financing, prescribed earlier by Bernstein for development of the economy, proved to be poisonous for the economy. But there was no going back from deficit financing. Gross fiscal deficit as a per cent of Gross Domestic Product continued to be high throughout the nineties and was 10% in 2001-02 and estimated to be 9.3% in 2002-03.[42] World Bank has already come out with the warning that Indian fiscal deficit is worse than in 1991.[43]

Let us see, when the deficit financing started getting out of control. Deficit financing, which had been liberally used for financing earlier plans, had given rise to extreme inflationary situation in 1973-74. 'Wholesale prices in 1973-74 soared by a fantastic 22.7% over the previous financial year, making it the largest ever rise in a single twelve month period. This means that the abnormal rise in prices which began well over two years ago continues and the Government's efforts to check inflationary forces have failed'. (*Statesman*, April 25, 1974). The same report goes on to say, 'What is disturbing is the share that various groups have contributed to the rise. Food prices in 1973-74 were up by 23.5% over the previous year, industrial raw materials by as much as 47% and manufactured goods by 16.7%'.[44] Inflation was running at a dangerous and unprecedented level in 1973-74, when the Fifth Five Year Plan was being formulated. Deficit financing which started in a modest way with the First Five Year Plan, became a major source of finance during the second plan. It is of importance to note that deficit financing started with the recommendation of the I.M.F. in its report in 1953. I.M.F. Mission, headed by Economist, E.M. Bernstein, invited by the Union Finance Minister, C.D. Deshmukh, in its report on 'Economic Development with Stability' strongly recommended, what it called safe deficit financing, i.e. deficit financing with control. There was no controlling the deficit financing, once it became an integral part of plan finance, under guidance from the IMF. Keynesian theory of easy money was introduced in the Indian Economy with disastrous consequences, which we have already seen. Bernstein had no hesitation in recommending the short-term and short-sighted Keynesian prescription to the Indian

Government. With this Keynesian prescription, India was launched on the path to Keynesian capitalism, although the ostensible policy was one of socialism. The moral of the story is that, you can not have socialism, with the tools of capitalisms. 'Many like Bernstein were essentially monetarists in practice even though they became Keynesians in theory'.[45] Rule of Keynesian economics became absolute over the economic policies of the countries on the way to development.

Although deficit financing was modest during the first plan period as a whole, the last year of the plan saw deficit financing to the tune of Rs. 212 crores, out of a total plan deficit of Rs. 532 crores. The first three years of second plan saw an increase in deficit financing, with the bulk of the deficit being concentrated on the first two years. This type of sporadic spurts in deficit financing, as in the case of Bangladesh war and the refugee problem created an unnatural situation in the Indian economy, as the economy had no time to adjust to such type of financing. The result was inflation and unbalanced economic development. According to Kaldor, 'Deficit financing imply a corresponding increase in privately owned wealth'.[46] Kaldor had however, advised deficit financing in the second plan to the extent of Rs. 150 crores a year. 'In my view (and this, I think, would be shared by most economists) the amount of deficit expenditure which the economy can absorb is not likely to exceed Rs. 150 crores a year, or, say, Rs. 800 crores in the five year period'.[47] (Nicholas Kaldor, Indian Tax Reform, from Reports on Taxation II). During the first two years of the second plan, deficit financing was to the extent of Rs. 635 crores, much in excess of Kaldor's recommendations and absorbing capacity of the economy. In the words of Kaldor, who was from Cambridge University 'My work consisted in applying Keynesian methods of analysis to assess the size of the "gap" that would need to be closed and the methods by which this could be achieved'.[48] To be fair to Kaldor while recommending limited deficit financing, he also suggested that 'the tax system is subjected to a through and comprehensive reform', as he found 'The present system of direct taxation in India is both inefficient and inequitable'.[49]

He had also warned, while bridging the gap of plan finances. 'It is essential that the additional burden that will inevitably be imposed (either through taxation or through an inflationary rise in prices) on the broad masses of population should be complemented by an efficient system of progressive taxation on the small minority of the well-to-do who in India number only about one per cent of the population. Without that, the rise in expenditure during the plan will inevitably increase the wealth of the richest classes disproportionately, and the distribution of the burden imposed on the community at large will be contrary to the sense of justice and equity of a democratic society'.[50]

GROWTH TARGETS AND INCREASING POVERTY

Central to Kaldor's recommendation was the Expenditure Tax, which was introduced in such a truncated fashion that it became ineffective and was withdrawn after a relatively short period. In his address to the Informal Consultative Committee of the Indian Parliament on 16th December, 1958, Kaldor said, 'Among the new taxes the expenditure tax and the gift tax are so heavily riddled with loopholes and exemptions that they bear only a superficial resemblance to the taxes, whose introduction I originally recommended'.[51] Again in the words of Kaldor, 'In the event, neither in India or Ceylon were the new taxes really "enforced"—they hardly yielded any revenue; and the particular tax on which the main hopes were based, the Expenditure Tax, was withdrawn in each country after a relatively short period. I have never found out whether the true cause of non-enforcement was the corruption of the officials or the connivance of Ministers'.[52] The answer to this is perhaps not so simple. The small per cent of the population, only about one per cent, according to Kaldor's estimate, was gaining further economic clout with economic growth. No elected Government can go against this powerful economic lobby which holds the levers of the economy. Through the plan process, there has been systematic transfer of public resources to private individuals. Since Government Projects are all implemented by private agencies, there has been huge transfer of public resources to private individuals. In fact, the growth of the economy depends on this small section. The economic growth figures depend on the growth of this sector only, as there is no concept of distributive justice in these figures. If the economic health of this sector is good, the growth figures are satisfactory and the IMF, World Bank and foreign missions give Indian Government a pat on the back, with few drops of tear thrown in for those below the subsistence level. 'It appears inevitable, therefore, that both the amount of privately owned wealth, and (in the absence of effective tax measures) the slowness of the distribution of that wealth should increase *pari passu* with economic growth. The more income and wealth grow, therefore, the more the inequality of wealth between individuals increases. (Kaldor, Indian Tax Reform)'.[53] So much for planned growth with equity.

National economic goal is measured in terms of growth targets. This trend started in Britain since the fifties, with the announcement by the British Chancellor of the Exchequer in 1954 'that a 3 per cent annual growth rate would double the national income per capita by 1980 and make every man and woman twice as rich as his or her father had been at the same age. Previously, national goals had been set in terms of specific (physical) targets. Henceforth, the primary goal would be economic growth. The ideological debate between left and right as to how a fixed pie would be distributed was largely defused'.[54] When an attempt was made to document these benefits in 1989, 'Problems only arose when I attempted to identify what they (the benefits) were, especially as it quickly became apparent that almost every social indicator had worsened over the third of a century the experiment had taken. Chronic disease had increased, crime had gone up eight-fold, unemployment had soared and many more marriages were ending in divorce. Almost frantically I looked for gains to set against these losses which, in most cases I felt, had to be blamed on growth'.[55] This relates to a developed country like Britain. 'We might apply a similar test to the five-fold increase in global output since 1950. Yet during this same period, the number of people living in absolute poverty has kept pace with the population growth:

both have doubled. The ratio of the share of the world's income that went to the richest 20 per cent and that which went to the bottom 20 per cent poor has doubled. And indicators of social and environmental disintegration have risen sharply nearly everywhere'.[56] The concept of economic growth is bereft of any distributive growth system. It is concentrated on visible and grandoise schemes. Pyramid and Taj Mahal syndrones continue to dominate economic thinking. 'It had built airports, supertankers and heavy goods lorries, motor ways, flyovers and car parks with many floors'.[57] But no effective steps have been taken for development of housing facilities for the low-income groups in urban areas, who continue to live in appalling conditions. Although super speciality hospitals have been built, but no steps have been taken to develop primary health care in most of the rural areas.

Notes and References

1. Friedrich Hayek and Milton Friedman are the main proponents of neo-classical school. Once banished out of mainstream economics, their theories now form the main theoretical base of New World Order.
2. J.M. Keynes, The General Theory of Employment, Interest and Money, p. VI.
3. J.M. Keynes, A Tract on Monetary Reforms, p. 65.
4. Michel Beaud and Gills Dostaler Economic Thought since Keynes, p. 26.
5. General Theory, p. 130.

6-9. Hartley Withers The Meaning of Money, (1931), p. 222.

10-13. General Theory, Keynes, pp. V, VI, 33, 18.

14. Schumpeter, History of Economic Analysis, p. 41.
15. Ragner Nurkse, Problems of Capital Formation in underdeveloped countries, p. 10.
16. Schumpeter, History, p. 42.
17. *Ibid.*, p. 42, quoting Keynes, General Theory, p. 250.
18. Sir Austin Robinson in D.E. Maggridge, Maynard Keynes, cover page.

19-20. D.E. Maggridge, Maynard Keynes, pp. 566-67.

21. Schumpeter, History, pp. 1127-28, footnote 11.
22. D.H. Robertson, Money, p. 155.
23. *Ibid.*, pp. 156-57.

24. *Ibid.*, p. 91.
25. *Ibid.*, pp. 158-59.
26-27 *Ibid.*, Keynes's Introduction, p. VI.
28. Eric Hobsbawm, The Age of Revolution, p. 30.
29. Money, Keynes's Introduction, in Robertson, Money, p. 30.
30. Keynes, General Theory, Preface, P. VIII.
31. Schumpeter, History, p. 1172.
32. J.R. Hicks, Critical Eassays in Monetary Theory (1967), p. 156.
33. Schumpeter, Hisotry of Economic Analysis, p. 1180.
34. *Ibid.*, p. 1181.
35. Eric Hobsbawm, Age of Extremes, p. 107.
36. Istvan Meszaros, Beyond Capital, Vol.2, p. 1003.
37. I.G. Patel, Glimpses of Indian Economic Policy, p. 18.
38. J.R. Hick, Critical Eassays in Monetary Theory, p. 168.
39-40 Hugh Dalton, Principles of Public Finance, pp. 186-87.
41. B.S. Minhas, Planning and the Poor, p. XIII.
42. Government of India, Economic Survey (2002-03), p. 41.
43. *Economic Times*, Kolkata Edition, dated 23.7.2003, quoting World Bank Report, India-sustaining reform, Reducing Poverty (2003).
44. *Statesman*, Calcutta Edition, April 25, 1974.
45. Patel, Glimpses, p. 27.
46-50. Nicholas Kaldor, Reports on Taxation II, pp. 43, footnote 1, 34-35, VIII.
51. Nicholas Kaldor, Essays on Economic Policy I, p. 217.
52-53 Kaldor, Reports on Taxation II, pp. IX, 42-43.
54. David Korten, When Corporations Rule the World, p. 39.
55. Richard Douthwaite, The Growth Illusion, in *Ibid.*, pp. 38-39.
56. Koreten p. 39.
57. Douthwaite, The Growth Illusion, in *Ibid.*, p. 39.

8

Economic Darwinism

BEYOND KEYNES

After the Keynesian system ran out of steam and deflation of the economy with continuous inflation posed serious problems, there was need to justify a changed policy. Now the guiding lights of economics are Friedrich Hayek and Milton Friedman, who had been marginalised throughout the post-war period. Their virtues were suddenly discovered, after the Keynesian prescriptions had run its full course of destabilizing the world economy in general and economies of developing countries in particular. These economists, who had little following except in the extreme right, were suddenly found to be paragons of wisdom. When the depression of the 1970s started raising its head in the western capitalist system, it was time to change guards and Hayek, a long discarded economist, was found suitable to fill this bill. It was about this time, i.e., in 1974 and 1976 respectively that Hayek and Friedman were awarded the Nobel Memorial Prize for Economics, for giving them credibility, which they had long lost amongst economists. Hayek's thesis is self-contradictory, as has been found by number of economists like Kaldor, Kalecki, Harrod, Schumpeter—to mention only a few. 'The presence of so many contradictory arguments is not accidental: it is due to the desire to demonstrate, at all costs, that the scarcity of capital is the great cause of economic crisis and a direct cause of unemployment. Hayek has been trying to prove this proposition ever since he first wrote on the subject. In the course of time the arguments became more ingenious and more complicated, but they brought him no nearer to proving it than he was at first'.[1] 'His ingenuity knew no bounds after he received official patronage of Margaret Thatcher and became the high priest of the free market system and 'barricaded himself behind the richly armoured battalions of the most reactionary propaganda organisations of the so-called free enterprise system'. According to Hayek's logic, capital is the origin of labour, not *vice-versa* and 'most of the western proletariat, and most of millions of the developing world, owe their existence to opportunities that advanced countries have created for them'.[2] This is a justification of domination by developed countries of the world economy. It lacks economic logic and smacks of imperialism of the highest order. Hayek does not believe in state policy and believes in the absoluteness of the market, quite forgetting that modern capitalism is a product of state power and not of free market. Only powerful states have prospered in this system, giving a lie to the spontaneity of market mechanism, which Hayek so passionately advocates Hayek's theory is not based on economic rationality and according to him 'are highly abstract, and are particularly hard to grasp for those schooled in the mechanistic, scientistic, constructivist canons of rationality that dominate our educational systems and who consequently tend to be ignorant of biology, economics and evolution'.[3] Hayek has taken a leaf from Adam Smith and tried to justify his theory on the concept of division of knowledge. According to him each individual or group with particular knowledge bring spontaneity in the market. In the modern society, knowledge of individuals and groups overlap and clash of knowledge and interest can hardly bring any spontaneity to the market. This is what Keynes had to say in his review of Hayek's 'Prices and Production' (1931), which was the basis of his theory, culminating in 'The Fatal Conceit: The Errors of Socialism (1988)', 'The book, as it stands, seems to me to be one of the most frightful muddles I have ever read, with scarcely a sound proposition in it beginning with page 45, and yet it remains a book of some interest which is likely to leave its mark on the mind of the reader. It is an extraordinary example of how, starting with a mistake, a remorseless logician can end up in Bedlam. Yet Dr. Hayek has seen a vision, and though when he woke up he has made nonsense of his story by giving the wrong names to the objects which occur in it'.[4] Hayek says that, 'a rational socialist economy, although theoretically conceivable, cannot exist in practice'.[5] Because knowledge is divided and nobody has the complete information about the economy. 'At a time of increasingly mechanised and automated business accounting, Hayek may have realised that this line of argument was not based on very solid ground. In his polemical pamphlet 'The Road to Serfdom' he therefore shifted the main emphasis of his argument into the sphere of politics'.[6]

Hayek seems to have been kept in reserve for such eventuality, which the Keynesian prescriptions brought about. Keynes found his theory interesting, but for wrong reasons. J.R. Hicks, who wavered between Keynes and Hayek, says that 'Hayek's diagnosis and prescription for the slump of 1931-32 in Britain could not have been worse'. But he goes on to say that since his prescriptions were wrong at that time, there is no reason it should always be wrong. If the economy has expanded more than its capacity and is held up by lack of savings, Hayek's theory is applicable. The developing countries are diagnosed as needing Hayek's prescription of expansion of credit through reduction of the market rate below the natural rate of interest. This practice has since been followed, but there has been no sign of revival of the economy. This is the opposite of Keynesian prescriptions. 'We have unquestionably learned from Keynes that control through banking is one-sided. . . . Banks can restrict expansion by refusing to lend; but they cannot force expansion just by offering to lend, on whatever easy terms'.[7]

Friedman believes in a currency system without any state control. In fact, he believes in a system of financial anarchy, which according to him produces best results. According to Frank H. Hahn, Friedman lacked precision and has a tendency to slip from empirical to theoretical.[8]

Friedman's study of U.S. monetary statistics, along with Anna J. Schwartz for the period 1867-1960, is an attempt to compare incomparables. The monetary systems during this period were different. From a closed economy with gold standard to paper currency in an international system are definitely not comparable. Moreover, according to Friedman-Hayek concept, knowledge is divisible and one cannot have full knowledge of what is happening and what happened. Statistics, howsoever comprehensive cannot have the complete date. Friedman's prescription of expanding the banking system during the depression of the thirties, would have only created bad debt and hit the depositors hard. He believes in natural rate of unemployment and advises the state not to meddle in such matters. Friedman tries to turn economics into a natural science from a social science, by theorising from imperfect and limited empirical date. Thus, while Hayek wants to make economics a biological science, Friedman wants to make it a natural science, in their quest for liberalism and ultimate withering away of the State. On the other hand, Keynes considered economics a moral science. According to him, 'economics is essentially a moral science and not a natural science. That is to say, it employs introspection and judgments of value'.[9] This tradition dates back to Aristotle and the Scholastics and was reaffirmed by Sidgwick, Marshall and J.N. Keynes. Economics, bereft of morality, spells danger for mankind. Economists will do well to be reminded of what Francois Rabelias wrote in the sixteenth century, 'Science without conscience spells but destruction of the spirit'.[10] Economists like Frank H. Hahn found Friedman's theory lacking in precision on the ground of his switching from empirical to theoretical and *vice versa*. He also finds Friedman's assumption of natural rate of unemployment unacceptable. In the true spirit of scientific enquiry, he 'holds that there remains an immense gap between the theoretical fields, in which scientific rigour is applicable, and practical economics, in which the economist still has little to say as a scholar'.[11] Franco Modigilani found that the neo-classical theory of Friedman, does not have much difference in the theoretical level with Keynesian economics, but has very deep political ramifications.[12] No doubt, Friedman was to Reagan, what Hayek was to Margaret Thatcher.

A perceptive observer can well see that Keynesianism and Hayek-Friedman's long neglected theories compliment each other. After the failure of Keynesianism, the latter theories reassured the Western countries that their socio-economic system of dominating the world economy can depend on the end of economics and beginning of biology theory offered by Hayek and currency school prescriptions offered by Friedman. Keynesianism was the 'go phase' of monetarism, while the latter is the 'stop phase' of Keynesianism.[13] The latter theory as propounded by Hayek is more than that. It is a theory of economic Darwinism based on the concept of natural order, as the West sees it through the vision or nightmare of Hayek. He has made an economist out of Darwin and a biologist out of Adam Smith'. From survival of the fittest to the survival of the richest—Hayek has made up, for his lack of economic logic, by drawing from diverse fields like biology, evolution and cybernetics. It is a thoroughly unscientific and illogical theory.

The World Bank and IMF have taken to Hayek-Friedman's theory like ducks to the water. Theories propounded by Hayek and Friedman and so easily accepted, can spell doom for the developing countries. To cite an example, Lawrence Summers, Economist and Vice-President, Research of the World Bank, in a study, 'offers a rational justification for the displacement of pollution and waste from the North to the South, where wages are lower, in terms of the relationship between the cost of a pollution dangerous to health and the profits absorbed by the growth of morbidity and mortality'.[15] This should be an eye opener to the third world countries, who are easily falling prey to half-baked economic theories offered through the courtesy of World Bank and IMF. Have we reached the end of economics? 'Today, as we face the great problems of our time, economic thought's broken wing has left the economist unarmed, with his knowledge fragmented, his analysis perfunctory, and helpless before the enormous void separating a theoretical edifice lacking coherence and a world in need of response and solutions'.[16]

CHANGE TO NEO-CLASSICISM

After having accepted the twin Keynesian prescriptions of easy money policy and Government intervention for development of the economy and running up huge internal and external debts, with persistent inflation and simultaneous economic slow-down, we have suddenly found virtue in a free market economy with a hands-off policy for the government. It is also strange that the hands-off the economy policy is followed by the government in a selective manner. This has sent confusing signals in the economy with GPreface government unable or unwilling to interfere when intervention was called for and intervening at most in-opportune times. This is particularly true of stock market scams, which have been plaguing the economy since the nineties. From the nineties, Indian economy had gradually become speculative, instead of productive. With the world depression of the 1980s, Indian industries gradually slid into stagnation and decline. Industrial recession in the West was transmitted into the Indian economy particularly the Industrial sector, due to the sudden opening up of the Indian economy to external forces at the worst possible time, when the western economy was going through a period of depression. The growing indigenous industrial sector of the Indian economy, which was developing in a protectionist system, to cater to the developing domestic market was deprived of the customs barrier on import of similar goods by the budget of 1992. This was done at a time when the Rupee was devalued twice during the course of the year and the Indian Rupee dipped to an all time low in relation to the British Pound, U.S. Dollar, German Mark and the Japanese Yen. This resulted in a situation of rising cost of the inputs of the nascent Indian industries, as the cost of imported capital goods like plants and machinery and the servicing charges of the same increased. Almost all the new manufacturing industries in India were set-up with foreign technology and foreign plants and machinery. Sharp devaluation of the Indian Rupee, led to the escalation of the cost of these industries and most of these industries became non-starter. Where the industries went into production with outputs geared to the export market, the increased cost of production due to the imported inputs, lost the cost advantage in the international market, which the devaluation of the Rupee was expected to bring in. The changing technology and the production pattern in the developed world, did not help in products of new industries set-up with huge investment, finding any assured export market. These industries were not also cost-effective for the domestic market and had little or no domestic market. With the sharp decline of the Russian markets in the wake of the collapse of the Soviet Union, and no substantial market-availability in the developed world, the Indian exports had to increasingly depend on their traditional markets in Asia, like Indonesia, Malaysia, Hong Kong, South Korea, Singapore, Thailand and Taiwan. Some of these countries were yet to recover from the depression of the last decade.

With the end of the cold war, decisively won by the U.S.A. and the West, there was shift in the economic strategy from heavy industries to consumer goods industries in the developed world. The existing industrial structure in the West particularly the heavy industries, viz., metal industries, chemical industries, hydel plants, nuclear energy, large dams came under increasing pressure from the environmental lobby. There was a shift of technology to keep up with the ever increasing environment standards. The old plants and machinery in the western world, had already outlived their utility, in the sense that the investments made on them had already been recovered with high profits and interests. The capital equipments of these industries had been caught in the cycle of obsolescence, which is a typical feature of the western concept of industrialisation. These idle plants and machinery were taking up valuable space and were badly in need of disposal. Indian Government liberalised the industrial sector in the nineties. The New Industrial Policy announced on 24th July, 1991, marked the watershed in government's policy towards the private sector *vis-a-vis* the public sector, which was dislodged from the commanding heights of the economy, where they have been placed by Nehruvian planning. The encouragement of the private sector was at the cost of the public sector, which had been denigrated for quite some time as a drag on the Indian economy. It is another matter that most of the criticism of the public sector was uninformed and an attempt to generalise from particular instances of a few unprofitable public sector undertakings. A false wind was blowing glamorising private sector and its managers and showing the public sector and its managers in a low light. The fact that the vision which had empowered the public sector in the early stages got dimmed with the gradual bureaucratisation. As the public sector units gradually lost out to their respective ministries in the matter of control and became mere departments of government, bureaucratisation was complete and the vision was completely lost. Technical leadership was downgraded and personnel, marketing and publicity were given greater importance in leadership. The management graduates of the IIMs, set-up by the government at public cost, were the glamous boys of the private sector, although they were the products of public sector institutes, run by the tax payers money.

Industrial de-regulation, which had started from eighties became a major policy of the Government programme of industrialisation. Henceforth, private sector was to occupy the pride of place in the Government's industrial dispensation. In its anxiety to give greater leverage to the private industries *vis-a-vis* the public sector banks and lending institutions, even the 'mandatory convertibility clause', which had been sparingly used by the banks, had been abolished in February, 1992 by the government. According to this clause, banks had the option of converting part of their loans into equity in case of default by new projects. The government's liberalisation drive was thus obviously at the cost of public sector financial institutions. The winds of liberalisation did not blow towards the public sector institutions, who were subjected to government dictat unfavourable to them. The government's policy was one of encouraging the private sector by scuttling the public sector. The Indian experiment with private industrialisation started with the banking sector and financial institutions under government control. The reform experiment, which in effect meant doing away with social control of the economy, was a half-way house with a nationalised financial sector. The experiment only helped in making the banking sector sick, with, a large portfolio of non-performing assets. While the private sector was liberated from all regulations, banks and financial institutions were subject to all sorts of pressure, political or otherwise, for financing non-viable enterprises. There was little or no accountability on the part of the private sector, whereas public sector banks and financial institutions were fully accountable. This type of arrangement was bound to be failure and it did not help either the private sector or the nationalised banks and financial institutions. Financial scams became the order of the day in the nineties and the financial sector had the worst of the bargain. At the end of the day, the private sector industries were left with number of non-performing units and the financial institutions with a huge portfolio of non-performing assets. The private sector units had to seek shelter under the Board of Industrial and Financial Reconstruction, another bureaucratic organisation, a by-product of the reforms process. The Board had been set-up in 1987 and has received 4930 references under the Sick Industrial Companies (Special Provisions) Act, 1985, from private sector units. The board has hardly been able to help the recovery of any sick unit and has provided a further hindrance to the financial institutions recovering their dues. Thus, the reform process has only added further bureaucratic institutions to the system like BIFR, SEBI (Securities and Exchange Board of India) and various other regulatory bodies in the banking, industries and services sectors. The architects of the Reforms process obviously could not trust the deregulation process they had ushered in. Thus, instead of a few regulatory bodies, we have a plethora of regulatory bodies.

The reason for sickness of new industries, started with foreign technology is not far to seek. Most of these units were set-up with out-dated technology and machines. Many of the technologies were in experimental stages and were tried in third world countries. Most of these technologies were being phased out from the developed countries and were imported in the craze for sudden industrialisation. Developed countries which were going through a period of recession, were keen to change their technology, along with the plants and equipments. The industrialisation drive in developing countries and the craze for foreign technology with export-oriented units, provided a golden opportunity for them to get rid of their industrial obsolescence at a huge profit. The new industrial units were caught like sitting ducks, when faced with international market forces in the globalisation drive. The changing technology and production pattern in the developed countries, away from basic heavy industries led to a situation where the intermediate industrial goods, the newly set-up industries were to manufacture, had no market. Change in technology also changes the market, particularly for intermediate industrial goods. Move in developing countries away from metal and metal-based industries led to complete market failure of export-oriented metal and metallurgical industries. The liberalisation process allowed the export of obsolete technology, along with the equipments from developed countries to new hopefuls intent on rapid industrialisation. Industrial deregulation provided excellent opportunity for the depression ridden West to dispose of their out-dated technology and pass on the burden of industrial depression to India. Thus, the policy of deregulation of industries in India was launched at a most inopportune time for the country, when the industries needed safeguard from the dumping of obsolete foreign technology. There was complete lack of any proper planning for technology import and technologies along with the machinery was imported on *adhoc* basis. Although, there are number of industrial research laboratories in India, no step was taken to start industries developed on indigenous technologies. If it was expected that foreign technology would integrate the Indian Industrial structure in the global economic system, the expectations were belied. The *adhoc* technology import, only helped in marginalizing the Indian industry in the global market. When we have depended on our own Research and Development Organisations, the result has been always beneficial. When technology for cryogenic engines for propulsion of Rockets, was denied to India by the Russian Government, our scientists could develop more powerful engines. In fact, denial of missile technology proved a boon for Indian space programme and proper technology could be developed by Indian scientists, which made India a powerful missile power and contributed enormously to Indian defence capabilities. It is unlikely that Indian missile programme would have been successful had we depended on foreign technology. The development in the field of atomic power and technology are other instances of India producing international standard technology. Countries like Phillipines which have imported nuclear power plants, have not been able to commission them, after decades. Industrialisation through borrowed technology is a misnomer and has not succeeded anywhere in the history of industrialisation. Technology should not be copied, but should be adopted and modified for indigenous use by indigenous scientists and technologists.

NEO-CLASSICISM IN THE FINANCIAL SECTOR

In India, huge portfolio of non-performing assets, which the banks are carrying are mostly loans to business-houses and fly-by-night operators, who wanted to benefit from the easy money policy, unleashed on the banks by the government. Little or no effective steps have been taken to recover any major part of this amount, in the fear of antagonizing the business community, particularly big business-houses. In the name of economic recovery, interest for loanees have been lowered and the depositors have been penalised with constantly sliding interest rates. Although interest rate for bank loans has been lowered, there has been hardly any improvement in the economic scenario. The industrial growth of 2.7 per cent during 2001-02 is the lowest during the last ten years. The failure to recover from industrial deceleration in 2001-02 is attributed to lack of external demand due to the fall out of the attack on the World Trade Centre in September 2001.[17] This shows the dominance of the events in the U.S.A., over the economy of India. Any shock-waive in the West will be passed on to Indian economy. Even mild tremors in the U.S. economy may cause an earthquake in the Indian economy. It is very clear that the industrial sector is suffering from recession due to

general slow down of economic activity, as government spendings on big projects have drastically come down. To expect that the private sector will revive on an easy money policy, is to indulge in wishful thinking. Easy money policy does not *per se* generate industrial growth, unless backed up by vigorous government spending in industrial and infrastructural projects. The private sector in India has mostly developed piggy back on Government projects. Whenever, there has been huge public expenditure on industrial and infrastructural development, private sector has prospered in India. With government spending in new industrial projects at a minimum, there is hardly any scope of private sector activity as contractors for such projects. The infrastructural projects with assistance from World Bank and other international agencies have turnkey contracts, with global tenders, where the Indian private sector has not been able to compete, unless linked up with multinationals. Since the World Bank demands international (western) standard in its projects, executing agencies have been mostly multinationals. This has effectively excluded the Indian private sector. While calling for latest western standard in foreign aided projects, the maintenance aspect is completely forgotten. The maintenance has to be done by local equipments through local technical know-how. Moreover, today's technology becomes outdated tomorrow. The project does not stand in isolation and unless the supporting system is upgraded, the project only becomes a show piece with little utility. For an international standard of road project, transport system has to be also internationalised. Moreover, unless the system of road network is rationalised, a single road developed according to the latest standard, will hardly have any impact on the economic development.

We can draw a parallel in the development of road-network in India with World Bank assistance, with the construction of railway net-work in India in the late nineteenth and early twentieth century with British capital and British engineers. In the case of building up of the railway system, it is the British shareholders in London, who benefited, whereas the entire loss was borne by the Government of India at the cost of Indian tax payers (both

direct and indirect), giving rise to the theory of 'Drain' of Indian wealth to England. 'Year after year the working of the lines shows a big loss to the Treasury, though it is true, no doubt, that private shareholders in these undertakings get a fair, if not a handsome, return for their money. Paradoxical as this state of things may appear—and strange as it may seem that, in a country where there is little or no competition between the different lines, the net earnings are not larger than they are found to be—the explanation is simple. The lines that have not been built with public money are practically owned by people in England and other foreign countries, who have made their investment on the guarantee of the Government of India that they will receive a certain rate of interest, apart from the question whether the lines make a profit or a loss'.[18]

Similar is the story of development of road net-work and other infrastructural projects with assistance from World Bank and other international loaning bodies. The entire loan burden of the projects, alongwith interest is on the Indian economy, whereas the profits are with foreign shareholders of the international banking agencies. We have already seen, how keen the IMF is to safeguard the interest of the international investors, at the cost of the loaning countries. The Indian situation is just the opposite with Indian government and financial institutions being soft on the creditors at the cost of the depositors. The creditors have become holy cows, as any punitive action against them is supposed to affect the growth process and development statistics, which are touted as index of achievements. The ability of the Indian populace to generate high savings, is now shown as anti-developmental in an atmosphere of blatant consumerism, with little regard for purchasing capacity or effective demand. The easy money policy of the government will only be used for speculative purposes and for buying up public sector assets, which are going up for sale in a big way. Thus, the public sector banks are loaning public funds for purchase of public property by private individuals. This is a paradox of present development policy, where the interest of vast majority of small savers, who form the bulk of the population, is sacrificed to boost up a small

business elite on public money. This policy is based on the neo-classical monetary theory prescribed by Friedman and Hayek. According to Friedman, expansion of bank credit is the remedy for economic depression. Such a prescription is worse than the disease and opposite of Keynesian prescriptions. Hayek had also offered similar solution of reducing the market rate below the natural rate.

This type of situation to create a private industrial structure on monetary policy, may not last too long. Banks and financial institutions are already showing signs of strain and financial scams have become the order of the day. With industrial recession gripping the world, expecting an industrial recovery on monetary policy alone, without substantial government spending in the industrial sector, is to indulge in wishful thinking. As the experience throughout the world has shown that the private sector can prosper only when there is substantial government activity in the industrial and infrastructural sectors. The depression of the seventies in Europe in the nineteenth century, was overcome by large scale public spending in laying down railway network on guaranteed return to private shareholders in Europe. World Bank and other international financial institutions are also following similar policy in development of road net-work in India, as was done by the Britishers at the end of the nineteenth century to develop the railway network in India. As the railway network in India was developed by European capital with British technology and engineers, subsidised by the government of India at the cost of Indian tax payers, the benefits went largely to Britain in the growth of engineering industries in Britain and prosperity of British shareholders. Lord Lawrence, Viceroy of India said in 1869, about the system of building railroads by private companies 'the whole profits go to the companies, and the whole loss to the government'.[19] The myth of private enterprise pioneering the Industrial Revolution in the nineteenth century is exposed clearly by a study of the economics of the construction of the Indian railways. 'The history of the Indian railroads illustrates the dangers of calling the nineteenth century an age of free enterprise. Empires were built and maintained by a mixed economy of state and private capitalism, a system designed to temper the efficiency and greed of the private sector with the inefficiency and social conscience of government'.[20]

BORROWED DEVELOPMENT

Funding of road projects in the name of development of infrastructure by the World Bank, when there is enough domestic savings available in the country, is paradoxical. No foreign technology is needed for road construction in India, particularly since, reputed civil engineering institutions have been in existence here, which have been developing technology suited to Indian conditions. The first engineering college was established in India in 1847 at Roorkee, followed by the starting of a civil engineering department at the Presidency College, Calcutta, which later became the Bengal Engineering College in 1880. Poona College of Engineering was formalised in 1859. Madras Surveyors' School functioning from 1794, became the Madras Civil Engineering College in 1862. Besides, since independence there has been significant development in India in development of road construction technology. India has enough technical manpower in this area and foreign technology is hardly required. Moreover, raw materials available for road construction are available locally. The machinery required for road construction is also available in India. In such a circumstance, it seems strange that we have gone for foreign loans in an area, where hardly any sophisticated technology is required. Government of India took up double-laning, four-laning and six-laning of National Highway system, in addition to construction of major and minor bridges. A considerable part of these projects (26%) are being funded by loans from the World Bank, Asian Development Bank and Overseas Economic Co-operation Fund (OECF), and Japan'.[21] Loan assistance means that these loaning agencies have exercised strict control over the technology of the projects, machinery procurement and selection of contractors. The question arises, once these projects are completed, whether foreign aid will be required for their maintenance. While taking up these projects, no attention has been given on their maintenance. Obviously, periodical foreign assistance will be required for their maintenance, as the construction required foreign technology and managerial ability.

David Korten in his book, 'When Corporations Rule the World', has analysed the aggressive loaning policy, which the World Bank proposed ostensibly for the development of the blacks who had been economically isolated, during the apartheid regime.[22] After the apartheid regime had come to an end in South Africa and the international sanctions had been lifted against that country, World Bank came up with a major housing project for the black townships. South Africa had low foreign debt and World Bank proposed a large loan programme for this purpose. Housing was a vital need for black townships, where slums and shanties existed in ghetto like conditions. But the question arises whether foreign loans are the best way of solving housing problem of the poor. Foreign loans generate very little economic activity at the local level and the supposed beneficiaries will have very little, if anything to do with these projects. World Bank aid in foreign exchange will import technical and managerial inputs in the form of machinery and foreign consultants. The project will have no lasting impact on the economy, particularly on the economic conditions of the weaker sections, for whom most of the foreign aid projects are ostensibly intended. No steps are taken to develop the technical skills of the local populace and ensure their economic involvement in the projects. These projects are artificial technological and managerial islands, which do not have any spread-effect on the surrounding ocean of under-development. In this way the foreign aided projects, have continued the colonial tradition and are an extension of colonialism. World Bank has kept the colonial flag flying.

Now the question arises, who pays for these technological and managerial extravaganza. The burden of payment of World Bank loans falls on the poor, the middle class and the small and marginal farmers, who are least benefited from the projects. Payment of loans will require mobilisation of greater foreign exchange and boosting of exports. The economy will have to be made export-oriented, instead of serving the needs of the local populace. As Korten has illustrated in the proposed South African case, the World Bank sponsored loaning and export-led economy, would have benefited the whites, who controlled all the levers of economic power. Fortunately, the new South African leadership, led by Nelson Mandela and Desmond Tutu did not fall for the trap laid by World Bank, ostensibly for the purpose of economic upliftment of the deprived blacks. The World Bank packages are marketed with powerful economic logic, which appears sound to the uninitiated. This so-called sound economic logic is based on premises, which do not take into account the economic interest of the large majority, who figure marginally or very little in the growth statistics of the World Bank.

Let us see the effect of export-led growth, which is the key economic agenda in the World Bank's loaning programme. Huge external loaning, will require mobilisation of a country's resources towards exports to attempt to pay-off the foreign loans. World Bank loaning ensures that a country is in perpetual debt. Whether one calls it debt-trap or not is immaterial. A country, which is constantly in debt to foreign loanees, obviously surrenders a part of its economic sovereignty. We have seen it in the case of various IMF debt-relief packages. The World Bank and foreign loans are tied-loans and the loanee country loses its sovereignty to the extent that the foreign agencies control the operation of the loan. Foreign agencies control the formulation and operation of the loan and this is certainly surrender of national economic sovereignty. Whether, this is a world-wide trend or supported by cooked up economic logic, do not make it less odious. It is certainly the same old colonial policy, followed by Britain. World Bank, Asian Development Bank, British aid and other loaning agencies identify our economic needs and give us tied-loans for the mitigation of the same. Conditions are laid down by these loaning agencies. The implications of such external aid in the name of development are serious indeed and will jeopardize our national sovereignty. World Bank has ushered in an era of corporate colonialism. The Bank represents the interest of the big American Corporations. Similarly, Asian Development Bank and various bilateral loaning bodies represent the interest of the private corporate sector in the developed countries. They are certainly not here for charity or for any altruistic purpose. They know World Bank loans and foreign loans have little or no accountability of the loaning agency or their selected foreign suppliers or executing agencies. John L. Seitz has quoted in his book 'Global Issues—An Introduction', from a study of World Bank experience of over forty years, how the World Bank imposes its suppliers along with technology on the loanee countries. 'When aid is tied to the supply of equipment from the donor country, ... freedom to choose an appropriate technology may be compromised'. (Warren C. Baum and Stokes M. Tolbert, Investing in Development: Lessons of World Bank Experience).[23] External aid is intended for marketing of goods and services of the loaning country, in the shape of supply of machinery and equipment, as well as consultancy services. The supposed benefit to the loanee country is marginal, if any. David C. Korten in his book, 'When Corporations Rule the World' has cited documentary evidence from World Bank's own internal reports that most of the projects have been failures. In the words of Korten, 'there is evidence that the majority of Bank Projects are failures, even by the Bank's own narrowly defined economic criteria . . . . The Bank bears no liability for its own errors'. (*Ibid.*, p. 171) The Bank is adept at passing on the blame to the loanees for their inferior work culture, lack of technical knowledge and managerial ability, corruption, etc.

CLASH OF KNOWLEDGE (TRADITIONAL *V.* INSTITUTIONAL)

Let me cite two examples of World Bank aided projects in India. From 1975, World Bank had taken up a major agricultural development programme in Orissa, with huge investment. It was intended to modernise agriculture and make it market-oriented. The various World Bank teams consisted of theoreticians, who had theoretical knowledge based on experience in their own countries. They were specialists in their own field, keen on implementing their own ideas in the field. They had little or no interaction with the cultivations, due to their flying visits, language and cultural barriers. Whatever knowledge, they had of local conditions, were obtained from the officials based in the State capital, Bhubaneswar, who themselves had superficial knowledge of the situation at the village level, gained from their occasional visits. A new market culture was sought to be created, forgetting that agriculture was a way of life in these places and not simply an isolated economic activity, based on the concept of supply and demand.

The World Bank Scheme went into a programme of mechanisation of agriculture. Huge earth-moving machinery and bull-dozers were brought in for clearing of village forests and taming of streams, quite forgetting that these village forests were part of the socio-economic structure of the village community and the streams, which were sought to be tamed were part of the major river systems. The stage was set for an eventual ecological disaster. No doubt, the scheme was a big failure. Destruction of the village forests ruined the delicately balanced village economy, where the villagers were dependent on the village forests for their economic wherewithal. Large number of unplanned minor irrigation projects, taken up haphazardly, destroyed the forest resources in the catchment area of major river systems. Village forests were the natural barrier between human habitations and reserve forests. These were intricately linked with the village economy, supplying firewood and other economic necessities like tamarind and various forest products. Villagers through generations were aware of the vital importance of village forest and took steps for its regeneration. Traditional knowledge of maintenance of forests, acquired through living with nature for generations, was ignored and is in the process of disappearing. One tends to forget that knowledge can also be acquired through interaction with nature. How can one explain large-scale depletion of forest resources within a short span of a few decades, when the same have been maintained by their forefathers for ages. This can best be described as clash of knowledge. The clash between theoretical knowledge and practical knowledge, proved an unequal one, as the former armed with the power of state and international agencies proved too powerful for the latter.

World Bank sponsored rural development programme

led to large-scale depletion of forest wealth in the span of a decade. A resource, which has been maintained for ages, was lost in a few years. The local populace deprived of the village forest, started making inroads on the Reserve Forests. Crash commercialisation of forest resources, which came in the wake of market economy, posed a serious ecological disaster. Treating forest resources as marketable commodity created serious threat to their existence. Natural resources like forest wealth can provide for the needs of a village community, but can hardly support market forces motivated by greed and blind profit. Opening up of these resources in the name of development, is bartering away the wealth built-up through ages. If this rate of depletion continues in the name of development sponsored by World Bank and International development agencies, in a few decades we will not have any forest resources left. This is the paradox of World Bank sponsored development we must face. After losing our forest wealth in these so-called development programmes, we are running to the same international agencies for creation of forests, as if foreign funds can create forests. Development of forests takes centuries and cannot be created by simply throwing money.

World Bank concept of development consists of introducing market economy. The rural communities are thought to be backward, as they have not been exposed to the urban market forces. Road to development consists of transforming the rural individual to economic man, motivated by greed, jealousy and selfishness. In this process it is quite forgotten that most of the rural societies, which are sought to be changed, have long tradition of co-operation. A basic cultural clash is sought to be introduced in rural communities by destroying the culture of co-operation and replacing the same by the culture of competition. This is based on the strong faith that competition brings out the best in the individual and the society. Western world has prospered due to the spirit of competition, whereas others have been left far behind. Industrial revolution occurred in the British Isles, due to the spirit of competition amongst the Britishers, in which the Spaniarards, the Dutch and the Portuguese were left behind. Even France, a country with the highest cultural tradition in Europe, was no match for the Britishers and were left far behind in this race. If the spirit of industrial revolution could be replicated in other societies, the same prosperity would come their way. It is the spirit of competition, jealousy and greed, which is lacking in the rest of the world, for which others are left behind. This is a very simplistic theory for a complex socio-economic situation, besides being a throwback on Darwinism. In this conflict between individual and individual, between society and society, between man and nature, only the fittest should survive. The fittest does not mean the best in human qualities but the most cunning, the most greedy and the most avaricious. We have already seen that in the conflict between man and nature, the latter is already extracting its revenge in a big way. It is now amply clear that the future of mankind lies in active co-operation with nature and not in conflict. The lesson should have been learnt by now that nature will not tolerate any exploitation of its resources. The market force of greed and jealousy which have been unleashed in areas, hitherto outside the purview of these forces, have already created serious damage to both nature and human society. The implications are very serious indeed and goes well beyond the pail of economics. The harmonious co-existence between nature and human society have sustained both for generations. Once this delicate balance is destroyed, it is inviting catastrophy for both nature and human society. The so-called Industrial Revolution has been achieved at a tremendous cost to nature and mankind and cannot be repleted elsewhere without destruction of mankind and the very planet itself, which we inhabit. If this appears melodramatic, we can read the report from National Geographic, September, 2002. 'Human impacts on the landscape are global in scale, on a par with volcanism or tectonic shifts. New data combining satellite imagery with historical records reveal that humans have planted, grazed, paved, or built-upon roughly 40 per cent of the Earth's terrestrial surface. . . . Population, consumption, and technology are seen by many, experts as driving the human impact on the planet'. . . . Half the developing world lives on less than two dollars a day, yet consumption and expectation for a better life continues to rise. Our large brain got us to this point. The question now, is, can they get us out?'[24] Technology and over-consumption are mainly responsible for this state of affairs. Industrial revolution in British Isles and the rest of Europe, led to huge explosion of population in these places, which they could partially solve by colonising three new continents, the two Americas and Australia. The scramble for colonies in the late nineteenth and early twentieth centuries by the European powers to emulate the British pattern of industrial revolution with captive colonial markets, led to two catastrophic world wars in the twentieth century. Fortunately, major part of the world remained territorially untouched by these catastrophic wars. This may not happen in future wars and the theatre of conflict is likely to be the so-called developing world. Sudden introduction of market forces has created a situation of conflict in areas hitherto untouched by these forces. This situation of economic conflict has not helped the economically weak, who have been marginalised. Economically weak will find it very difficult to survive this drive for commercialisation of natural resources. Sudden commercialisation of basic needs will price these out of reach of the majority of population. Market forces are breaking up the basic structure of the community and the village communities are fast disintegrating. We are already seeing the results in large number of starvation deaths in places, where foodgrains are available in the market. The market prices, which are determined by well organised urban centers, working on the basis of profit, will be out of the reach of the large number of population in rural areas. The marketisation of basic necessities will pose a serious problem for those failing to attain economic viability.

Notes and References

1. Nicholas Kaldor, Professor Hayek and the Concertina Effect, in *Essays on Economic Stability and Growth* (1980), p. 176.
2. Istvan Meszaros, Beyond Capital (Vol. I), p. 131.
3. F.A. Hayek, The Fatal Conceit: The Errors of Socialism, pp. 88, 131.
4. Maggridge, Maynard Keynes, p. 534.
5. Marz, Schumpeter, p. 108.

6. *Ibid.*, p. 108.
7. J.R. Hicks, Critical Essays in Monetary Theory (1967), p. 169.
8. F.H. Hahn, 'Professor Friedman's Views on Money', *Economica*, Vol. 38, pp. 61-60.
9. Michel Beaud, *et. al.*, Economic Thought since Keynes, p. 25.
10. *Ibid.*, p. 158, note 79 quoted from the Complete Works of Rabelais.
11. *Ibid.*, p. 259.
12. *Ibid.*, p. 350.
13. Meszaros, Beyond Capital, p. 125.
14. Hayek, Fatal Conceit, p. 144.
15. Beaud *et. al.*, p. 151.
16. *Ibid.*, pp. 153-54.
17. Government of India, Economic Survey, 2001-02, p. 161, 2002-03, p. 129.
18. Editorial in the Statesman, Calcutta, September 1, 1893. Reproduced in *Statesman*, Calcutta, September 1, 1993, under the caption 100 years ago.
19. Daniel Headrick, Tools of Empire, p. 186.
20. *Ibid.*, p. 187.
21. Government of India, Economic Survey, 2002-03, p. 194.
22. David Korten, When Corporations Rule the World, pp. 169-71.
23. John L. Seitz, Global Issues, p. 170.
24. State of the Planet, Supplement to the National Geographic, September 2002.

9

Corelation between Technology and Economy

Technology of an economy at any given time is a product of the economic environment of a particular country and unless the economic conditions are similar, a simple transfer of technology from one economic environment to the other, will not be beneficial. In the history of economic development, no country has been benefited from a simple transfer of technology from another country. This clearly shows the relevance of technology transfer *vis-a-vis* the circumstances in which each country is placed. Technological innovation is not universal but relevant to the socio-economic conditions. Science and innovation are different and one need not be confused with the other. Laws of science may be universal, till unchallenged, but economic success of scientific knowledge, when put in the form of technology depends on numerous variable conditions, socio-economic situation being the major factor. 'Innovation is essentially a two-sided or coupling activity . . . . On the one hand, it involves the recognition of a need or more precisely, in economic terms, a potential market for a new product or process. On the other hand, it involves technical knowledge, which may be generally available, but may also often include new scientific and technological knowledge, the result of original research activity'.[1] Spectacular industrial development of Germany and

Japan after the Second World War, was not due to the transfer of superior technology of the victor to the vanquished, but due to adaptation of technology to indigenous circumstances. A detailed analysis of the German war economy after the defeat of Germany in the Second World War reveals that the basic infrastructure of the German industry remained intact and was not destroyed by the war. A detailed study entitled 'The Effects of Strategic Bombing on the German War Economy', shows that there was sufficient reserve in the German economy, which could be used with advantage after the war. This study shows that Germany did not commit her entire resources—both manpower and industrial to war effort and instead used the resources of the occupied territories to advantage. It was this economic strategy of limitations in her war effort, that kept the German economy both elastic and resilient in meeting the post-war challenges.[2] In short, the war could not damage the basic structure of the German economy, it was obviously the sound economic infrastructure, together with the will to economic victory, spurred on by military defeat that led to industrial resurgence in Germany.

IMPORTED TECHNOLOGY PROVES NON-STARTER

In the case of Japan, destruction wrought by the Second World War could not destroy the basic infrastructure of the Japanese economy, as the process of industrialisation was gradually weaved in the Japanese economic, social and cultural fabric. A study of Japanese industrial development prior to Second World War reveals that the displacement of workers was minimal and the process of industrial transformation much less painful than in other countries. 'Yet this (process of modernisation) did not prevent a substantial section of Japanese industry from preserving in essence its former character, nor indeed from developing upon lines not vastly different from those of Tokugawa period (1603-1868). The preservation of the familiar, however, seldom attracts the attention excited by the appearance of the novel and the strange'.[3] The most characteristic feature of Japan's industrialisation has been that the process of industrialisation takes a deep root in the country's socio-economic structure. The Japanese term for this is 'namawashi' (root binding). Japanese industrial development has not been due to a transfer of technology from scientifically advanced countries, but due to the building up of the technology in the economic system itself. This has been in sharp contrast to the former Soviet Union, where a heavy industry economy was built-up on largely peasant economy.

In India since the mid-fifties, there has been large-scale technology import in the heavy industries sector. Huge investments were made in this direction, as capital formation and development of industrial infrastructure through import of technology, were supposed to usher in an era of sustained industrial development. 'Capital formation' was the key to our industrial planning since the fifties to the eighties. This was also justified by the economic theories of that period. Since the latest technology was not available within the country, the only solution appeared to be importing the same to make up for the lost time. This technology import was mostly in the heavy industries in the public sector. Today most of these technologies have become outdated and need modernisation at a huge cost. One of the main reasons why such technology became outdated before the investment incurred on them could be recovered, was due to the fact that most of such industries are products of the Second World War. Heavy industries got a boom during the Second World War and the years following it due to the need of the massive reconstruction in the aftermath of the war. Once the situation changed, the developed countries diversified their manufacturing away from heavy industries to electronic and pharmaceutical industries. Decline of the Soviet Union in the economic field, was particularly due to the fact that it remained wedded to the heavy industries and lacked the flexibility of diversifying its industrial structure.

The gradual shift from heavy industries to high technology value-added items by developed countries, has changed world industrial situation. In the changed world economic situation, the heavy industries on which we had invested, became out-dated. It is obvious that if any country desirous of development, hitches its economic bandwagon to foreign technology and foreign markets, it will always remain a few steps behind in this race for industrial and technological development. Whereas the technology acquired by us may not be suited for the high-tech international markets, we can use it to advantage for our domestic markets, with its huge potentiality. The modern technological developments in the fields of micro-electronics, computers and telecommunications equipment are suited for development of countries with limited manpower and natural resources. India with its vast manpower and natural resources should try to evolve technology which can gainfully utilize both these basic resources. Technology should help to develop a country's human and natural resources. Mere pursuit of technology, howsoever glamorous, should not be an end in itself.

Developed countries as world leaders in technology can switch over their technology according to their convenience and change the market situation drastically. It is the technology which controls the market and not *vice-versa*. 'When from the 1960s onward, world manufacturing began to shift away from traditional heavy goods toward high-value-added, knowledge-intensive, and consumer-driven industries—computers, software electronics, automobiles, civilian aircraft, pharmaceuticals, communications—the Soviet Union was unable to follow suit'.[4] It was not only that the Soviet Union was unable to follow suit, the entire developing world, consisting mostly of countries, which had just thrown away the colonial yoke was affected. Most of the developing countries, particularly India launched itself in a course of development of heavy industries in the core sector with iron and steel in the forefront. From the Second Plan (1956-1961) onwards under the influence of 'Mahalanobis strategy' of development, emphasis on planning shifted from agriculture to heavy industries. Bulk of the plan funds were committed to heavy industries with large steel plants having the pride of place. Thinking big was the order of the day—gigantic steel plants were planned for producing huge quantities of steel, which will be required for the infrastructural development of the country. It was thought that to transform India into a major industrial power, there will be continuous need for steel for the next fifty years or more. It was thought inconceivable that India, with its vast manpower and huge untapped potential will ever be lacking in demand for steel. Steel was the basic commodity needed for transforming the country to an industrial super power. The Architect of Indian planning, Jawaharlal Nehru, saw in the giant steel plants, 'The temples of Modern India', which would transform the sleeping Indian economy to an economic giant.

The giant multipurpose projects like Bhakra-Nangal, Hirakud, Damodar Valley projects and various other multi-purpose projects occupied the pride of place in India's first two plans. These multi-purpose projects were to transform the agricultural economy of the country by harnessing the water resources, going waste to the sea. They were also designed as power-houses to make cheap power available for a modern economy. It was a bold vision for development of the Indian economy, based on its abundant resources in terms of water, mineral, land mass and above all manpower. It appeared strange that in India with its huge water resources and fertile land mass, its people should depend on other countries to feed them or suffer from periodic famines. India with its abundant mineral resources and skilled manpower need not depend on other countries for her manufacturing requirements. When the basic needs of mankind are more abundant in India than anywhere else, Indians need not remain poor. This was the basic concept of planning. India's early plans, particularly the first two plans were documents of vision. But vision must match with economic reality to produce a purposeful and effective plan. Vision and reality must match at a particular point. It is a great tragedy for India that Nehru's 'Temples of Modern India' became the proverbial 'White Elephants' bleeding the Indian economy continuously. The vision of the early Indian plans, crashed on the consumer-driven international economic scenario created by the U.S.A. and Britain. The seeds of consumerism were subtly sown in the economy from the sixties onward, till the craze for newer and newer consumer gadgets overcame the economy from the eighties. The mighty Soviet Union collapsed under the onslaught of Western consumerism and an orderly society degenerated into the anarchy of the market. Basic industries (iron and steel) were meant for improving the living standard of the masses by creating huge infrastructure for transportation, housing and all round development. Harnessing the water resources with dams across huge rivers, was meant to stabilise food supply and provide abundant cheap electric power for the people, as well for development of small-scale industries in a massive scale. This would have transformed the life of the millions. These are all slightly long-term planning and needs vision for its implementation. Benefits would have taken sometime to flow in and during the intervening period some sacrifices would have been necessary. But 'Consumerism' thrives on greed and jealousy and does not recognise higher values like sacrificing a little today for a better tomorrow for the masses. Consumerism aims at the economic elite and encourages the masses to fritter away their hard-earned earnings on trivialities. Rich and powerful are the models of 'Consumerism' and those who cannot make the grade must suffer permanent privation.

A theoretical justification of this is not far to find. Keynes, the most influential Economist, who dominated the thinking of generations of influential Indian economists in government circles, had this to say, 'For my own part, I believe that there is social and psychological justification for significant inequalities of incomes and wealth, but not for such large disparities as exist today'.[5] Keynes in his 'General Theory' has quoted extensively from a number of writers from the sixteenth century onwards, who have been advocating great inequality of income and conspicuous consumption by the rich. Once the theory of inequality was propounded, there was no going back from it. Inequalities have been rising over the years throughout the world, since Keynes wrote his 'General Theory' in early 1930s. Number of billionaires and millionaires are growing throughout the world, whereas absolute poverty is increasing. Even in India the achievements of billionaires and millionaires have been blown out of proportion by the Media. They are projected as modern heroes and achievers. Economic theories have taken a neat somersault over the years, where blind pursuit of wealth is glorified beyond all proportions. The theory seems to be that these heroes of today should be emulated by the new generations for elimination of poverty. While touting such a theory, we forget that the world's resources are limited and concentration of wealth in the hands of the few, will only increase the absolute poverty of the many. It is not that an anti-rich economic climate should be created, but economic thinking should not go overboard with anti-egalitarianism, as it had earlier gone head over heels about socialism. There is need for a balanced and pragmatic approach in economic thinking, instead of being carried over by dogmas and short-term success stories. One thing is however obvious, that increasing the number of millionaires and billionaires, will not reduce the level of poverty in India.

This shift of world manufacturing activities away from basic to consumer and information-oriented industries marks a clear departure from the development pattern, in which a country like India had planned to develop her strength by investing heavily in core industries like steel, mineral industries and giant multipurpose project. This was also the basic strength of the Soviet economy. Change in world economic development pattern made the projects in which India had invested bulk of her resources, completely unviable in the world market. Almost all these industries were developed on imported foreign technology and as such their products had no international market, when the economic production activities in the Western countries shifted and a new international demand pattern was created. Western countries with their absolute control over technology could control the world technological profile and consequently change the market conditions, where the products of the industries from the developed countries could be marginalised in the international market. Shift in economic activities from basic industries to electronics, computers, robotics, bio-technology, marks the change of work force from an army of skilled and semi-skilled work-force with bargaining power to a small group of well paid, technically qualified work-force with no job security or bargaining power. The fate of this work-force is left to the tender mercies of the market forces, which is an euphamism for the power to hire and fire by the employer at this sweet will.

The working life of this work-force is likely to be short, as the skills of today will be outdated tomorrow and drastic change of technology is likely to make the skilled work force of today obsolete within a period of ten years. Today's technology is based on the principle of quick change in the guise of improvement and modernisation. Technology is ever changing and yesterday's technology must be inferior than today's. Market is controlled by technology, instead of it being, the other way round. This is like the proverbial 'tail wagging the dog', instead of 'dog wagging the tail'.

Need for obsolescence of machine and work-force is the basis of the present western economic system. The redundancy of work-force will affect the highly skilled technologists of today, as much as it affected the blue collar workers of yesterday. The highly placed work-force of today, who are bred on the philosophy of competition and individualism and have no bargaining power, will face greater hardship than the unionised workers of yesterday, who had the union to fall back upon. A smaller and younger work-force, trained in new skills will replace the present work-force, who will become less cost effective. The Silicon valley of the U.S.A. has already reached saturation point and job cuts have already started. Information technology has already reached its peak and there is no way that this industry can progress further without substantial economic activity, which is already in the decline. Information technology is only a managerial tool for achieving greater efficiency and productivity in any sphere of activity and not an end in itself. Recessionary tendencies in the world economy have been pronounced since the 1980s. Reported unemployment rate in the United States was as high as 9.7% and 9.6% during 1982 and 1983 respectively and from 1980 to 1986, the unemployment rate was never less than 7%. Economic growth was negative during 1980 and 1982. These figures are quoted from the Economic Report, 1988 of the President of the U.S.A. placed before the Senate. The World stock market crash of October 1987, wiped out a lot of small investors throughout the World. 'On October 19 the New York stock market plunged by 22.6 per cent, the largest drop in 73 years, even larger than the worst single day fall in 1929.

This crash had its echoes throughout the world with huge stock market losses in Japan, Australia, Hong Kong, Mexico, Spain, Canada, Brazil, Britain, France, Italy, West Germany, and elsewhere'.[6] We are all too familiar with the collapse of 1997 of the emerging South-East Asian economies. 'The financial collapse in Asia was followed by an economic collapse. In Indonesia, for instance, most of the gains in living standards that accumulated during 30 years of Suharto's regime have disappeared'.[7] Russia has suffered a complete financial and economic breakdown by an abrupt U-turn from a Government controlled system to market capitalism.

The position in Western Europe was no better. Throughout the eighties there was serious unemployment even in countries like Britain, France and Germany. 'In 1986 unemployment rates reached post-war highs in Britain (13.4 percent) and France (10.5 percent); in Germany, industrial production declined at an annual rate of 6.5 percent in the first two quarters, generating an unemployment rate of 9 percent. Western Europe as a whole suffered an unemployment rate of over 11 percent, signaling a serious recession'.[8] This trend continued through the nineties. 'Over 11 per cent of the work-force in the European Union was unemployed in 1997'.[9] Germany, the power house of Europe, had an unemployment figure of 13 per cent, with France 12.6 per cent and Spain over 20 per cent. The erstwhile colonial countries like the U.K. and the Netherlands had figures of 6.1 per cent and 6.2 per cent respectively. This situation is continuing and even in 2004, the European Union has an unemployment rate of 8.8 per cent, with Germany as high as 10.2 per cent. At present, France has an unemployment rate of 9.7 per cent and Spain 11.2 per cent. Britain, which had an unemployment rate of over 13 per cent in the mid-eighties had a much lower figure of unemployment. In Britain, the unemployment percentage has further come down to 5 per cent by 2004, whereas Netherlands has an unemployment rate of 6 per cent compared to 4.4 per cent last year. The United States has been able to bring down its unemployment rate, varying between 4 to 5 per cent during the nineties. In recent times again, it has shown an upward trend and stands at 5.8

per cent in the beginning of 2004. Obviously, U.S.A. and Britain have been major beneficiaries of the globalisation process, whereas countries of Western Europe, which had the comparative advantage in metal industries lost out. This is mostly due to fall in developmental activities throughout the world which created constant demand for machinery. Britain which had lost comparative advantage in these industries, had little to lose from this downturn. Ship-building in Britain, due to the excess capacity created by the war, accounted for over half the gross tonnage produced in the world. In a period of 'rapid growth of the industry, British output stood still, and then in a dozen years (1975-87) plunged 96 per cent. Wipe-out'.[10] British auto industry was in constant decline during the post-war period. Even a state subsidy of £ 2,400 million between 1975 to 1984, during the Tory laissez-faire period failed to bail out the British auto industry'.[11] Britain's industrial production has been lagged behing in the present decade with negative growth. At the beginning of 2004, the industrial growth figure stood at—0.8 per cent. Britain lacks a system of training workers. 'Technical colleges still have low status, and there is no well developed apprenticeship system as in Germany. . . . The British work-force is well behind in education and skills compared with that of many other advanced nations'. This is also applicable in case of India, where no steps have been taken to train up the industrial work-force. In Britain, 'Even engineering has been treated in a theoretical way at the leading Universities. . . . There is a shortage of managers trained in technology entering manufacturing industries, and a technical background has been uncommon in top managemnt'.[12] In this case also, the Indian situation is a reflection of the British model. Sidney Pollard and David Landes ascribe the main reason for British failure in post-war industrialisation to lack of entrepreneurship in both public and private sectors. British automobile industry, which was entirely in private hands, failed to upgrade its technology and its policy of setting up one group of workers against others through a policy of differential wages backfired. 'The group was only as fast as its slowest member.'[13]

The sharp decline in industries in post-war Britain, is

failure to cope up with a non-colonial countries like Germany and Japan. Britain, whose industrialisation was based on a colonial structure of captive markets and cheap raw materials found the situation uncomfortable in the new situation and slid into economic decline. Many economists have wondered, why Britain, the pioneer of industrial revolution, failed to keep up in the science and technology-oriented industrial situation of the post-war of world. The reason is not far to seek. Whereas development of scientific knowledge in Britain has not been lagging behind other industrially advanced countries, there has been little application of science to industry. In fact, the British industrial revolution was not the product of combination of science and industry, but of division of labour, which means not only the factory system of production, but also international division of labour, where the colonies serve as cheap sources of raw material, as well as captive markets. 'Friedrich List (1841) believed that Smith underestimated the importance of science and technology and over stated the division of labour argument'.[14] Smith based his theory firmly on his observations of the actual changes taking place in Britain. The industrial revolution was pioneered by artisans and man lacking any formal education for their professions. James Hargreaves, a carpenter; Richard Arkright, a barber; Samuel Crompton, a cotton spinner; were the pioneers of industrial revolution. Long used to a colonial system of dependencies and assured markets, Britain lost out due to failures in the field of production technology, design, industrial relations and entrepreneurship. Britain is still obsessed with defence requirement. 'In 1987, for example, 50 per cent of government R & D was for defense purposes compared to about 12 per cent in Germany, 5 per cent in Japan, and 34 per cent in France'.[15]

Faced with a sliding economy, Britain has gone back to its erstwhile colonial markets. Due to the English language, Britain has strength in financial services, financial journalism, legal services and financial advertising and public relations. 'London is solidifying its position as Europe's financial center'.[16] Having lost the race in the manufacturing industries, Britain has switched on to service industries, where they have strength due to the language and historical ties of colonialism. The developing countries, with financial problems provide a captive market for accounting and consultancy. Indian public sector and financial institutions are heavily dependant on British consultancy firms for financial and managerial restructuring. Major part of the British aid to developing countries is tied to the purchase of British goods and services. 'Aid has been used to assist structural adjustment since it helps recipient countries to make reforms relevant to investors'.[17] Thus, the British aid is closely related to marketing of British goods and services. The institutions, which have taken British aid for their restructuring programmes, will be permanently dependant on British goods and services. We have seen it in the restructuring programmes in the power sector. Efficiency in public sector undertakings and banks, has become synonymous with British managerial consultancy. Private sector is also liberally using such services. This is rather paradoxical, as Britain's own industrial decline has been attributed to managerial failure. 'Here is Sidney Pollard: [In addition to government policy], other factors in the decline have been poor management, complacency, poor industrial relations, an over-fragmented industrial structure, unhelpful financial institutions and a relatively stagnant home market'. And the first of all was poor management another way of saying poor entrepreneurship. Britain had to depend "on the financial resources, design and production technology, managerial methods, working practices and approaches to industrial relations" of American, French and especially Japanese multinationals'[18] to save its automobile industry from extinction.

INDIA'S EDUCATIONAL SUBSIDY TO U.S.A.

A considerable portion of the work-force in the U.S.A. and the Western countries, as well as in India working in the Information Technology Sector for the foreign multinationals, is from the Indian technical and management institutions. Huge resources had been invested in technical education in successive plans to build up technical manpower in India. This huge investment at the cost of Indian taxpayers (both direct and indirect taxpayers), has benefited the Western economies, particularly the U.S.A. In fact, the investment in technical education in India has acted as a huge unaccounted subsidy for the U.S.A. and other Western economies. Obviously the technical man-power planning and development was such, for which Indian economy committed to basic industries, had limited or little demand. While the Western World and their cheer-leaders in India are crying hoarse about food and agricultural subsidies being against economic norms, there is no mention of this huge subsidy by a developing economy to the developed world. It was expected that the technical manpower trained in India at public cost would help in the development of India. Substantial investment has been made at Indian tax-payers cost for higher technical education. The large-scale migration of trained personnel from India, for working in the U.S.A. and the developed western countries, constitute a major indirect subsidy to the industries of these countries. In India, higher technical education was fully funded by government and still continues to be government funded. A great part of this investment has benefited development of industries in the developed countries. There has been considerable mismatch between higher technical education and the economy, resulting in under utilization of such manpower. Technical education at public cost is not an end in itself and must serve the economy which provides it. Such migration is one of the ways of transfer of resources from one country to another. This mismatch has occurred, as the technical education was concentrated in providing theoretical education. Little or tardy steps were taken to build-up a cadre of technicians and skilled workmen to support the industrial development. As Kaldor had said in 1969, 'In many underdeveloped countries too much is spent in providing high-level education of a theoretical kind, and too little in creating a cadre of qualified managers, engineers and technicians'.[19] The mismatch of technical education and the economy is glaringly apparent in the fact that upgradation of technical education did not lead to upgradation of technology, which had to be again borrowed from the West.

IMPOSED TECHNOLOGY STIFLES LOCAL INNOVATION

Attempts to transform the Indian economy to an electronics and computer-oriented economy will be counter-productive and will destroy the basic economic structure. Economic activities based on electronics, computers, telecommunications, information technology and consumer-driven entertainment industries do not create a base for economic development and must have a basic economic base to stand upon. Basic economic activities like agriculture, agro-based industries, road development, cheap mass transport system, power generation and irrigation activities provide the base for industrial development. Although investment in these sectors has been quite substantial in successive five year plans, no attempt has been made to develop a viable agro-industrial base in India. Schemes conceived in a different milieu, under laboratory conditions, have been super-imposed and have failed to take proper roots. Mere financial planning without proper socio-economic planning, has not given the desired result and funds have gone astray. Planners have not been able to take into account the various socio-economic forces released by pouring in huge sums of money without detailed planning. Plans are conceived in the Planning Commission without detailed ground level planning. These plans are transmitted from the national level to the block and village level. There is little or no interaction between the national level planners and those at the executing level. The gulf between the planners and the executing agencies is enormous in social and official status, educational level, mobility level and economic level that any meeting of mind is impossible. Over the years this gulf has widened and the planners tend to cover up the deficiencies in their planning by blaming the executing level for corruption and inefficiency. It is not that the people at the executing level are a bunch of angels. At this stage, there is no point in entering into a puerile polemical exercise, as to whether planning was faulty or execution faulty. Obviously, the failure has been on both these fronts, but the greatest responsibility lies with the planning process itself for not taking into account the ground realities and for imposing something which is not workable.

A development process imposed from above, however well-intentioned will create several distortions in the economy and the society. It is not, perhaps realised that imposition of technology from above creates job losses and reduces the area of economic activity. While land reforms was an important creed with the Planning Commission and the Government, there was no attempt to develop an appropriate and cost-effective technology, which would help small farmers with limited resources. For irrigating small fields, human-operated or animal-operated techniques, which are being used for generations, can be improved. Instead of going for centrifugal pumps operated by diesel or electricity, it would be easier and more beneficial for small farmers to go in for improved variety of manual water-lifting devices. Imposition of technology from above has made the rural artisans, who were an integral part of the village-economy, completely redundant and has added to the unemployment problem. Skilled or semi-skilled work-force has been added to the huge unskilled category of work-force. Herman Kahn, a perceptive observer and analyser of the world economic scenario noted the innovations in the agricultural sector, worked out by the rural peasantry. 'All the bullock carts now have ball bearings—and many have rubber tires. Such things may not seem exciting to visitors but they are terribly important to Indian peasants. In the long-run, the economic picture is also not without encouragement'.[20] Kahn, the founder, director of the Hudson Institute, a foremost think tank of the 1980s, was rightly impressed by this small example of technological development from below, which saves on the energy and prevents damage to roads and highways. Had such small innovations been followed widely, rural sector would have been much more self-sufficient than it is today. Similarly, fitting small engines to cycle-rickshaws and rickshaw-trolleys, which are universal in almost all cities, towns and villages in India, would have made this means of transport more viable and improved the quality of life of the workers in the unorganised sector, who operate this means of transportation. A gradual upgradation of technology would have been more user friendly and cost effective. This will also avoid the technological shock inherent in super imposition of technology. The basis of development should be building-up on the existing techniques already available with the people. A development process imposed from above and built-up without any foundation, is unlikely to take any deep root in the economy and society. Technology developed from below will be more broad-based and will ensure greater equity in development. Technology imposed from above and imported from a different milieu, will only help those with economic power. Technology is not neutral and has a tendency to help the rich and powerful. Technology, built-up on the existing know-how, is unlikely to be spectacular, but will certainly help in implanting the seeds of equitable development deep in the rural economy. We cannot expect miracles through importing costly technology, which can benefit only the rich and powerful.

TECHNOLOGICAL HEGEMONY

Technology is the guiding deity of today's economy and has replaced various 'Isms' like Socialism and Communism. With the rapid developments in the field of transport and communications technologies, the world is shrinking fast. According to *The Economist*, 'The death of distance as a determinant of the cost of communications will probably be the single most economic force shaping society in the first half of the next century'[21] (twenty-first century). Whole world is likely to become a global village, with the march of technology, but such globalisation is unlikely to encompass the entire population of the world. The process of globalisation is likely to make the concept of nation state as a geographic entity more and more redundant. Globalisation is likely to transcend the international boundaries of countries and States will have to surrender portion of their national sovereignty to be a part of a global economic system. Necessity of immediate enactment of the ordinance to amend the Indian Patent's Act as a conditionality for India's membership of the World Trade Organisation, clearly indicates the price of such globalisation a country will have to pay. Integration of the world in a single economic unit transcending state boundaries, will usher in an era of great prosperity for those who are able to take advantage of the economic miracle. This economic paradise will however by-pass the great majority of the people. High technology creates an island of artificial prosperity within a sea of economic deprivation. High technology is not labour friendly and is highly labour displacing. With high technology has come terms like golden handshake, labour rationalisation, etc. This does not augur well for the labour market and with more and more labour displacing high technology, we will be seeing a gradually shrinking labour market. An analysis of the employment figures in the U.S.A. shows that employment has been declining in absolute terms since the early eighties. Only recently there has been some marginal improvement. Great Britain has been facing continuous industrial recession. Germany, the economic power-house of Europe, is facing severe unemployment, leading to riots against guest workers (migrant workers from other countries). European Union, as a whole, had a serious problem of unemployment with percentage as high as 8.8 per cent at the beginning of 2004.

There is little doubt that the developed countries will have to gear up their economic policies to combat this situation. Technology transfer is one of the devices for transferring older technology from developed countries to developing countries. Countries like India provide an excellent market for second-hand technology. Our craze for modernizing our economy by trying to keep up with the western technology has provided an ever expanding market for western technology transfer. Ostensibly, such technology transfer is to bring the Indian technology at par with the technology of advanced countries and make the Indian industries more competitive. Transfer of technology in the field of industry from developed country to less developed country, is one of the accepted forms of development. It is assumed that such transfer of upto-date technology, will bring the technology of transferee country at par with the technology of transferor country. Till the nineties, such technology transfer was mostly on a government to government basis. Such technology imports from friendly foreign countries enabled us to set-up our steel industry in the public sector. These were all done on the basis of bilateral government to government negotiations. All these plants faced the need for modernisation within a period of ten to fifteen years, before the capital invested in the old technology could be recouped. This shows that the dependence on foreign technology is not economically viable, as the expenditure on investment incurred could not be recouped. There are of course other parameters of such investment, like development of the core sector, for all-round industrial development of the country. But the fact remains that on the touchstone of economic viability such investments cannot be supported. The reason for our running a losing race for keeping up with modern technology, inspite of spending a huge amount on importing the same needs to be analysed. There is no doubt that most of the technology, which we have imported from foreign countries, was the outdated technology of yesterday. We imported technology in the hope of increasing our export potential, but the obsolete technology imported at a huge cost had no takers in the international market. History of technology transfer in India is replete with cases of import of out-dated and rejected technology. Failure to develop a strong R & D system to support the industrial development has made us over-dependant on foreign technology at every stage of industrialisation.

The Western capitalistic countries well understood that the strength of a developing country like India lay in heavy industries like iron and steel, metal industries, mining industries, hydel-power and agriculture, with considerable mineral, water and human resources. Economic development based on these resources, is most suited to a highly populous country like India, where human resource should be given top-most priority. Oil crisis of 1971, when the prices of petroleum products sky-rocketed, in the world-market provided a rude jolt to India's industrialisation programme. Main beneficiary of this price rise was the Big Western Oil Companies. Countries like Iran and Iraq, which are major oil producers have not benefited from this price rise. Oil Cartel, which started operating from 1971, was certainly not a product of the market forces, but an *ad hoc* decision which was a *fait accompli* for a country like India. Had India worked out bilateral trade agreements with some of the more friendly oil producing countries, the shock of the oil price rise could have been avoided. India should have worked out an agreement with the Soviet Union, which had sufficient oil supply. A deal could have been worked out with Iraq, which maintained cordial relations with India and did not show any tilt towards Pakistan, as some of the other countries in the region did.

The Oil Crisis (the sudden dramatic rise in the price of petroleum products) of 1971, marks a transition of the world economy from basic industries like steel-making, mineral industries, cement, machine tools, textiles, multipurpose irrigation-*cum*-power project, to electronics, computers (both hardware and software), bio-technology, entertainment industries and communications. The trend was visible from the 1960s onward, but it came into sharp focus from the 1970 and overtook the world market from the 1980s. World export of high-technology products is entirely controlled by the U.S.A., West Germany, Japan and U.K. In the field of Micro-electronics, computers, Telecommunications equipment, Machine Tools and Robotics, these countries have a dominant role. According to the CIA handbook of Economic Statistics, for the year 1989, quoted in Paul Kenedy's 'Preparing for the twenty-first century', in the global exports of eight high-technology items, U.S.A. topped the list in the fields of items like Computers (24%), Aerospace (45.7%) and Scientific Precision Equipment (25.2%). U.S.A. comes a very close second in items like Microelectronics (21.9%) and Organic Chemicals (15.5%). Japan leads in the field of Microelectronics (22.1%), Telecommunication Equipment (24.7%), Machine Tools & Robotics (23.3%). In Aerospace industry, erstwhile West Germany, U.K. and France had shares of 12.5%, 10.9%, 10.2% respectively. The major countries in export of high-technology products are U.S.A., erstwhile West Germany and Japan; with U.K., France and Sweden having small share of the market. Other than Japan, the only Asian country figuring in the list of top five are Malyasia and South Korea with a market share of 8.9% and 7.4% respectively in the field of microelectronics and Taiwan having a market share of 5.8% in computers. Both South Korea and Taiwan were new entrants in the field, as they did not figure amongst the top five in any of the items in 1980. Except Japan; Singapore and Malyasia had a market share of 10.1% and 8.9% only in microelectronics in 1980.[22]

These statistics indicate a complete dominance of U.S.A., Japan and a few West European countries in the field of high technology items. The close relation of Japanese economy with the U.S. economy has made it possible for Japan to be an important player in some of the high technology items. This close relation of Japan with the U.S. economy is both a boon and a bane. The recessionary tendencies in U.S. economy is transmitted to the Japanese economy, which in turn is transmitted to economies of South Korea, Thailand, Philippines, Hong Kong, Indonesia, Malyasia and Singapore. Asian stock market crash of 1997, which originated in U.S. and Japanese economies led to serious recessionary tendencies shattering the economy of Indonesia; created serious industrial depression in Korea and wiped out almost all the small shareholders from the market in all these countries. The high-technology products are monopolised by a few developed countries, with countries like South Korea, Taiwan, Singapore and Malyasia playing subsidiary role. The high-technology products are mostly electronic items like microelectronics, computers, telecommunication equipment, machine tools and Robotics and Scientific and Precision equipments. Even aerospace industry, which is an important high technology item has a large component of electronic equipments. Aerospace industry, which is a strategic industry has no Asian player, including Japan. U.S.A. controls nearly 50% of this market, with Germany, U.K., France and Canada being other major players.

ELECTRONICS: A CONTROLLED REVOLUTION

The seeds of the 'Electronics Revolution' or 'Second Industrial Revolution' were sown with the invention of the semi-conductor (transistor) in Bell Telephone Laboratories, U.S.A. by William Shockley, John Ardeen and Walter Brattain in 1947. The transistor principle had to be developed further, before it could be used in computers, which were previously using the electron tube. The transistor being much smaller and faster, galvanised the computer industry from 1960s. While the electronics revolution was taking shape in American laboratories, India had been investing heavily in the industries of the first industrial revolution. Thus, the Western economies through their complete control over the technology will be always a few steps ahead of the developing world. It is time that countries like India should decide whether we should blindly follow western technology to be mere camp followers of western economies. Besides Japan, countries like South Korea, Malyasia, Singapore, Thailand, Taiwan, Indonesia and Hong Kong benefited in the short-run by being an early climber on the bandwagon of electronics revolution. In fact, the myth of Asian Tigers, is built on the industrial structure created for the manufacture of electronic components. The phenomenal rise of the Korean economy was in being a major manufacturer and exporter of the semi-conductor, micro-processor, the single most important component in electronics industry. In 1990, Korea was the thirteenth-largest trading nation in the World, with World Bank forecasting that it will become one of the richest countries in the twenty-first century. All this rosy predictions turned into nightmare with the change of technology.

First commercially successful micro-processor chip, 8080 which was introduced in the market in 1974 by the Intel Corporation had only 4,800 transistors. There was enormous demand for this vital component for computers, robots, calculators, toys, video games and home appliances like refrigerators and air conditioners. There was tremendous boom in the market for these commodities, as mass production of electronic goods targeted at the urban middle class and the rural rich, ushered in large-scale consumerism throughout the world, particularly in the developing countries of Asia. Korea, Taiwan and even Japan geared up their economy to the manufacture and export in the booming market of semi-conductors. The unprecedented development of Korea, primarily an agricultural country in the 1960s to an important industrial country was based to a great extent on capturing the market of semi-conductors. The market for micro-processor shrank dramatically with the change in technology by the introduction by Intel Corporation of

America in 1993 of the microprocessor Chip Pentium, with 3,200,000 transistors against the previously used microprocessor chip with 4,800 transistors. This market innovation in the field of manufacture of this important component, completely upset the industrial growth of countries, which had concentrated on the large-scale manufacture of microprocessors. Once the Pentium Chip was available in the market, computers and other related electronic equipments became cheap and the market for electronic hardware declined sharply. There was no need of large-scale manufacture of microprocessor chips, when a single chip could do the job of thousands. The countries which are at the receiving end of technology, always run the risk of their economic calculations being upset by labour displacing technology in the name of innovation. Had the developing countries been in control of the technology, they could have innovated qualitative products without going in for displacement of labour and existing manufacturing activities.

While from the 1990s, the Asian countries were planning and preparing for several decades of large-scale manufacturing activities in computer hardware and other computer-related electronic equipments the Silicon Valley switched its activities from further development in the field of computer hardwares to software development and marketing. The rapid development in the field of software had far-reaching impact on the computer hardware industry. Earlier, the computer manufacturer had their proprietary rights on their computer operating system. This was completely changed from the 1990s, with the introduction of a system in which software companies developed proprietary rights over their products and software developers took complete control of the computer market. Previously software used to be developed, as a part of the computer hardware. With the proliferation of software companies, and their patenting over software, computer manufacturing became a subsidiary activity to software development. Computer industry in the U.S.A. was changing over their technology in a big way from computer hardware development to research and development of computer software throughout the 1980s, when some of the Asian countries were adjusting their economies to be the powerhouse for the electronic revolution, so-called second industrial revolution. 1990s saw development and complete control of the computer industry by software developers. New multibillion dollar worth software companies like Microsoft, Oracle, Sun Microsystems located in the U.S.A. became powerful players in the computer market. Older American companies like IBM, Motorala, Apple diversified their activities to software development. Software companies were valued at billions of dollars, although they had hardly any assets. The valuation was done on the basis of software developed and patented. Information industry or knowledge industry became powerful players in the world market and their founders like Bill Gates, who had developed the technology in their garage, after being college dropouts, became world heroes.

It was not that this development was accidental. Inclusion of the Intellectual Property Rights in the GATT agreements in 1990, in which India was a signatory, was a clever ploy, which created the ground of patenting of software; price of which was notionally fixed at a very high level in a monopolistic market controlled by a few American companies. The concept of patenting was extended to information, and software companies became worth billions of dollars, without having any real assets. Software companies became powerful players in the computer markets, with the computer hardware industry playing a secondary role. The might of the software companies was built-up not on assets like machinery, but on intangibles like computer operating methodology, worked out by American Software firms, which were patented. Control of the computer market by American Software Companies led to a similar oligopolistic situation in the computer hardware market in which the research in software and hardware proceeded in tandem. 'By moving into open systems, each computer manufacturer loses the uniqueness of its operating system and must compete primarily in price or performance within thin profit margins. For survival, computer manufacturers try to team up with others, sharing one common operating system to lure more customers. They prefer to form a small group of manufacturers, because competition within a large group becomes too great'.[23]

JAPAN: THE TECHNOLOGICAL WINDOW OF U.S.A.

Rapid industrialisation of the East and the South-East Asian economies, was due to the close relation of some of these countries like South Korea, Taiwan, Indonesia and Philippines, with the U.S.A., due to their strategic defence requirements with the latter. Hong Kong was a British Colony till 1998. Even Malyasia had to depend on the U.S.-British alliance to counter the communist threat. Japan, due to historical reasons, since the Second World War, became an important ally of the U.S.A. in Asia and gradually came to depend on the latter in various ways, particularly for its defence and allied requirements in a bipoloar world. Japan became the window for the U.S.A. to the Asian countries, particularly those with historical and other ties with Japan. This was the background in which the economies of these countries prospered during the late 1970s and 1980s. Models of the Asian tigers were touted by the market savvy economists and India was berated for not taking the path of the Asian tigers. Throughout this period, India's relation with the U.S.A. was a troubled one, particularly due to India's proximity to the U.S.S.R. and her leadership of the non-aligned movement. Moreover, the geographical area and population of India, make it impossible to be too closely aligned with any particular economy. Even in the heydays of colonialism, Indian economy could not be a subsidiary of the colonial power.

Electronics revolution or the second industrial revolution was the basis of industrialisation of these Asian countries; with the U.S.A. as the technological headquarters. In the early stages, U.S.A. encouraged these countries and helped in the development of electronic industry, particularly semi-conductors, for which there was a proliferating market due to large-scale demand for computer and allied products. Asian countries restructured their economies for a sustained period of industrial development, based on an ever growing market for electronics industries, which thrived on their novelty and not on any intrainsic value of their products. 'In the early years (of electronic industry), curiosity and naivete caused private consumers and corporate purchasers alike to buy products which were ill-conceived and offered little real benefit to their users'.[24] They could not foresee the change of technology, which was engineered in the U.S.A., which pushed the manufacturing activity as a subsidiary of software development. With the change of technology in the electronics industry and the dominance of software and data processing industries over manufacturing, the electronics industry suffered a major setback in the Asian countries. George Soros in his 'The Crisis of Global Capitalism' while analysing the Asian financial crisis of 1997, followed by economic recession mentions 'exports were concentrated in a limited number of commodities where the increased selling pressure drove down prices. Semi-conductors, in which Korea, Taiwan, and, to a lesser extent, Japan vied for the world market, were particularly hard hit'.[25] This situation has carried itself into the present century and countries depending for their development on export-led growth of high-tech items will have to do so as subsidiary of the U.S.A. 'Prospects for many developing countries in East Asia in 2001 are closely linked to the high-tech cycle in the United States and the movement of their currencies against the dollar and the yen. Growth in the sub-region depends to a large extent on external demand for electronics, and would therefore be hit by any declaration of global demand. The rate of increase in new orders received from the United States for electronic goods had already declined by half in October 2000. The outlook is for further declines as inventories in the United States continue to increase, and there were clear signs of declining semi-conductor prices in early 2001'.[26]

LAWS TO ENSURE TECHNOLOGICAL HEGEMONY

The change of technology by the U.S.A. multinationals with their powerful Research & Design facilities, as well as close collaboration with the American Universities, was not the only weapon with which the U.S.A. was fighting the Asian economic ascendancy, from the 1980s. Reaganomics became a dominant tool of America's economic warfare. In the book 'Eagle Defiant', published in 1983, 15 leading experts analyse the dominant role envisaged by Reagan administration in the world affairs, particularly world economy. 'Throughout the Reagan administation's first eighteen months, Trade Representative Brock sought to focus the upcoming GATT meeting (scheduled for November 1982) on plans for a new round of multilateral negotiations aimed at liberalizing the movement of capital and services such as banking, insurance, data processing, engineering, shipping, and telecommunications—all areas in which the United States, as the world's leading service-industry economy, could be expected to benefit disproportionately. And to back up this approach, Brock also formally asked Congress to strengthen his bargaining hand by authorizing retaliation against countries that discriminate against imports of "invisibles" or investments from the country'.[27] This was the tone of the U.S. representative in the GATT Conference of 1982. The U.S.A. was thus preparing for a massive export in invisibles like computer software, investments, telecommunication technology, entertainment products and insurance. Export of computer software and data processing industry could be built-up on the basis of patenting the same. With the decline in the market for traditional goods, in which the developing countries were becoming self-sufficient, it was necessary to build-up new markets by creating new demands. The U.S. Government and industry were quick to realize that with the abolition of informal sector and gradual formalisation of the economy, the developing countries are bound to be baulked down in their decision-making process by a plethora of facts and figures, which have to be analysed. With the availability of the computers, it is possible to develop appropriate methodology locally. Once such methodology or software is developed locally, the export market in computer hardware and software will gradually reduce for the U.S.A. There was therefore urgent need for patenting of computer software and data-processing. Intangible items were for the first time sought to be brought under trade agreements.

'Intellectual Property' was a new concept in the field of trading and trade agreement between the countries. This is not a concept which can be easily defined and has the potentiality of creating serious complications in the field of trade. There has to be mutually acceptable adjudicating bodies to determine, what is an 'intellectual property' and who is the rightful owner of the same. Without a detailed discussions of the various implications in national forums, the matter was internationalised and India became a signatory to the "Treaty of Intellectual Property in Respect of Integrated Circuits", adopted at Washington on 26 May, 1989. With the signing of this treaty, 'Intellectual Property' became a tradable commodity. From here it was but a short step to India being tripped into TRIPs (Agreement on Trade-Related Aspects of Intellectual Property Rights), which was a part of the General Agreement on Tariffs and Trade (GATT) 1994. It is matter of serious concern, whether such matters of wide ranging implications, which affect the Indian Polity, can be adopted without the approval of the Indian Parliament. By creating a monopoly in the field of computer software, by a new set of U.S. Multi-nationals, a veritable, Pandora's Box has been opened up, which will have far reaching implications on the Indian economy in years to come. The concept of 'Intellectual Property Rights' goes much beyond protection of 'Computer Software', which had already been achieved by the U.S.A. through the Treaty on Intellectual Property in Respect of Integrated Circuits, signed in Washington on 26 May, 1989. It seeks to create a monopoly on knowledge by the Developed Countries. Technology and its application will be tightly controlled by the Developed Countries and the development of Appropriate Technology by the Developing Countries will not be possible under a technology control regime, which is sought to be ushered in by the Washington Treaty on Integrated Circuits in 1989 and the GATT Agreement of 1994 on Trade Related Aspects of Intellectual Property Rights. While the U.S.A. and the other Developed Countries, have a well developed and well documented system of Patenting, India and most of the Developing Countries have no such system of documentation of products and processes. There are various indigenous methodologies in medicine, food processing, human and animal power technologies, which are not documented.

Under the onslaught of a technology control regime, innovations in agriculture and industrial field will die down. The indigenous processes, developed through ages, will completely wither away. This has already happened to a great extent by invasion through foreign technology. Withering away of indigenous methodologies, which have evolved and have been widely used, will make the Indian economy a technological subsidiary of the American economy.

Patent laws vary from country to country, even amongst the developed countries. 'In some countries patents are granted without examination for originality, whereas in others there is an examination procedure'.[28] OECD countries and the U.S.A. have built-up a strong patent regime since 1970s, when the clouds of economic depression were already on the horizon. Even among these countries, patent laws and administration are far easier in U.S.A., U.K. and France than in Germany, the Netherlands and Sweden. Patents are granted more easily in the former three countries than Germany. U.S.A. is the leading country in registration of patents. Between 1975 and 1995, 'the number of patents registered in the U.S.A. increased from 76,800 to 113,600, i.e. by 48 per cent' of these 'in the more' knowledge-intensive sectors, patenting rose from 16,827 to 47,533, i.e. by 183 per cent.[29] Japanese firms had imported technologies and improved on the same. This was because of their own strength in R & D. Under the new technology control regime, it will be very difficult to amend or improve any existing technology to suit local needs. A monopoly of technology by the West will have serious repercussions on the industrialisation of developing countries. India has not been able to develop a R & D system of international reckoning. Patents have hindered development of a proper R & D system. Unlike the Japanese, we have not been able to improve on the foreign technology imported at a heavy cost, due to the control exercised by these countries. Technology imported was tied technology and fully under the control of the exporting country. Japanese experience was, however different. 'Japanese firms, which were importing many technologies from Europe and North America, were apparently exceptionally good at the improvement of both processes and products but they could only do this because of their own strength in R & D. These will not necessarily be recorded in patent statistics, both for reasons of secrecy and patentability'.[30] A patent control regime will curb the R & D activities in developing countries. World monopoly of technology through the patent control regime will ensure the dominance of the West at the cost of Asia, Africa, Latin American countries and Eastern Europe.

FAILURE OF PUBLIC SECTOR TO ACHIEVE TECHNOLOGICAL INDEPENDENCE

The restrictive role of patenting in not allowing the development of technology in India and in throttling the development of R & D (Research and Design) system in India was highlighted in a Planning Commission document in 1978. Draft Five Year Plan of 1978-83, prepared by the Planning Commission under the Deputy Chairmanship of D.T. Lakdawala, expressed serious misgivings about the restrictive role of proprietary rights and trademarks in not allowing the development of indigenous R & D. This Planning Commission document of 1978 says, 'Measures for minimizing the baneful influence of restrictive privileges like trademarks and proprietory names, which have hampered the normal development of R & D, and its utilization, have to be given careful consideration.'[31] Transfer of technology has been only screwdriver technology and not R & D technology. Development of R & D, from the beginning of India's industrialisation has been held up by foreign trademarks and proprietary rights. This has been clearly admitted in the Planning Commission document, but no steps have been taken for its rectification, as had been promised. Foreign assistance, mostly for technology transfer went up sharply from 1980 onwards. External assistance between 1979-85 was to the tune of Rs. 17,700 crores, as against Rs. 9,653 crores between 1974-79 and Rs. 4013 crores between 1969-74. (Report on Currency and Finance, 1984-1985, Vol. I, Reserve Bank of India). During the period from 1985-86 and 1989-90 (upto September, 1990) approvals for external commercial borrowings for public sector were to the tune of Rs. 12,000 crores, whereas Rs. 1,300 crores were the approval for the private sector.[32]

No attempt was made to develop indigenous technology. Instead, easy route was taken to the importation of screwdriver technology to the utter ruination of the Public Sector. The Planning Commission document of 1978, reads, 'The Public Sector had also neglected Research Design and Development (RDD) until recently. This lacuna is now sought to be corrected by purposeful inputs for setting up/enhancing the in-house R & D capability in various public sector undertakings. The large size, technological complexity and potential growth of public enterprises offer exceptional opportunities'. (Draft Five Year Plan, 1978-83, p. 260). Again the document states, 'Self-reliance is not a distant goal, but an attitude and a strategy towards decision-making right now. In Science and Technology (S & T) it implies a judicious mixture of indigenous R & D and imported know-how, in such a manner that the initiative is always in our hands'. (p. 261) Bold and noble sentiments indeed. But subsequent facts completely belie these noble intentions. No attempt was made to develop self-sufficiency in technology. Whatever, the development goals were, self-sufficiency in technology was certainly not one of them, as subsequent events have proved. Self-sufficiency in technology is now a joke in poor taste, with the ushering in of a rigid patent regime. The Planning Commission document of 1978 had rightly pointed out, restrictive privileges like trademarks and proprietory names had not allowed the growth of any indigenous R & D and its utilization. Public Sector Units were not allowed to develop the technology, transferred from external sources, as the foreign agency transferring the screw-driver technology, maintained a rigid control over the technology and did not allow any R & D activity on the part of the transferee on the ground of proprietory rights over the manufacturing process.

This is in sharp contrast to the Japanese practice, which prospered on improvement and modification of imported technology. Modification and improvement of an existing technology require as much, if not more, originality and scientific knowledge and technological process as the original technology. Development of technology and its industrial applicability is more an evolutionary process than a revolutionary one. Technology evolves through industrial applicability, which varies from country to country and situation to situation. Patent regime ushers in monopoly in technology. Litigation in such matters in International Tribunals will be time consuming and will help the firm or country claiming monopoly to continue with the same till it becomes obsolete, due to the lengthy process of litigation. This will only benefit countries, who are in control of technology. Japanese obtained the existing technology and developed on the same. They could not have carried out their research and development activity in a technological vacuum. 'It must always be remembered that after the introduction of a new process or the construction of a new plant, many minor technical improvements will be made. Japanese firms, which were importing many technologies from Europe and North America, were apparently exceptionally good at the improvement of both processes and products but they could only do this because of their own strength in R & D. These will not necessarily be recorded in patent statistics, both for reasons of secrecy and patentability'.[33]

The reason, why India could not develop on the technologies imported, inspite of having adequate scientific and technical manpower, when Japan could do it may not be too far to seek. India, newly independent from the British rule, had the British system of jurisprudence and prided itself in playing the game according to rules laid down by the Britishers, while Japan, which had industrialised itself, inspite of foreign opposition, suffered no such moral compunctions and played the game according to their own rules. Strictly observing a patent regime and having foreign control over their technology, would not have allowed the Japanese to achieve the leadership in industrial technology, which they have done. After the industrial revolution in Britain, Britishers tried to have a monopoly over technology. But this could not be possible, as other European countries and the U.S.A. were determined to industrialise and employed all sorts of techniques, including industrial espionage. 'Bourbon France had a well-established tradition of industrial espionage, which was intensified when new technological progress was achieved in Britain from the 1760s onwards'.[34] This continued throughout the Napoleonic Wars (1793-1815), when the British Government had put a strict ban on the transfer of technology. During the post-1815 period, 'Government had given up industrial espionage, but private enterprise stepped in: there were agencies which obtained from England machines which it was prohibited to export and also procured English workmen'.[35] In the case of German industrialisation, 'A major innovation, initially developed abroad, presents itself for local exploitation and quickly seised upon by dynamic entrepreneurs'.[36] Had the patent regime, as envisaged by developed countries today, been followed in the nineteenth century, European continent and the U.S.A. would not have been industrialised and industrial revolution would have been confined to Britain alone. Today, the developed countries, by bringing in the patent regime, are trying to do to the developing world, what Britain was doing *vis-a-vis* Europe and U.S.A. The future of industrialisation in the developing world, will depend on, whether they are able to develop their own technology, in spite of the patent regime, as Europe and U.S.A. had done, inspite of the restrictions imposed.

CLASH OF INTEREST IN INDUSTRIALISATION

Let us see the views of some of the foreign countries particularly Britain, on India's industrial programme. I.G. Patel in his book 'Glimpses of Indian Economic Policy', writes about his experience, when he attended the Colombo plan meeting in New Zealand, as India's representative. 'I was to learn within a day or two of my arrival in Wellington that the British were on the war path against India. They were peeved by Suez; and by our flirting with a bold plan of industrialisation and with socialism and by our acceptance of Soviet aid. . . . According to Rumbold of the British delegation, this had to be stopped and India must be taught a lesson. He was trying to work on others to support this line in the meeting of the donors. The Americans were sympathetic to this line of thought.'[37] Regarding India's industrialisation, Philip Openheim, Editor of business magazine, British Member of Parliament, 'acknowledged trade and industry expert, and a fierce opponent of free trade barrier', writes 'The establishment of some form of Steel Industries has traditionally being regarded by most developing countries as indispensable to any nation with serious pretentions to industrialisation. So countries like Brazil and India have piled in, more than doubling the number of steel producing nations between 1950 and 1985—a process which has only been encouraged by steel plant equipment suppliers from developed nations, who are themselves often subsidised with state-provided export credits.'[38]

While admonishing countries like India and Brazil for daring to be steel producing countries, which is the monopoly of developed countries, he lets us know, the interest of the developed countries in setting up steel mills in developing countries, with huge public investment of scarce resources. It is no coincidence that the period of investment in setting up of public sector units in developing countries, was also the period of high growth and prosperity in developed countries. The period from the 1950s to the middle of 1970s, was the peak period of investment in new projects and industries in developing countries, in an attempt to replicate the Western pattern of industrial development. This was also the period of economic prosperity for the West. The excess capacity created in industries, particularly heavy industries like Steel, for meeting the ever increasing demand for production of armaments, was utilised gainfully by the West for setting up plants and machinery in the developing world with pre-Second World War technology. No doubt, the plants, set-up with this technology, became out-dated, even before they could go into production. Germany had huge excess capacity in machine tool industry at the end of the Second World War. German machine tool industry 'remained, on the whole, underutilised throughout the war, 30 per cent of its capacity having been converted to direct munitions production.'[39] German 'machine tools were of the universal (multipurpose) type which could easily be converted to purposes of war production.'[40] Britain and U.S.A. expanded their machine tool industry during the war and was working almost in full capacity. 'It is even better shown, however, by the fact that in contrast to British and U.S. experience where the machine tool industry was very much expanded and strained to the Utmost to meet requirements, German machine tool production had hardly expanded after 1939.'[41] U.S.A., Britain and Germany had huge excess capacity in machine tools after the end of the war. Britain and U.S.A. had increased their machine tool capacity tremendously during the war, whereas Germany had considerable excess capacity in machine tools during war. Erstwhile U.S.S.R. had also increased its industrial capacity during the war.

At the end of the Second World War in 1945, huge excess capacity in industries in the belligerent countries, posed a serious problem of depression. Report of the Delegation on Economic Depressions, titled, 'Economic Stability in the Post-War World', subtitled 'The Conditions of Prosperity After the Transition from War to Peace', published by the League of Nations, Geneva, 1945 says, 'For certain industrial products, world excess capacity became common when the industries of the belligerent countries were released from war employment. . . . We may anticipate, however, that for a considerable number of years the urgent desire of the less advanced states to acquire capital goods for the development of their industries will provide a potential outlet for part of the output of the mechanical industries which have been so greatly expanded during the war in the highly industrialised belligerent states.'[42] The developing countries eagerly fell into the trap of industrialisation in the name of developing their own industrial power and the developed countries were successful in getting rid of their excess capacity by transferring out-dated pre-second war technology.

This vital post-war document had addressed itself most seriously to the problem of maintaining full employment in developed countries. With the experience of depression of the thirties and the consequent world war, fresh in their minds, the authors of the document were keen to avoid any economic slow down and unemployment in Europe. The constant war between the European nations for economic dominance throughout several centuries culminating in two major wars in quick succession in the first half of the twentieth century, had to be put a stop to and for that economic welfare of the developed countries, who were also the major belligerents, had to be ensured. It did not matter, whether the economic interests of the under-developed world, were sacrificed at the altar of this noble cause of avoiding any conflagration in Europe.

The main priority of the document is maintaining full employment in 'the great industrial states', i.e. Western Europe and the U.S.A. The document warns of the 'war' between less developed countries and developed countries. 'At the same time, it would seen certain that the changes in world industrial structure will render trade uncertain and unstable unless a high degree of employment can be maintained in the great industrial countries. The exact nature of the effects of this war can not be foreseen; but there is every reason to believe that the drift away from the relatively simple exchange of raw materials against manufactured products that characterised the trade of the early and middle nineteenth century will continue, and it is possible also that there will be a very rapid industrial development in countries with low labour costs. But there is no reason for believing that in the long-run trade will be reduced on this account; on the contrary it should increase with the rising standards of living of these peoples, and, as we shall endeavour to show, its ultimate stability is likely to depend mainly on the extent to which policies designed to maintain full employment are successfully applied in the great industrial states.'[43]

The Western world did not take kindly to India's plan for industrialisation, but used the opportunity to dispose of their excess capacity in plant and machinery alongwith obsolete technology. It was in fact on the large-scale industrialisation programme of the newly independent countries that the Western countries to a large extent built-up their post-war economy and enjoyed a period of economic boom, as long as the technological honeymoon with the developing countries continued, throughout the sixties. The World Bank and IMF ably followed the guidelines laid down by the League of Nations in keeping the western economies running at the cost of the developed world. After having duped the newly independent countries in transferring second-hand technology, the next phase in the global attempt to keep the economies of the developed countries afloat is to turn the third world countries into huge consumer economies. This will destroy the producer-consumer relation in these countries altogether. The globalisation and commercialization of agriculture will spell the doom of preasantry in India, as we have seen happening in early phase of industrialisation in Great Britain. There will be no new continents for migration for the Indian peasantry, thrown out of their traditional occupation, as happened in colonial Britain.

NEED FOR TECHNOLOGICAL INDEPENDENCE

This eloquently indicates the attitude of the erstwhile colonial power and the hegemonistic powers towards industrialisation of India. The incident cited by Patel is not an isolated one and clearly sums up the ambivalent attitude of British imperialism towards industrialisation of India, particularly steel and heavy industries. It was clearly realised that an independently developed steel industry will break the monopoly of British capital over India. Unfortunately, we did not go for development of indigenous steel mill with the available know-how in India of over fifty years. India, already had modern steel industry in Tata Iron and Steel Company (started in 1907) at Jamshedpur; Indian Iron and Steel Company (started in 1908) at Burnpur; Mysore Iron and Steel Works (started in 1923) at Bhadrabati, with trained manpower. But instead of building up steel mills on the basis of technology available in India, we went for borrowed technology, which was redundant pre-Second War technology, which had survive due to the unnatural demand on the Steel Industry during the Second World War. This dependence on borrowed technology from the West, was one of the hangovers of long colonial rule. Socialistic fashion, imported from Britain, played its part in the government of the day is not having anything to do with the technological know-how available with the Indian private sector, although the socialistic pretensions did not prevent us in importing technology from foreign private sector. Indian steel industry, both in the private sector and public sector, should have complimented each other. Instead they worked at cross purposes, creating sickness, first in the private sector in the profitable Indian Iron and Steel Company and then in the public sector. Indian Steel Industry had already come of age, when the public sector steel plants were set-up in the fifties with foreign collaboration. There was no need for going for borrowed technology, when we had skilled manpower and technologists within the country. Regarding the usefulness of the Indian Steel Industry, we have the testimony of Lord Chelmsford, the Viceroy 'And in the last War (First World War), the usefulness of these industries was strikingly manifested. "I can hardly imagine", handsomely acknowledged Lord Chelmsford, "what we should have done if the Tata Company had not been able to give us steel rails, which have provided, not only for Mesopotamia, but for Egypt, Palestine and East Africa," and even, he might have added, for the Salonica front.'[44] By the end of the First World War, Indian Steel Industry was not far behind British Steel Industry. 'In 1921 the *Asiatic Review*, an imperialist journal, compared the Indian Steel Industry favourably with that of Britain, noting that the raw materials needed to make a ton of pig iron cost half as much in India as in Britain and that Indian labour, though still inefficient was improving'.[45]

While tracing the development of iron and steel industry, Pillai has noted the world-wide tendency in steel industry to combine the upstream and downstream operations in steel manufacturing, right from mining to end products. 'The history of that industry, elsewhere, has shown that its extension has always been accompanied by combinations of firms dealing with the material in all its successive stages, from the crude ore to the most perfect machinery. . . . The operations of the English firm of Vickers range from steel to ordinance, motors and battleships, and the American Steel Corporation and the German Stahlwerksverband are other examples of the integration of the iron industry. With the completion of the proposed extensions in the Bengal and Tata Companies, India will also take a step towards such an integration. The new alterations will revolutionise the engineering industry of the country, and the production of steel in plates and sheets and other required forms will give a great fillip to the ship-building, engine-building and constructional steel industries.'[46] India was well on the path to industrialisation at that time and had we built-up our industrial structure on the existing industrial base, the story of post-independence industrialisation would perhaps have been different. Although, India had adopted the mixed economy approach to development, the plans were drawn up in economic vacuum, completely disregarding the existing industrial and economic structure. The planners made no attempt to integrate the new industrial structure being built-up through the public sector, with the rest of the economy, although suitable technology in iron and steel was available in the country or could have been developed according to domestic requirement. The history of industrialisation was not taken into account and available technology, which had developed over a hundred years was completely disregarded. The planners were in a hurry and a public sector created with foreign technology was sought to be superimposed on the country. Too much reliance was placed on two dimensional models, instead of technology and marketing. It was expected that public sector will rule the commanding heights of the economy and the rest of the economy will be subsidiary to it. The essential inter-relation between different sectors of the economy and co-relations of industries within the same sector was not taken into account. It was thought that public sector would function in isolation, quite forgetting that we had adopted the mixed economy approach, instead of the Soviet system of economy, whose planning methods were adopted. Too much of ideological baggage in economic planning, without taking into account economic realities, when major portion of the economy was with the private sector, created serious imbalance in the economy, with huge public resources being committed to the plan projects.

The ambiguous attitude to the private sector, under socialistic dogma and the failure to spell out its role clearly in sectors, where it was in direct competition with the public sector, did not create a healthy attitude towards harmonious development of the economy. 'Given the natural sensitivity of private enterprise to India's avowed socialist goods, it is particularly important to have concrete and explicit statements of Government policy toward private business'.[47] The concept of public sector industrialisation was one of an integrated structure, with an inter-linked system of demand pattern. Heavy Engineering Corporation was set-up in Ranchi to provide machinery for the steel plants which in turn supply steel to the former. Thermal and hydel plants were set-up in the public sector to cater to the public sector requirement. Heavy Electricals Plant was set-up at Bhopal to meet their requirements, as well as to create demand for the steel mills. Conceptually 'the steel mills supply material to the heavy engineering installation at Ranchi and, in turn, receive equipment from them. Both the mills and Ranchi require electric power, and thermal plants are built to supply these needs. The thermal plants need equipment, and the heavy electrical equipment plant at Bhopal is established and, in turn, secures its supplies from the steel mills. All these enterprises require coal, and the government opens new mines, thus creating a demand for heavy mining equipment from Ranchi'.[48] It was envisaged to build up a self-sufficient public sector, with both vertical and horizontal linkage between different production activities. In this, the planners had correctly followed the English, American and German system of combination of different industrial activities. The Indian public sector was envisaged as an integrated entity, with each unit supporting the other from production to marketing. Working of such a gigantic integrated industrial structure, required a high degree of central planning and control. There was need of a super ministry to control such an industrial structure. It was probably expected that the Planning Commission under the direct control of the Prime Minister would fill this role. This would have required enormous concentration of power in a single body, which was hardly possible in a democratic set-up. In actual practice, the public sector undertakings, which were under various ministries, had little co-ordination and each acted independently of the others.

'Leading sector' hypothesis of German industrialisation, which was later followed by the Soviet Union, obviously influenced the early planners, in building up a gigantic heavy industrial structure. In this type of industrialisation, 'building costs are typically underestimated and cost over runs endemic, related financial difficulties as well. A clear cyclical pattern of boom and bust emerges, but on an upward trend of investment activity which continue for decades'.[49] This is with regard to German industrialisation of the nineteenth century, but aptly sums up the position regarding Indian industrialisation drive with the public sector. There is no doubt that the industrialisation programme envisaged had an 'electrifying effect on the other branches of the economy. Coal mining, iron production and mechanical engineering made particularly rapid progress during that period. At a later stage most sectors of the consumer goods industry were caught up in the momentum of the upswing'.[50] This is again with reference to German industrialisation, but can be again said of the Indian industrialisation through the public sector.

Notes and References

1. Chris Freeman and Luc Soete, The Economics of Industrial Innovation, p. 201.
2. Nicholas Kaldor, The German War Economy in Collected Economy Essays (Vol. 4), pp. 203-32.
3. G.C. Allen, A Short Economic History of Modern Japan, p. 56.
4. Paul Kennedy, Preparing for the Twenty-first Century, p. 232.
5. J.M. Keynes, General Theory, p. 374.
6. Ravi Batra, The Great Depression of 1990, pp. 6-7.
7. George Soros, The Crisis of Global Capitalism, pp. XI-XII.
8. Batra, p. 15.
9. David B. Andretsch; Knowledge, Globalisation and Regions in Regions, Globalisation and the Knowledge-Based Economy, Edited John H. Dunning, p. 64.
10. David Landes, Wealth and Poverty of Nations, p. 456 foot note.
11. *Ibid.*, p. 463.
12. Michael E . Porter, Competitive Advantage of Nations, pp. 497-98.
13. Landes, p. 462.
14. Freeman and Soete, p. 35.
15. Porter, p. 498.
16. *Ibid.*, p. 502.
17. Earthscan, The Reality of Aid 1997-98, p. 145.
18. Landes, p. 464.

19. Nicholas Kaldor, Advanced Technology in a Strategy of Development, in *Collected Economic Essays*, Vol. 6, p. 153.
20. Herman Kohn, World Economic Development, 1979 and Beyond, pp. 424-25.
21. *The Economist*, 30 Sept. 1995, The Death of Distance; in John H. Dunning edited, Regions, *et. al.*, p. 64.
22. Kennedy, p. 153.
23. The New Encyclopaedia Britannica, Vol. 16, p. 648.
24. Michael Connors, The Race to the Intelligent State, pp. 18-19.
25. George Soros, Global Financial Crisis, p. 149.
26. United Nations Conference on Trade and Development, Trade and Development Report, 2001, pp. 20-21.
27. K.A. Oye, *et. al.*, edited Eagle Defiant, p. 122.
28. Freeman and Soete, p. 135.
29. Denning, edited, Regions, etc., p. 9.
30. Freman, p. 120.
31. Government of India, Planning Commission, 1978, Draft Five Year Plan, 1978-83, p. 261.
32. Bimal Jalan, India's Economic Crisis, p. 156, note 51.
33. Freman, p. 120.
34. Francois Crouzet, France, in The Industrial Revolution in National Context, edt. Mikulas Teich, *et. al.*, pp. 37-38.
35. *Ibid.*, p. 39.
36. *Ibid.*, p. 103.
37. I.G. Patel, Glimpses of Indian Economic Policy, p. 53.
38. Phillip Oppenheim, Trade Wars, p. 100.
39-41. Nicholas Kaldor, The German War Economy, in *Collected Economy Essays*, Vol. 4. pp. 207-08.
42. League of Nations, Economic Stability in the Post-War World, pp. 37-39.
43. *Ibid.*, pp. 39-40.
44. P. Padmanabha Pillai, Economic Conditions in India, pp. 231-32.
45. Daniel R. Headrick, The Tentacles of Progress, p. 292.
46. Padmanabha Pillai, pp. 227-28.
47. Gerald M. Meier, edited, Leading Issues in Economic Development, p. 739.
48. *Ibid.*, p. 741.
49. Richard Tilly, German Industrialisation, in *The Industrial Revolution in National Context*, p. 103.
50. Marz, Schumpeter, p. 43.

10

International Capitalism and India

The honeymoon period Indian economy with continuous deficit financing and huge external aid continued till 1991. It was only when the external debt reached the four digits in billions (Rs. 1215 billions) and near default in foreign obligations in July 1991, that the Government of India woke up to the alarming situation of living on foreign debt.[1] The huge partfolio of external debt led to newly discovered economic wisdom of a complete turnaround from established economic policies. However, such wisdom had no prescription for reducing the mounting debt burden. The pre-budget economic survey reports prior to 1991-92, while fully aware of the mounting debt problem, have not addressed itselves to a policy of reducing the external debt, while being highly conscious of internal debt. They had been lulled into passive submission by the World Bank IMF assurances. The Economic Review of 1989-90 says, 'Despite the significant growth in external debt, India's position *vis-a-vis* other developing countries continues to be satisfactory. According to estimates published by the World Bank, India's debt-GNP ratio in 1988 was a little over 22 per cent compared with around 54 per cent in 19 highly indebted middle-income countries and over 111 per cent in 27 severely indebted low-income countries'.[2] Such comparisons between countries, which is the practice of IMF-World Bank reports, serve little purpose, as countries are different entities with different problems. Even the IMF reports of 1985 were non-committal on India's debt status. IMF report of 1985 places India and China in separate category, although both the countries qualify in the indebted category of countries. In the case of China invisibles in the shape of remittances from overseas Chinese contribute to a large extent in reduction of the debt quantum. Even a country like Somalia, which has been cut-off from external aid due to American misadventure, has not suffered due to large scale remittances from expatriate Somalis.[3] In the case of India, decline of invisibles contributed to a large extent in bringing about the debt crisis of 1991. 'Invisible surpluses have traditionally financed a large part of India's trade deficits. However, the trend has been on the decline in the eighties on account of a fall in gross invisible receipts, as a per cent of GDP, from 4.3% in 1980-81 to 2.8% in 1987-88, coupled with an increase in invisible payments from 1.2% of GDP to 1.9% of GDP, respectively, during this period. The decline in gross invisible receipts relative to GDP is mainly accounted for by a leveling-off of private transfer receipts. Private transfer receipts, representing mainly remittances by non-resident Indians have leveled-off in the last few years'.[4] Non-resident remittances, which had increased during the initial years of gulf boom, tapered-off. Between 1980-81 to 1987-88 interest and service payment on foreign loans and credit expanded at 31.8% per annum.

WORLD BANK IMPERIALISM AND U.S.A.

During the initial stages of India's forays into foreign debt, a rosy picture of management of foreign debt was given through assurances of easy credit policy. International Development Agency was set-up in September 1960 to provide a 'soft loan window', with low interest rate and long-term maturity. During the 1960s and the 1970s, India received the bulk of IDA assistance, which became 40% in 1980 and was further reduced to 16% in 1988.[5] This is primarily because U.S.A., which is the single largest creditor of the I.D.A., switched the Agency over to a policy of promoting American business interests in the debtor countries under

Reagan administration. 'The Reagan administration's natural impulse was to turn the Agency for International Development into an instrument to promote the private sector . . . IDA officials announced that they would concentrate not on income redistribution but on wealth generation, not on inefficient and coercive public sector projects but on private sector development'.[6] It was not that the IDA had not financed private sector projects in India, but the bulk of the investment had gone to the public sector and other government projects. There was a complete turn around in the policy of Multilateral Development Banks like World Bank and other regional development banks in the wake of Reaganomics, in which bankability of the project was more important than poverty alleviation. 'Governments judged unwilling to work harmoniously with private capital would receive less aid. IDA spokespersons claimed that their main focus was the indigenous private sector, but a least some programmes were interested in promoting joint ventures with American capital. While some of these directions were not entirely new, the swerve away from projects oriented directly toward the poor majority was striking'.[7]

The world Bank's main focus shifted to promoting American business interests in debtor countries, instead of development of the economy of these countries. Reagan 'administration also wanted to curb the use of "performance criteria" under which host countries require foreign investors to use local components and meet prescribed export targets'.[8] According to Reagan's agenda, prosperity and development of the U.S.A. was synonymous with economic development of other nations. Reagan said at the IMF-World Bank meet of 1981, 'No American contribution can do more for development than a growing, prosperous U.S. economy, . . . And as the world's largest single market, a prosperous, growing U.S. economy will mean increased trading opportunities for other nations'.[9] Reagan administration marked a complete turn around in U.S. policy, in which America, as the major user of world's resources, no longer had the moral compunction of helping the third-world countries in their fight against poverty, as a world strategy to contain communism and spread of Soviet influence. U.S. had recovered from the scars of Vietnam debacle and Soviet influence was on the decline with communism no longer offering a panacea for the world's poor. The ideological war, which dominated the Cold War period, was gradually running out of steam. Reagan administration was the first to realize that the battle for world dominance has shifted from the ideological front to the economic front and tailor its policies accordingly. Rhetoric of communist ideology had given place to economic realities and in this battle U.S. realised that with its world net-work of transnational corporations and control over technology, it had a distinct advantage over the rest. Rhetoric of ideology was replaced by the rhetoric of market place. 'As Reagan stated: "The societies which have achieved the most spectacular, broad-based economic progress . . . [are those that] believe in the magic of the market place." The administration tended to equate market mechanisms with private ownership'.[10]

Reagan administration chose the Multilateral Development Banks, IMF and GATT for pursuing its policy of 'America first' theme. Earlier U.S. administrations of Ford and Carter resisted any attempt to democratize international financial institutions. 'Both, for example, maintained American voting shares in the international financial institutions and preserved the jurisdiction of these institutions over vital international matters'.[11] Economic power was closely retained in the specialised agencies, like IMF, World Bank and GATT, which were dominated by the developed countries and not in the more democratic U.N. General Assembly. World Bank and IMF, which had so far been not directly interfering with the policies, while at the same time pursuing the interests of the multinational corporations, were asked to take a harsher stand against the developing countries not fully taking the line of international capitalism and suffering from socialist pretensions like having a public sector for industrialisations, tariff protection for infant industries, poverty allevation programmes, subsides to correct the imbalances and other measures, which had become intrinsic in managing the economies of developing countries. Overtly, World Bank was advocating income redistribution and even its former president, Robert Mc Namara was accused of fostering socialism in the third Word. 'High level Reagan appointees came to Washington with a strong suspicion of the multilateral development banks. . . . They also tended to view the World Bank and the smaller regional development banks as welfare handouts'.[12] This was the perception World Bank and other multilateral development banks had created as international do gooders. Even the higher levels in the U.S. polity had this perception of World Bank, which had marketed this benevolent image in the third world countries, most of which fell for this trap in a big way. India had been a major debtor of the multilateral development banks, as the planners believed in financing all development programmes through foreign financing. This was the easy way out for all concerned. The line of least resistance taken in the matter of development financing would not prove beneficial to the country in the long-run.

It took a major study by officials of the Reagan administration to find out the true facts about the World Bank operations, so cleverly it had camouflaged its actual agenda of promoting American interests. U.S. Treasury Department officials in their report after a major study of the multilateral banks, came to the conclusion that these institutions were fully supporting American economic and political interests. The report 'United States Participation in the Multilateral Development Banks in the 1980s', leaves no doubt that multilateral development banks like World Bank and other regional banks are an extension of the U.S. administration. 'Indeed, the official report was unusually candid in its discussion of American clout in the banks . . . The report concluded that the Multilateral Development Banks contribute to American global economic objectives by encouraging developing countries to participate more fully in an international system based on liberalised trade and capital flows. American commercial objectives were served by the expanded opportunities for American exports, investment and finance'.[13] No doubt, 'It is said that the international capitalist economy has developed an imperialism of its own' and this has been made possible through 'World Bank imperialism of proliferating the principles and institutions of good capitalist management into little brother's organisation'.[14] This was till

1980 done covertly. Reagan administration started the era of doing it overtly, as the third world countries had last their voice by that time by falling into debt trap and failure to reconcile their differences. This was the time to tighten the economic noose. Developing countries by living through debt for development, had failed to set their houses in order. U.S. Treasury Department asked the Multilateral Development Banks (MDBs) to coordinate with the IMF, which was required to follow a more rapid adjustment programme of external debt and balance of payment deficit. The close coordination between IMF and MDBs, was to ensure a stricter debt regime and push through U.S. Treasury policies in the financial administration of debtor countries.

Indian government, which was so far basking in the MDBs liberal loaning policy, was suddenly called to order by the IMFs rapid adjustment programme. This programme 'meant sharp devaluations, tight credit, lowered government spending, falling wages, and other austerity measures to correct balance of payments disequilibria and slow domestic inflation'.[15] Indian government, suddenly faced with a sudden turn around of its long practiced policies, had to find a scapegoat for the faulty planning and management of the economy, leading to a crisis situation. The Indian Public Sector, a captive body of the government, offered itself as a ready-made whipping boy for all and sundry, particularly for the failure of economic planners and policy-makers. 'About 90 per cent of the approvals for external commercial borrowings (in value) were given to meet public sector requirements during 1985-86 to 1989-90'.[16] Public sector was saddled with external borrowings to the extent of Rs. 12,000 crores during this period. This was done with the ostensible purpose of upgradation of technology of the public sector enterprises to international standars, as their sales were mostly for the domestic market and only two per cent of the total sales was exported. The public sector units were sought to be made export-oriented to bail out the government from the balance of payments crisis, which was already showing signs of reaching alarming proportions. Public sector had been designed for the core sector of Indian industrialisation to build-up the infrastructural system. If, it was to be diverted from its main purpose, to cater to foreign markets, this was not the best way of doing so by getting them further indebted and risking their viability. When the government was fast losing its faith in the public sector, it does not stand to reason, why such heavy foreign exchange bill was loaded on the public sector in the name of modernisation. Since the mid-eighties a serious disinformation campaign had been launched against the public sector, highlighting its drawbacks and completely ignoring its achievements in the industrialisation of the Indian economy. The government, particularly the economic and administrative bureaucracy seems to have been losing faith in the public sector and holding it more and more responsible for the economic ills facing the country. However, when the policy of disinvestment of public sector, was on the anvil, imposing a huge foreign exchange bill on this sector, in the shape of dubious foreign technology, was to say the least suspect.

CHANGING TECHNOLOGICAL BASE OF AMERICAN CAPITALISM

So-called modernisation or up-gradation of technology of the public sector undertakings, was taken up at a time, when the Western economies were going through a recession and was in the process of changing their basic economic structure from metal and basic industries to consumer-led industries. 'Pentagon Capitalism' was taking a different form in the wake of Vietnam debacle. Military spending had switched-off from building up military stockpiles in the shape of hardwares to sophisticated electronics technology, missile and space programmes. Demand for steel was coming down from the late seventies. Defence was becoming more technology-oriented with the U.S. defence strategy shifting to the concept of a short, swift and decisive war after the military debacle in the long drawn Vietnam War, in which commitment of men and material was too heavy. This strategy proved effective in the Gulf Wars of 1991 and 2003. With the arms race between the U.S.A. and the Soviet Union being gradually called-off since the eighties and altogether ceasing in the nineties, stockpiling of military hardware became a thing of the past. Demand for steel and metals, which was already showing declining trend from the late seventies came down sharply in the U.S.A. and other Western economies. Lawrence Klein, Chairman of the Council of Economic Advisers observed regarding the U.S. economy in 1976, 'If you analyse the present recovery, it's definitely consumer-led'.[17] Similarly, *Business Week* observed in September, 1976, 'In the U.S. capital spending is still running some 9% below the peak reached more than two and a half years ago, in the second half of 1973. In Japan, Capital spending is some 24% below the rate of this late 1973 period. In the four major countries of Western Europe—Germany, Britain, France and Italy—the shortfall is some 11%'.[18] U.S. News and world report lamented in July 1976, 'The absence of a widely predicted burst of business spending on new plants and equipment (which) should sustain economic growth for a still longer period . . . After adjusting for inflation, this type of investment is considerably lower today than it was when the economy touched bottom in early 1975'.[19] It is obvious that depression in the western economies in the mid-seventies was sought to be countered not by investing on plants and machinery, but by huge expenditure on military-related industries, energy and environment. Lawrence Klein observed in U.S. News and World Report (August 23, 1976) 'you have to remember that a lot of investment, instead of raising capacity, is now directed at energy problems, and they are going to take a long time to solve. And a lot of investment is directed towards protecting the environment'.[20]

The U.S. economic boom from World War II was due to huge military expenditure, which created a system of 'Pentagon capitalism with a military-industrial complex'. 'World War II had provided the impetus for a massive industrialisation effort in the U.S. When the war ended, this capacity, the world's biggest, was intact and ready to churn out products of all types in any volume. The U.S. became the number one peacetime industrial power overnight . . . . The jump that the U.S. got on every one-else due to the war lasted well into the 1970s'.[21] The first serious warning about the military industrial complex was sounded by President

Eisenhower in his famous farewell speech, 'We have been compelled to create a permanent armaments industry of vast proportion'. Then again 'I began to feel more and more uneasiness about the effect on the nation of tremendous peace-time military expenditures . . . Unjustified military spending is nothing more than a distorted use of the nation's resources'.[22] The leaders in the U.S.A. had already become alarmed by predominant role of the armaments industry in the economy. They understood that this legacy of the Second World War, boosted by the Cold War, could not continue indefinitely. This stage of American capitalism blew out of its steam by the 1970s and reached its lowest point by 1975 in the wake of Vietnam disaster, with official unemployment at 10% in the U.S.A. and other OECD countries (and by some unofficial estimates double that number). Second phase of post-war Pentagon capitalism was already taking shape in huge Federal expenditures in military-related industries. 'Pentagon Research and Development expenditures provide the seed money that creates new technology and industry. Federally funded science complexes, have given birth to a whole range of modern science and engineering businesses including computers, calculators and magnetic recording. Private industries producing everything from transistors to lasers grew up largely in the wake of the technological advances pioneered by federal programs in nuclear physics and modern electronics'.[23] In 1975 the sunbelt states (California, Texas, Georgia, Florida and North Carolina) received 40% of the 86 billion Federal military budget.

The first phase of post-World War II, American capitalism was based on the momentum for industrialisation provided by the war. This continued till the seventies with the American military commitment in major theatres of war in Korea and Vietnam. The cold War with the Soviet Union ensured continuous stock-piling of armaments, with both sides trying to keep ahead of each other in the balance of power, which during the cold war period meant quantitive superiority in armaments, as technological knowledge in conventional, nuclear and space technology was more or less evenly balanced between the super powers. Steel and metal industries were the basic supporting industries for manufacture of war-ships, arrmoured cars, tanks, air-crafts, air-craft carriers, missiles and missile launchers, guns of different caliber, submarines and various defence-related hardwares. Strategic Arms Limitations talks in the 1970s and the strategic Arms Reduction Talks of the 1980s, also effectively slowed down the arms race. The lessons of Vietnam proved the futility of conventional warfare based on superiority of military hardware. United States had learnt the lessons of Vietnam war, even before the end of the war and gradually changed its military strategy to high technology-oriented short and decisive war. Mid-1970s is the water-shed point from which the American capitalism changed over from steel and metal-based heavy industries to electronics and scientific-based industries. Shift in technology required transformation in production processes and inputs from coal, iron and steel-based industries to oil, gas, aluminum, electronics and service-based industries. Development of the Silicon Valley, in the U.S.A. which became the nerve-centre of electronics and computer industry throughout the world started from the 1970s. In fact, this is a single major development which averted a major depression, knocking at the portals of the U.S. economy at least since the early seventies. 'Federal expenditures in military-related industries has had a powerful impact on the expansion of the Sunbelt economy. By awarding extensive military contracts to private industry, the Federal Government augments private demand in key Sunbelt manufacturing industries, such as electronics. Furthermore by socializing the costs of technological innovation and the costs of training the required technical labour force, the Federal Government lowers the costs of these production inputs (and therefore the costs of production) which private industries eventually absorb'.[24] This picture of the formative years of electronics and electronics-related industries in the Silicon Valley, clearly shows that technology was mostly developed in military research laboratories and passed on to private industries. Thus, the basic input of technology was made available to private industries at government cost, which gave a head start to electronic and electronics-based private industries. Steel Industry was already facing severe depression in the 1970s and was the single most important factor causing recession in the U.S. and the Developed World. There was no new investment in steel industry in the U.S.A. and the investment shifted from coal, iron and steel belt of the north-eastern States to the southern States. This is also reflected in the declining population of New York City, Cleveland, St. Louis and Pittsburgh, compared to the rapidly growing population in Houston, Miami, Dallas, Atlanta and San Diego. The decline in investment in Steel Industries from the seventies led to the decline of the North-eastern steel belt in importance, ceasing to be the economic hub of the U.S.A. There was also rapid decline of Steel Industry in western European countries. As to the investment sensitive and indicative Steel Industry, the press reports "the French Steel Industry faces a deep depression . . . and West German rolled steel orders show further fall."[25]

EXPERIMENTATION IN PUBLIC SECTOR WITH FOREIGN TECHNOLOGY AND MANAGERIAL PRACTICES

When there was all-round recession in steel industry in the developed countries and no new investment or technology was forthcoming in this sector, the decision to import obsolete technology and equipment for the public sector steel industries in India with the ostensible purpose of modernisation was tantamount to technological hara-kiri. The public sector steel plants which had some teething problems initially due to the difficulty in absorption of foreign technology had increased their capacity utilization and productivity. The Integrated Steel Plants in the Public Sector, was set-up to meet the domestic demand for steel. The major such demand was coming from the building construction sector in the country. In view of this, the need for modernisation does not stand to reason. Moreover, the technology in steel industry was certainly not at a lower level than the technology in the other sectors of the economy. The Integrated Steel Plants were basically meant for meeting growing domestic demand in a developing economy. The technology in the steel industry, which was of the late fifties and sixties, could not have become outdated in such a short period of twenty years. A steel plant with gigantic investment and long gestation period, has to function on basic proven technology, which cannot change overnight. After committing huge resources of the country with the best available technology, the entire plant and technology can't be declared obsolete. There was no major development in manufacture of steel during this period, when the steel industry in the west was in decline.

The new technology supposedly required new managerial technology, in addition to technical know-how. Annual Economic Survey (1989-90) reads 'another item which has recorded substantial increase in payments in the 'miscellaneous' group which covers payments on items like technical know-how, management fees, office expenses, and other professional services and technicians' fees'.[26] Managerial techniques grow on the job and are not transplanted. When the public sector undertakings were started, managerial techniques were not imported and it was thought that Indian management was good enough. Import of managerial inputs for office management, added to the external debt burden. Foreign management techniques are tailored to their particular conditions and are unlikely to be useful elsewhere. In the history of industrialisation, no country has successfully imported management technique. Japan has devised its management techniques, so also, South Korea, close business partners of U.S.A. No major country has gone in for foreign management techniques by inducting foreign advisors and consultants for putting their house in order. This was part of the globalisation drive, in which foreign consultants and advisors have to be imported at a heavy cost. Foreign consultancy and services are areas in which U.S.A. and Britain, being world's leading service providers were benefiting disproportionately. When the initial enthusiasms regarding the public sector was over and actual operational problems surfaced, instead of handling them ourselves, we turned to foreign advisors and consultants to bail us out, when we were not lacking in trained manpower ourselves. Invisibles like consultancy and service industries were becoming more important in the new economic dispensation, when basic industries were in the decline. The market for invisibles had already been created in developing countries, after they ran into difficulties in their industrialisation through borrowed technology and western blue-print for development. There was now demand for foreign consultants and advisors as well as foreign service industries. As we have seen, during the late eighties, import of invisibles had become an important feature in India's foreign exchange budget. Reagan administration realised the importance of trade in invisibles and services and wanted to preserve its dominant position, together with its close ally Britain. It was also strategically necessary to take Britain along, as it had first hand knowledge of most of the developing countries as an erstwhile colonial power. As a colonial power, she had traditional trade links with its erstwhile colonies, which she had developed to her advantage during colonial rule. The British Prime Minister, Margaret Thatcher, who was the 'ideological soul mate' of Reagan supported Reagan's policies throughout, although there were opposition from major European countreis.[27] Britain, which had declined as an industrial power, but had strength in consultancy and service industries, mainly due to the English language, stood to benefit from Reagan's policies. It is of interest to note that English language proved a major factor in export of invisibles like consultancy, office management, service industries from Britain and America to India. 'Throughout the Reagan administration's first eighteen months, Trade Representative Brock sought to focus the upcoming GATT meeting (Scheduled for November, 1982) on plans for a new round of multilateral negotiations aimed at liberalising the movement of capital and services such as banking, insurance, data processing, engineering, shipping, and telecommunications—all areas in which the United States, as the worlds leading service—industry economy, could be expected to benefit disproportionately. . . . For many of President Reagan's officials, what was even more importantly at stake was the general interest of the nation as a whole in a system that seemed to them increasingly discriminatory against American Industry and agriculture'.[28] Indian's economic policy during this period coincided with the American Policy, which was in the latter nation's interest. Public sector units, which were under government control, proved to be ideal for putting Reaganomics in practice.

After the initial euphoria regarding high and unrealistic expectations from giant public sector units was over, an impression based on disinformation was gaining ground against the basic concept of Public Sector. There was mismatch between management and labour. There was mismatch between islands of high technology and the surrounding villages with much lower level of economy. Expectations of the local populace from the project was too high, which were not possible to meet. In fact, there was a huge *crisis of expectations,* once the initial euphoria was over. This was a proverbial case of killing the goose that lays the golden eggs. Everybody wanted his share from the project, before it could go into operation. A conflict situation developed between the management and labour; between the surrounding populace and the project. A cold war situation existed between the project authorities and local administration about the role of each other regarding various administrative matters, since the very inception of the projects. Large number of unskilled workers, who were brought by the contractors during the construction phase for early completion of the project, stayed back in the hope of a better life, instead of going back to their villages. A situation of inter-group rivalry between different interest groups, was certainly not conductive for the healthy growth of public sector projects. There were slippages in the execution of the projects, for which alibi had to be found for satisfying the bureaucratic and political masters. A situation like this was fraught with dangers for the Public Sector, which was a new concept and had to be given sufficient time to prove its efficacy. The management practices in the public sector were the same as in private sector, which were based on constant conflict between the workers and management. The success of projects of this magnitude depended on co-operation, rather than conflict, which was the very basis of management techniques developed in western countries. The essence of the 'science of management', as developed by F.W. Taylor and others can be found in the writings of Charles Babbage, whose ideas on management science preceded that of F.W.

Taylor by eighty years. The superiority of machine over man, is the fundamental of scientific management, as developed in the Western countries. 'Babbage constantly insists on the importance of precise measurement and verification, trying to optimize the productive advantages of machinery by superimposing its power of control on the human agency. This is how he describes the process involved: One great advantage which we may derive from machinery is form the check which it affords against the inattention, the idleness or the dishonesty of human agents. . . . Perhaps the most useful contrivance of this kind, is one for ascertaining the vigilance of a watchman. It is a piece of mechanism connected with a clock placed in an apartment to which the watchman has not access; but he is ordered to pull a string situated in a certain part of his round once in every hour. The instrument, aptly called a tell-tale, informs the owner whether the man has missed any, and what hours, during the night'.[29]

It is no coincidence that Babbage is also regarded as the father of computers. This was scientific management compared to the crude process of exploitation of the Industrial Revolution of nineteenth century Britain and is perhaps a formalised beginning of control of man by machines, which were gradually taking over the role of Supervisors. It is perhaps thought to be more humane than the old system of Overseers, who were depicted to be cruel tyrants, at least due to the influence of literature, the foremost of which were the novels of Charles Dickens in English language. This theme was taken up by different writers in different languages, particularly in Indian languages, where the influence of English literature was pronounced. Literature managed to create a demonic image of the overseer in public mind. The literature was as market-oriented as any commodity or service and found a new theme in its search for the demon *versus* innocents, which is an age old ingredient of literature. The people were getting tired of old demons, who looked too stereotyped and hackneyed. A new demon had to be found and who else could fill this vacuum than the new class of overseers and supervisors in industrial and commercial establishments.

People educated or otherwise, are likely to sympathises with the under dog as depicted in literature. It is another matter that the demon and under dog are the perennial and most commercially successful theme of literature. Charles Dickens was a great commercial success in the field and instituted a scheme of public readings of his own works on a professional basis, which was a great financial success and ultimately contributed to bring about his untimely death, due to over-strain.[30] The same system of bullying and tyranny by senior boys over young and new boys was prevalent in the famous English Public Schools, in the name of character building.

Practical men must distinguish between literary myths and reality. The system of control over workmen was developed through supervisors, who were themselves workmen. This was a system of incentive through promotion as well as control. As the supervisor was himself from the ranks, he had the control over workmen through confidence. Being human, he was probably a bit partial towards good workmen. Naturally, this created discontent amongst the lazy and shirkers. The mechanization of supervisory work effectively scuttled development of any leadership amongst the workers. The old system of industrial organisation, which produced leaders from the shop floor, became a thing of the past. In the early days of American industrialisation, most of the leaders of industry and management worked their way up from the shop floor. Thomas J. Watson, Senior (1874-1956) who built-up the computer giant IBM from a scratch, was a travelling salesman.[31] He used his knowledge of ground level salesmanship to market computer, which was a completely new product. Business machine or computer was the ideal product for salesmanship and linkage of market and technology. With the upgradation of technology in various types of computer hardware, the rate of obsolescence was high. It was a close linkage between technology and marketing. Technology was moving fast and so was the market. It required the genius of a door to door salesman to unravel the seemingly perennial marketability of the computer.

Andrew Carnegie (1835-1919), the pioneer of giant Steel Industry, who became a millionaire many times over, started as a bobbin boy in a cotton factory, then a telegraph messenger and telegrapher. During his years of apprenticeship in lowly jobs, he could visualize the future of steel industry and developed acute business sense, which helped in establishing American steel industry and made America an industrial power, overshadowing European economies. Similarly, the pioneer of modern management practices, Fredrick W. Taylor (1856-1915) started his career as a machine shop labourer and subsequently shop clerk. This practice of shop floor to Board room and industrial democracy were the characterization of American industrialisation, which was quite different from British pattern. Thus, each country has to follow the management practices suited to its own social ethos, instead of mechanically implanting management practices, which had proved successful under different conditions in another country. The management practices must develop from below, instead of being superimposed.

The Indian industrial culture, mostly copied in the initial stages from the British industrial culture, did not encourage development of leadership from below. Technological leadership imposed from above did not take into account the ground realities. Had a proper industrial culture been allowed to develop through a policy of co-ordination, without outside influence, the health of the public sector would have been certainly better. Machines were gradually taking over the jobs of the supervisors. The earlier management concept of workers and supervisors became a misnomer. Machines had graduated from punch cards to computerised integrated control system for the whole plant based on the hierarchical control philosophy. Maintenance through computer-managed maintenance information system, became the order of the day. Technology in the developed countries was changing to computers and robotics from the seventies, which accentuated the unemployment problem. There was need for marketing these techniques and developing countries, which had proved a fertile ground for export of outdated and obsolete technology from the West, proved an equally fertile ground for experimenting on labour displacing management techniques, completely lacking in originality of outlook. These management techniques, which were in the initial stages, had not been tested for their efficacy and were in experimental stages.

Untried and untested management techniques in the western countries, were thought to be panaceas for increasing managerial efficiency and improving the performance of public sector undertakings. After import of initial engineering technology, the second phase of import of managerial technology started in a big way. There was no move to upgrade the efficiency of the workmen. Obviously, the system did not have any faith in its workmen and thought improved managerial techniques could change the situation. This was like putting the cart before the horse. The efficiency of an undertaking depends on the strength of its workmen. Instead of trying to improve the efficiency of the workmen, spending huge amounts of scarce foreign exchange on management technology, proved short-sighted. These imported, unproved managerial technology did not give the desired results and dragged the public sector units into huge debt traps, making them unviable. This in a nutshell is the sad story of modernisation of Indian public sector. The so-called third world countries wanting a magic formula for development have proved to be dustbin of obsolete technology. No doubt, the results have been unsatisfactory.

We should have taken the hard road to development, instead of putting our faith in magic formula from so-called developed countries. Instead of being dazzled by foreign technology, we should have analysed and studied its long term impact, before importing them. We should have studied the Japanese and German examples of re-building their economy after the Second World War. Japanese management practices were entirely indigenous, developed to suit changing economic requirements. Japanese never went for import of foreign management techniques, but developed their own techniques based on their own tradition and experience. This is perhaps the key to Japan's post-war economic success. This is not an economic miracle, as some economic analysts have tried to make out on a superficial study of the situation. The miracle, if anything, lies in the Japanese ability to adopt their own traditional culture to the new industrial culture. Japanese did not adopt the western management practices to manage their industries but developed their own managerial culture on the basis of their own traditional organisations and culture. The strength of the Japanese industrialisation lay on its maintenance of the integrity of its own economic structure, instead of allowing its entire economy being assimilated in the western international structure, as a part of the globalisation exercise, which some people feel inevitable for development. Once, Japan gets assimilated in the western economic structure, it will cease to be the economic giant, which it is till today. The basic reason for the failure of the Koreans to continue with the industrialisation drive on the way to overcoming the Japanese, was their inability to adopt the new industrial culture to their own culture and value system. The series of labour and social unrest and corruption at high places, were symptomatic and outward manifestations of this failure. These were not the causes, but the effects of the failure to integrate the modern industrial culture needed for industrialisation to Korean's own culture and traditional practices. This is like an old Greek tragedy, where countries, which have been too long under foreign domination, fail to develop an independent managerial and administrative ethos of their own, when they are able to break away from foreign political shackles.

The same thing has happened in the case of India. As we have seen in the process of industrialisation through the public sector, we were not content with importing technical know-how, there was large scale import of managerial techniques, quite unsuited to Indian conditions. In fact, the public sector units were never allowed to develop their own R & D units, to keep the technology updated. Even, if a fraction of what was spent on import of foreign technology, could have been allotted for development of R & D in public sector, there was no need of running up a huge foreign exchange bill and the results would have been certainly better. This is amply illustrated by the fact that when the Indian missile development programme, which was with Soviet collaboration, got a jolt in the early nineties, due to the sudden stoppage of technology transfer, for Rocket engines needed for propulsion of rockets. This was due to the demise of the Soviet Union and the pressure of the Western Government on the successor state, Russia. In fact, this proved to be a great boon, as Indian scientists, without any foreign interference, could develop world class missile technology, updating India's defence capabilities in missile to international standards. This would certainly not have been possible, had we been dependent on Russia for transfer of out-dated missile technology, as the progress in the development of missile technology in that country had come to a standstill since the mid-eighties with the advent of Perestroika and subsequent disintegration of Soviet Union. In the field of nuclear technology, India has been able to develop its own technology without any foreign assistance, in fact in the teeth of opposition from nuclear powers. If in such advanced scientific fields like missile technology and nuclear technology, Indian Scientists and Technicians can develop the requisite advanced technology, without foreign technological assistance, there should be no difficulty in developing suitable technology in steel-making, where India had a long tradition and no dearth of technical manpower. The history of foreign collaboration in technology development is replete with failures. The public sector industries should have been allowed to be technologically self-sufficient, instead of being constantly technologically dependent. We should have explored our own strength, instead of copying others blindly.

PRIVATE SECTOR SURVIVES ON PROTECTION AND SUBSIDY

It is of interest to recall that Indian steel industry in the private sector could not have survived without protection against cheaper steel import. Ironically, this protection was provided by the British government after the First World War, for development of steel industry in India for defence of the British Empire. After the First World War there was a huge glut in steel production due to increased production by Germany, Belgium and France. After the First World War, 'peace ended TISCO's cozy monopoly of the Indian steel market. The competition, however, was no longer from

British but from German and Belgian steel . . . . After the war, TISCO turned to the government for protection against its dangerous new competitors . . . . The result was to build a high wall around the Indian steel market, behind which TISCO proceeded with its greater extensions'.[32] TISCO (Tata Iron and Steel Company), which first started commercial production of steel in 1913 enjoyed near monopoly position during the First World War, due to the dislocation of supply from European and American markets. 'Had it not been for the almost complete and highly profitable monopoly of the home market during the war, it is very much to be doubted whether the Steel Industry would have survived till 1924, when it asked for and obtained public assistance in the form of protective tariff as well as bounty (subsidy)'.[33] Tata's was the only steel producing concern in India at that time and its profits went up manifold during the war years. Encouraged by such windfall profits, Tata's went in for an ill-considered pan for expansion during the war, when the supply position of new tools and plants was highly doubtful, on account of the disturbed conditions due to war. 'The available evidence on the subject shows that the project was originally taken in hand owing to the exceptionally favourable prospect of manufacturing steel at a profit, and not at the suggestion of the Government of India'.[34] However, the company found itself in great financial crisis immediately after the war, due to this misadventure. The production cost of steel by TISCO went up and large orders were placed by importing firms for cheaper foreign steel. The unfair advantage which TISCO enjoyed during the war, ended with its conclusion.

The Steel Industry (Protection) Act was passed in June 1924, incorporating heavy import duties for imported steel. 'The result, in short was the imposition of duties averaging about 33 per cent *ad valorem*, that is practically what had been demanded by Tata's'.[35] Additionally, bounties were granted on the manufacture of steel rails, fishplates and railway wagons, to bail out TISCO from the contract entered into with the railways, for supply of these items at fixed prices. This bounty was given at a time of serious budgetary deficit of government of India. Even this measure was not sufficient to ensure the viability of TISCO and Tatas applied to the Tariff Board for supplementary protection due to its inability to compete with imported steel. Tariff Board recommended almost doubling the duties. 'It would be noticed that in less than six months the extent of protection necessary was found to be between 70 and 105 per cent higher than was originally granted'.[36] The additional duties would involve a burden of about Rs. 2 crores on the economy, while the benefit to the company was estimated at Rs. 50 lakhs. In view of this the Government of India increased the subsidies to TISCO. Tatas continued to apply and receive protection for their steel till 1941, when again they benefited from rising prices of steel and absence of competition from foreign steel.

Manufacturing cost of steel in TISCO had increased due to high overhead costs and outdated machinery. Technology in steel manufacturing had advanced in the continent, particularly in Germany and high quality of steel was available at considerably lower cost. 'In the post-war period, very great progress has been attained, specially in Germany, in introducing technological improvements particularly in respect of fuel cosumption'.[37] The practice of manufacture of steel in TISCO through basic Open-Hearth steel furnaces became out of date soon after the First World War. Duplex plant (combining the Bessemar and Open-Hearth processes) was not successful. The tariff Board recommended complete overhauling of technology. Foreign supervisory personnel, managing agency system, overstaffing and ill-timed plan to expand when the cost of machinery and transportation were at its highest increased the overhead costs. The protection of the Tata steel works was at the cost of the Indian consumers and the economy in general. In determining 'fair selling price' the Tariff Board made *adhoc* calculations favouring the company, which called for serious criticisms. One of which was 'it is a dangerous principle to hold that the manufacturer, instead of being left to suffer for the inferior quality of part of his output, should be fully compensated for the same at the expense of the general tax payer'.[38]

H.L. Dey in his; 'The Indian Tariff Problem' had examined in depth the various protective measures and subsidies to keep TISCO afloat throughout the 1920s and 1930s, 'While examining the sequence of events that led to the demand for, and grant of, protection to the Indian Steel Industry, we found that the real purpose of protection was to help a particular firm (TISCO) to tide over the financial difficulties that had been brought about largely, if not wholly, by its own mistakes, miscalculations and misfortunes . . . . It is therefore, essential to examine whether that firm is endowed with a sound organisation and efficient management'.[39] He then goes on to comment on the absentee management of the firm. Tata Sons Ltd., the Managing Agents, who have a complete control over the financial and commercial business of the firm, were located at a distance of over 1000 miles at Bombay, whereas the plant is at Jamshedpur. There is nobody among the Board of Directors or Managing Agents having 'a first-hand knowledge of the intricate details of organisation and costs in a gigantic steel factory of modern times. The result is that the business and financial heads of the steel works are absolutely powerless in checking the costs of production. This ineffectiveness of control over the costs of production is also due to the fact that not even one member of the Managing Agents or the Board of Directors is resident at Jamshedpur'.[40] The criticism is further confirmed by the statement of Sir M. Visweswaraya, the eminent engineer and administrator, who had just been appointed to the Board as a Director. 'Sir M. Visweswaraya publicly stated that there were many directions in which technical improvements could be made and where technical advice was needed, that there was no budgetary system at the works, that there was too much secrecy in the figures given to the Board; that the system of management at the steel works at Jamshedpur was antiquated; and the Board had no control over it'.[41] While examining the composition of Board of Directors of Tata Irons Ltd., Managing Agents for fourteen major Tata concerns, it is observed that 'the firm has only nine Directors in all, of which at least five (possibly six) appear to be blood relations'.[42] It is obviously impossible to extend any control over fourteen major industrial undertakings, two of which are at a considerable distance from Bombay. As early as 1899, General R.H. Mahon,

Superintendent of the Government Ordinance Factories, in a report had laid down clear guidelines for promotion of iron and steel industry in India. This was one of the reports, on which TISCO was founded. Regarding management, General Mahon had stated that it must combine expert knowledge and local experience. As we have seen, this advice was not followed. He had advised that technology should be up to date. In this case the technology became out-dated within a few years. Fair selling price of steel, on which the protective measures were taken in favour of the firm, was determined by the costing figures supplied by the beneficiary (TISCO). No steps were taken to verify the cost of production in competing countries. TISCO was also overstaffed, as was found during enquiring by the Tariff Board.

It is necessary to analyse the reason for such generosity of the British Indian Government in protecting the Indian steel industry, particularly that of Tata. The protection was given at the cost of the economy through higher selling price to the Indian consumers. Subsidies were given directly from the budget. The effect was to tax heavily the unsheltered industries and the agricultural sector, who had to bear the higher prices, as well as suffer from depressed conditions while selling their products. Subsidies and tariff protection in steel industry, led to compensatory subsidies in engineering industries, which were old and established. It may be no accident that the period of industrial subsidies coincided with a period of agricultural depression, leading to agrarian unrest, culminating in the Bengal famine of the forties. The terms of trade became highly unfavourable to agricultural products, *vis-a-vis* industrial products. The policy of British Indian government towards the Indian steel industry, was one of protecting it form competition from the superior quality of continental steel, particularly German, Belgian and French and not from British steel industry, which was stagnating due to failure to upgrade the technology, as was done in the continent. Britain was thus protecting its own steel industry, in the guise of protection of Indian steel industry. Cutting-off the continental steel industry from the Indian market, was sought to give the British steel industry the required time to reorganise itself and upgrade the technology. It was also in the interest of British national security to check the growth of highly efficient German steel industry. We have seen earlier, Britain had thrived on a policy of *laissez faire,* when it suited its commercial interests. 'The war had swept away the traditional British belief in free trade and *laissez faire*'.[43] Britain turned protectionist when it suited its interests.

Another reason for British Indian Government's protection of Indian steel industry, was one of strategic one, to protect the Eastern Empire in the case of future war. Tariff Board had observed in its report in 1924, 'the strategic advantage of basing the campaigns in Mesopotamia and East Africa on steel supplied by India far outweighed any money saving, and could not be estimated in terms of money'.[44] During the First World War TISCO provided steel rails, also to Egypt, Palestine and Salonica fronts. Establishment of steel industry in India, proved to be strategically important for Britain in conducting their operations in the eastern empire. TISCO had been nurtured with a view to the strategic interests of the empire. 'If in some future war, the Suez canal be blocked, and India cut-off from the Mother country, it may well be that works like Tata's may serve as arsenal for the outlying parts of the empire, and enable then to defend themselves till communications are restored. The political and military significance of such an enterprise is by no means to be cast into shade by its direct industrial results'.[45] No doubt, the British imperial interests coincided with that of the Indian iron and steel industry. As such, this was protected, whatever the cost to the Indian economy. Consumers have no effective way of protecting themselves against the organised pressure of the manufacturer. And 'If, on top of that, the financial system of the government is organised in such a way as to coincide with the aims and purposes of the large-scale manufacturers, then the consumer and taxpayer would undoubtly become absolutely helpless in protecting himself'.[46] In this case, the interests of the government and industry coincided. The policy of the British Indian government was to prevent the expansion of steel industries in the European continent, particularly Germany and they used the protectionist policy effectively. The policy of imperialism in trade and industry was camouflaged in such a way, as if it was protection of India's national interests, although it was far from any such altruism. Few in India at that time could see through the policy of protectionism, although it seriously affected the agricultural sector and the unsheltered industries, which were to bear the burden of protection and subsidies. The imperial power took advantage of the public opinion in favour of national industry. Tata steel industry satisfied all the protectionist pleas, such as economic nationalism, infant industry, basic industry and military necessity. Employment of psychologically effective phrases and arguments such as 'the national industry in danger', 'the wickedness of the foreigner in selling his goods at a low price with a view, to killing the indigenous industry', 'the right of the home industry, to supply the home market and so on',[47] came in handy for the imperial government to support particular firms, in their own military interests as well as a matter of policy in controlling the international market.

GLOBALISATION AND POWER POLITICS

The interest of the developed western countries lies in controlling the world economy to their own advantage, at the cost of the third world countries. This problem was discussed at length in a document entitled 'Economic Stability in the Post-War; World Report of the Delegation on Economic Depression'. The document allays the fear of the European countries, which suffered from depression and then plunged into war. The main economic challenge was expected to be from the newly industrialised countries, which were diversifying their economy from being merely producers of primary goods. The document warns 'up to a certain point the diversification of the sources of national income is likely to prove stabilizing factor as regards the economy of the newer countries . . . . On the other hand, this development has probably tended to increase the instability of the older industrial countries'.[48] The document anticipates a full capacity utilisation of the mechanical industries in the developed states for a considerable number of years, to meet the demand for machinery from the newly industrialised countries. The document is concerned with maintenance of full employment in industrialised states, but does not talk of any employment policy for the newly industrialised states. It talks of 'the rising standards of living of these people',[49] which is not the same thing as full employment. There has certainly been rise in living standard in the developing countries, but it has by-passed the majority. This rise has certainly created increased demand for consumer goods. The policy prescription is for international economic stability by assuring full employment in the industrialised states. Industrialisation of the developing countries has been viewed in the context of maintaining full employment in the developed countries. The crux of the problem is employment, which alone can raise the living standard. Rising living standard without full employment is a contradiction in terms. The document clearly states 'ultimate stability is likely to depend mainly on the extent which policies designed to maintain full employment are successfully applied in the great industrial states'.[50]

It advises the developed countries to maintain their economic strength through an active policy of foreign lending to the under-developed countries in their industrialisation drive, as otherwise they may develop industrially on their own resources and get out of the stranglehold of the developed countries. 'If no outside assistance is forthcoming, it is likely that many of the economically under-developed countries will aim at producing at home the industrial equipment of all types they require for their industrialisation, with consequent adverse effects on the flow of international trade and the loss of benefits of the international division of labour. On the other land, if the economic development of economically under-developed areas is assisted by foreign investment, it can proceed more quickly and with smaller risk of fostering *autarkic tendencies* inimical to the healthy development of a world economic system'.[51]

The document warns against development of any autarkic tendencies in the industrialisation of under-developed countries. The world *'autarky'*, according to the Oxford Dictionary, means 'economic independence or self-sufficiency'. This vital report, contains the ideas, which were discussed at Bretton Woods Conference (1945) which led to the formation of IMF and IBRD (World Bank), two institutions which control the world's finances. League of Nations' Report (1945), which is a blue print for post-war international economic structure, warns the industrialised countries to ensure that the newly industrialising countries do not break away from their economic stranglehold and become economically independent. After the Second World War, it was realised that it would no longer be possible to continue with the nineteenth century pattern of colonialism, in which both political and economic control were possible. The economic clout of the developed countries can be continued through international division of labour, which is an euphemism for continued economic superiority of developed countries, through their technological advantage. This advantage was to be maintained through control of international finances and technology.

Today's market economy and international division of labour are the product of industrial revolution. The anarchy of the market, which is emerging as the dominant international doctrine, can be controlled by centralised power and not by decentralisation of power. The myth of self-regulating market forces has been amply exploded by the British colonialism and gun boat diplomacy of the nineteenth and early twentieth centuries, as well as the U.S. dominance of the world economy in the post-Second World War period. This has become further acute with the end of the Cold War. 'As Karl Polanyi demonstrated, enforcement of market rules required the existence of military or police power'.[52] There has been a proliferation of regulatory bodies both at the national and international level with globalisation and liberalisation. Since economy is closely connected with national security, such control at the international level has serious security ramifications. 'Economics and politics are different analytical sectors of a single reality'.[53] If economic power is lost, the loss of political power will follow. Global capitalist system is kept in place by threat, either implicit or explicit. 'Any show of resistance designed to opt for an alternative developmental strategy can be countered by a series of measures, beginning with a cut-off of credit and progressing through political destabilisation to culminate in covert and ultimately overt military attack'.[54] The developing countries have been so far kept in line by controlling their foreign credit. The situation is summed up in one sentence by one of the votaries of liberalisation. 'Robert Gilpin, for example, unblushingly remarks that: Unfortunately, the world had to suffer two world conflicts before an American-centered liberal world economy was substituted for a British centered one'.[55] The earlier world economic structure of U.K.-centric colonialism is replaced by U.S.-centric globalisation, through two World Wars and Cold War.

GLOBALISATION AND THE POOR

The present world system of production and exchange, powered by technological obsolescence, require global integration, as the third world countries will be the consumers of a technological system, in which fast obsolescence of technology is the key. Technology is simply market-oriented, instead of welfare-oriented. In this relentless march of technology, today's technology is redundant tomorrow and the race is programmed by its authors in such a way that third-world countries always remain a few steps behind and the technological masters are always the lead players. The system has been designed to ensure that these countries spend their resources to obtain technology from the developed West. This technology obtained through scarce resources, will become outdated by the time the technology goes into stream and is ready for production. This in short is the story of technological transfer from advanced countries to developing countries. India has run up huge external debts in pursuit of technology, which became outdated even before the gestation period of the project was completed. The country was thus left with a huge external debt and a museum of obsolete western technology.

In the normal course the technology of yesterday, should suit third world countries in meeting the demands of the domestic market and in economic development. This technology could very well be the intermediate technology, which will help in the development of less developed countries. But the present world economic dispensation calls for technological integration, where there is no scope for intermediate technology. Developed countries have kept a tight control on technology. Technological integration of the world, will marginalize the third world countries with the majority of population in these countries being in the economic periphery. Whether` developing countries should embrace the chimera of globalisation and start dismantling their economic system in the name of economic reforms, needs to be debated seriously in different fora, before it becomes too irreversible. The inevitability of economic reforms and stopping any arguments on the grounds of perverted economic logic, is dangerous for the country's future. The pendulum of economic thinking has swung all the way from socialist dogma to free market policy of the survival of the fittest and elimination of the unfit. Such swing in thinking from one extreme pole to another, is unprecedented in any other discipline. This has serious implications both for the individual and the State. It will mean servitude and ultimate elimination of all those who fall behind this rat-race in the altar of the market. To accept the Darwinian implications of the market glibly, will spell disaster for mankind, not only in the developing countries, but also for the poor in the developed countries.

'One need not go to some remote corner of Africa to experience the disparities. I see it daily within a block of my apartment in the heart of New York City. Shiny chaufferred stretch limousines with built-in bars and televisions discharge their elegantly coiffed occupants at trendy, expensive restaurants while homeless beggars huddle on the side-walk wrapped in thin blankets to ward off the cold'.[56] David Korten in his book exposes the hypocracy of the World Bank and the International Monetary Fund bureaucracy. He has quoted from Journalist Graham Hancok's account of what gala affairs World Bank, IMF meetings are 'I had come (to Washington, D.C.) simply to attend the joint annual meeting of the Boards of Governors of the World Bank and the International Monetary Fund—two institutions that play a central role in mobilizing and disbursing funds for impoverished developing countries . . . . The total cost of the

700 social event laid on for delegates during that single week was estimated at $ 10 million . . . A single formal dinner catered by Ridgewells cost $ 200 per person 15'.[57] Hancock then goes on elaborating the lavish and ostentatious menu of the dinner and how the Washington limousine companies were doing a roaring trade, providing costlist transport for the delegates. David Korten further highlights the hypocracy by quoting from the keynote address of the President of the World Bank, Barber Conable, a former U.S. Congressman, exhorting the members to 'look at our world through the eyes of the most under privileged'.[58] Such exhortations sound hollow in the face of such ostentations. The World Bank and IMF are in the business of poverty and getting rich dividends from the same. Rightly, they have been called 'Lords of Poverty' by Graham Hancock in his book of the same name. 'Far from encouraging delegates to see the world through the eyes of the poor, the organizers of the World Bank-IMF meetings take great care, to shield them from the specter of poverty'.[59] David Korten goes on to show the length to which the Governments of the developing countries have gone to get certificates from the World Bank and IMF, who are the 'leading proponents of economic rationalism and free-market, export-led growth strategies',[60] that they have arrived in the higher economic strata. Government of Thailand, which hosted the World Bank-IMF directors meet in 1991, pulled out all the stops to ensure that the world economic czars certify the arrival of Thailand as a full member of the elite club of newly industrialised nations. 'To ensure the desired impression, a shiny new convention complex was rushed to completion in downtown Bangkok to host the conference. Two hundred families were evicted from their homes to widen roads to and from the site. A nearby squatter settlement was leveled so that the delegates would not be troubled by unpleasant views of Bangkok's poverty. Schools and Government offices were closed to limit traffic congestion and help clear the air of emissions . . . English-speaking engineers, doctors and lawyers were pressed into service as drivers for the delegates; nurses and teachers waited tables in the conference restaurants to ensure that instructions were understood and that no need of a visiting dignitary would go

unmet . . . . The World Bank-IMF meeting in Thailand was a fitting metaphor for the illusion within which the world's power holders live'.[61]

While we need not begrudge the crusaders against poverty, their lavish life-style when hunger and poverty exist in their backyard, we should not fail to note unheard of ostentation which has become the order of the day. This is an example of globalisation at its worst. Rich and powerful enjoying unprecedented life-style in the history of mankind due to technological advance while technology has failed to touch their backyard. Former will be assured of lavish life-style from Washington to Bangkok, while abject poverty exists in the side-walks of the American Cities and amidst the share croppers in the U.S.A., not to speak of development of slum and squalor in geometric progression to the World Bank-IMF sponsored development programmes in third world countries. Globalisation is creating islands of unheard of affluence powered by technology, inhabited by the rich and powerful. Such islands are growing in affluence with the progress of globalisation and exist in all parts of the world—developed and developing. Only the size of the islands and the degree of prosperity vary from nation to nation, depending on whether they are classified as developed or developing. Market competition is between these islands and the economic growth indicators are on the basis of increase in prosperity of this small sector. The rest of the population will only count marginally. The major feature of globalisation is that, no country will be bereft of such islands, however small it may be. The bigger islands will be existing in developed countries, with comparatively less acute degree of poverty and deprivation alround. All the same, poverty will increase proportionate to the growth of affluence, which will make the rich the richer and more powerful. No doubt, the Trade Unions and Labour Organisations in developed countries, are up in arms against such globalisation. It does not require any great economic sense to understand that allocation of resources as practiced by World Bank-IMF due is skewed in favour of the rich and powerful. Technology does not increase the World's resources, it merely increases the transfer of resources from the many to the few and globalisation is a process of accentuating the same. Technology mostly by-passes the masses and concentrates riches in the hands of the few—both in terms of nations and individuals.

The islands of affluence, which are sought to be created by free trade and export-led growth, in all nations, which accept World Bank-IMF dictate, will be linked through technology more and more sophisticated air travel, telecom-facilities, computers and internet. These islands would only compete amongst themselves and would be the index of development. Rest of the world will have to depend on charities—religious or otherwise. Presence of the poor, would also help the rich in assuaging their conscience. Creation of enclaves of rich and powerful in a world of poverty and deprivation, which is being sought to be done in the name of development, is a frightening scenario. It will make the world a much more dangerous place to live in, than it has ever been. Bernard De Montferrand, Ambassador of France in India, while talking of terrorism in the wake of September 11, 2001, has rightly observed, 'The world is a dangerous place to live in and will never stop being dangerous. But the international society, as it appears after the 11 September terrorist strikes, offers as many positive opportunities as risks. In the last resort it depends on us to be active, to take our responsibilities and work for the betterment of the international society, or to retreat and abstain'.[62] Although this is in a different context, particularly that of terrorism, it will be equally applicable in the economic context. It is high time to break the stranglehold of World Bank-IMF over the world economy. Let us not create a situation, where, 'This troubled planet is a place of the most violent contrasts. Those that receive the rewards are totally separated from those who shoulder the burdens. It is not a wise leadership'.[63]

World Bank Projects are drawn up in consultation with bureaucracy and experts and never in consultation with village communities, which do not find any place in the decision-making process. The local self-Government or Panchayat Raj machinery had became non-functional in most of the states and had no role in formulation of the World Bank Projects, which were bureaucratic and technocratic exercises. World Bank Schemes involved a huge multiplication of bureaucracy and technical departments, which had little or superficial contacts with the local community. World Bank always links its loaning programme with technology transfer from the developed loaning country. Aid tied with technology for the project financed by the World Bank, had led to the distortion of the economy. No steps have been taken to develop an appropriate technology, but technology has been imposed from above. Technology imposed, has no spread effect on the economy and does not even benefit the particular project for which it is intended. As when the World Bank aid is stopped, technology cannot be sustained, due to lack of adequate supporting infrastructure. World Bank Scheme involves transplanting of imported technology for even the most backward areas. This has resulted in mismatch between technology on the one hand and society and environment on the other. Imported technology has not taken root in a different environment and has led to waste of scarce resources. The World Bank Projects, while being formulated, have not taken into account the existing know-how available in the area, which, however primitive it may appear to an outsider, has evolved over ages, through knowledge acquired from generation to generation. The close linkage between man and environment in agriculture has not been taken into account. Even today, the Western concept of Environment does not take into account the close linkage between agricultural and pastoral society and environment. There has been a definite clash of value systems with market-oriented values clashing with values of a traditional self-contained society. This has resulted in the destruction of the old value system, while the market-oriented value system has not worked due to the failure of the development schemes. Moreover, market cannot develop in such communities overnight and bulk of the people, who were taken care of by the previous system have not found their place in the market system and have become economic non-persons. These are the victims of short-sighted development projects, who have been increasing in the countryside. Pathetic tales of poverty, which are being highlighted in media and different forums are the results of short-sighted and lopsided development. The community system, which was the backbone of tribal and pastoral communities have broken down due to the onslaught of the market forces in the countryside. The result has been that those who have been marginalised by the market forces have no safety-net to fall back upon. Market does not conceive of a safety-net and those who fail to be part of the system must perish. The old, infirm, widows and orphans must fend for themselves. Besides the market system which is in the initial stage is not big enough to absorb the entire able-bodied population in these areas and a large number of them will have to shift to the already overcrowded urban areas to add to the urban poverty. The World Bank Schemes are classic examples of good intentions going hay-wares. It was thought that introduction of institutions from a developed society, will automatically bring in development in backward communities. This has not happened, as the socio-economic conditions are vastly different.

Resources, particularly natural resources, available to a community is limited and has to be used by future generations. The maintenance of natural resources like soil fertility, water resources, plant and vegetation, which constitute forest cover, water bodies and water resources, have to be preserved from generation to generation and each generation has the burden and sacred duty to preserve it for future generations. To treat these resources as marketable commodities is a basic flow in the developmental concept. The resources available in a particular village community are natural resources and have to be preserved, rather than marketed. Once the concept of marketability of natural resources comes in, there is depletion of forest cover and scarce water resources. Introduction of market element in management of scarce natural resources, has led to large-scale denudation of forest cover. Unplanned irrigation projects, specially minor irrigation projects have played havoc with the ecology of the area. The natural resources, which are held by a village community, are in the shape of a trust for generations and are beyond the concept of market economics. To treat the natural resources, as marketable commodities, will disturb the delicate ecological balance between man and environment. This is exactly what has happened through the introduction of World Bank sponsored market concept in self-sustained rural economies. The forest wealth, which was suddenly turned into marketable commodity, was denuded and within a short span of a couple of decades, village forests, which formed part of the village economy and protected the environment, completely vanished. Rapid disappearance of forest cover within a decade has been the price of World Bank sponsored development. The World Bank sponsored agricultural programmes in a big way in the seventies.

The World Bank sponsored programme in Orissa for increased food production in the mid-seventies, with huge investment in creating a bureaucratic superstructure for management and monitoring of agriculture in a parallel line to industrial management, did not yield the desired result in increased agricultural production. In fact, according to the statistics available from the Bureau of Economics and Statistics of the Government of Orissa, the food-grains production remained static and showed no improvement in spite of huge World Bank intervention. The technological know-how transferred from different agro-climatic zones, were not easily accepted by the farmers and only succeeded in confusing them. In the field of agriculture, a revolution like the industrial revolution is not possible, without seriously disrupting the socio-economic structure. The agrarian economy, however, inefficient it may appear to an outsider, coming from a market-driven society, supports the population of a particular area. Once, this support base is withdrawn, by commercializing the entire production process, majority of the population would became economic non-persons. We have seen the cost of British industrial revolution in the form of complete displacement of British peasantry and making the small and marginal farmers wage-slaves. Colonisation was an essential feature of industrialisation. Agricultural operations, which support a huge population in a country like India, if organised on similar lines as industry, will break up the entire socio-economic structure, which has developed through generations. No alternative structure has been envisaged, which can support the entire population. A small group will certainly become more prosperous by over-utilising the natural resources, while majority of the population will become redundant. Such large number of unemployed able-bodied population without any employment opportunity, spells danger for the society. The urban areas, where the job opportunities are drying up, will not be in any position to support further migration from the countryside. It will not be wise to plan for a society, where majority of the population at the mercy of the market forces are marginalised and become economic non-persons. Nature can provide for everybody's need, but not for everybody's greed. Once greed and avarice are introduced in management of nature's resources, the delicate balance of rural societies will break down, leading to serious chaos. Development has to be with nature and not against it. Most of the theories of development, developed under colonial hegemony, was to treat the resources of the colony as exploitable. This has led to the development of a theory of Man *vs.* Nature.

The notion that trade and commercialization are necessary for development has no basis in fact. In fact, sudden exposure of the isolated rural economy to outside trade and commerce creates an unfavourable terms of trade for the village *vis-a-vis* urban areas. This unfavourable terms of trade leads to drain from rural areas to urban areas and fast depletion of natural resources, which are the basic capital of rural areas. In the name of development, economy of self-sufficient communities have been broken up. This self-sufficiency may not measure up to any high standard of economic development, but at least it is able to meet the basic needs of the community and provide a safety-net for the economically indigent. Even in Europe, there are self-sufficient economic communities, who have not merged their economy entirely into the market economy and have remained self-sufficient at least in basic needs. Basic needs of the community have to be taken care of by the community as far as practicable and possible, whereas for luxuries they have to depend on the market economy. The concept of luxury has certainly changed over time for those who benefit by the development process, but basic needs have not changed much over time. Economists and policy-makers have to concern themselves with basic needs, particularly since a large number of people are left out of the developmental process. The method of economic development envisages the concentration of resources in the heads of the few, whereas the resources earlier belonged to the community. Resources in the rural community basically constitute land, water and forest resources. These resources are not renewable and are for use for generations. In case, a particular generation uses up all the natural resources, it will be depriving future generations, their wherewithal of survival. Mankind is at cross-roads, as never before. With two dimensional economic logic should we jeopardize the lives of future generations, as well as millions of people, who will be deprived of their livelihood by concentration of resources in a small island of economic prosperity?

Notes and References

1. Government of India, Annual Economic Survey, 1991-92, paras 5.1-5.3.
2. Government of India, Annual Economic Survey, 1989-90, p. 129.
3. National Geographic, July 2002, pp. 59-60.
4. Annual Economic Survey, 1989-90, p. 111.
5. *Ibid.*, p. 133.
6. K.A. Oye, *et. al.*, edited, Eagle Defiant, p. 151.
7. *Ibid.*, p. 152.
8. *Ibid.*, p. 154.
9. *Ibid.*, p. 137.
10. *Ibid.*, p. 141.
11. *Ibid.*, p. 136.
12. *Ibid.*, pp. 156-57.
13. *Ibid.*, p. 157.
14. R.E. Robinson, The Excentric Idea of Imperialism with or without Empire, in P.J. Cain, *et. al.*, edited Imperialism (Vol. 2), p. 355.
15. Eagle Defiant, p. 158.
16. Bimal Jalan, India's Economic Crisis, p. 132.

17-20 A.G. Frank, Mainstream Economists as Astrologers, in *U.S. Capitalism in Crisis*, pp. 9-15.

21. William Lareau, American Samurai.
22. Anthony Sampson, The Arms Bazzar, pp. 102-03.
23. Brad Heil, Sunbelt Migration, in *U.S. Capitalism in Crisis*, p. 100, footnote 66.

24. *Ibid.*, p. 92.
25. A.G. Frank, Mainstream Economists as Astrologers, in *U.S. Capitalism in Crisis*, p. 14.
26. Annual Economic Survey, 1989-90, p. 112.
27. Eagle Defiant, pp. 118, 120, 134 and 143.
28. *Ibid.*, p. 122.
29. Istvan Maszaros, Beyond Capital, p. 847, note 29, quoted from Charles Babbage, on the Economy of Machinery and Manufactures, pp. 54-55.
30. Charles Dickens, Great Expectations, Rupa & Co., 1989, p. 7.
31. William Rogers, THINK: A Biography of the Watsons and IBM, Stein and Day, New York, 1969.
32. Daniel Headrick, The Tentacles of Progress, pp. 292-93.
33. H.L. Dey, Indian Tariff Problem, p. 160.
34. *Ibid.*, p. 162.
35. Vera Anstey, Economic Development of India, p. 246.
36. Dey, p. 211.
37. *Ibid.*, p. 232.
38. *Ibid.*, p. 221.
39. *Ibid.*, pp. 228-29.
40. *Ibid.*, p. 230.
41. *Ibid.*, p. 230, footnote 1.
42. *Ibid.*, pp. 230-31, footnote 2.
43. Headrick, Tentacles of Progress, p. 293.
44. Dey, p. 160.
45. Pillai, Economic Conditions in India, p. 232.
46. Dey, p. 236.
47. *Ibid.*, p. 187.

48-51 League of Nations, Economic Stability in the Post-War World, pp. 39, 40, 191.

52. Robert W. Cox, Global Restructuring: Making Sense of the Changing International Political Economy, in Stubbs and Underhill, edited Political Economy and The Changing Global Order, p. 54.
53. Barry Buzan, The Interdependence of Security and Economic Issues in the "New World Order", in Stubbs and Underhill, p. 89.
54. Robert Cox, p. 55.
55. Barry Buzan, People, States and Fear (1983), p. 147.

56-61 David C. Korten, When Corporations Rule The World, pp. 20, 104-106.

62. *U.S.I. Journal*, April-June 2002, p. 164.
63. David Korten, p. 103.

Bibliography

Anstey Vera (1952), The Economic Development of India, Longmans, Green and Co., London.

Alternative Economic Survey, 1993-94, Public Interest Research Group, Delhi.

Alternative Economic Survey, 2000-2001, Rainbow Publishers Ltd., Delhi.

Asian Development Outlook, 1994, Asian Development Bank, Oxford University Press.

Babbage Charles (1835), On the Economy of Machinery and Manufacture, Charles Knight, London.

Baldwin Richard E., Cohen Daniel, Sapir Andre and Venables Anthony (1999), Edited, Market Integration, Regionalism and the Global Economy, Cambridge University Press, Cambridge, U.K.

Batra Ravi (1988), The Great Depression of 1990, Dell Publishing, New York.

Beaud Michel and Dostaler Gilles (1995), Economic Thought Since Keynes. Routledge, London and New York.

Bernal J.D. (1954), Science in History, Watts and Co., Fleet Street, London.

Bhaduri Amit and Nayyar Deepak (1996), The Intelligent Person's Guide to Liberalization, Penguin Books, India.

Brandel Fernand (1993), A History of Civilizations, Penguin Books.

Buzan Barry (1994), The Inter-dependence of Security and Economic Issues in the "New World Order" in Stubbs and Underhill Edited, Political Economy and the Changing Global Order.

Buzan Barry (1983), People, States and Fear: The National Security Problem in International Relations, Wheatsheaf

Books Ltd., Sussex.

Cain Peter J. and Harrison Mark (2001), Edited, Imperialism, Critical Concepts in Historical Studies, 3 Volumes, Routledge, London.

Cain P.J. (1980), Economic Foundations of British Overseas Expansion, 1815-1914, Oxford University Press, New York.

Chossudovsky Michel (2001), The Globalization of Poverty, Impacts of IMF and World Bank Reforms, Other India Press, Goa.

Clark Ian (1997), Globalisation and Fragmentation. Oxford University Press, Oxford.

Connors Michael (2001), The Race to the Intelligent State. Oxford Centre for Innovation, Oxford, U.K.

Cox Robert W. (1994), Global Restructuring: Making Sense of the Changing International Political Economy, in Stubbs and Underhill Edited, *Political Economy and the Changing Global Order*.

Currie Bob (2000), The Politics of Hunger in India, Macmillan India Ltd., Chennai.

Dalton Hugh (1936), Principles of Public Finance, George Routledge and Sons Ltd., London.

Dey H.L. (1933), Indian Tarrif Problem: In Relation to Industry and Taxation, George Allen and Unwin Ltd., London.

Dunkel Report, General Agreement on Tarrifs and Trade (GATT, 1994), Vidhi Publishing, New Delhi.

Dunning John H. (2000), Edited, Regions, Globalisation and the Knowledge Based Economy, Oxford University Press, Oxford.

Dutt Romesh (1906), The Economic History of India under Early British Rule, Trubner's Oriental Series, Kegan Paul Trench Trubner and Co. Ltd., London.

Dutt Romesh (1906), The Economic History of India in the Victorian Age, Trubner's Oriental Series, Kegan Paul Trench Trubner and Co. Ltd., London.

Eckans Richard S. (1967), Techniques and Functions of Indian Planning, reprinted in G.M. Meier, *Leading Issues in Economic Development*.

Economic Stability in the Post-war World: The Conditions of

Prosperity after the Transition from War to Peace, Report of the Delegation on Economic Depression, Part II, League of Nations, 1945.

Feis Herbert (1931), Europe, The World's Banker, 1870-1914, Council on Foreign Relations, Yale University Press.

Feldstein Martin, Refocusing the IMF, *Foreign Affairs*, Vol. 77, No. 2, March/April (1998).

Fifty Years of Indian Parliamentary Democracy, Lok Sabha Secretariat, New Delhi, August 1997.

Frank Andre Gunder (1978), Mainstream Economists as Astrologers: Gazing through the Clouded Crystal Ball, Published in U.S. Capitalism in Crisis by The Union for Radical Political Economics.

Frank Andre Gunder (1998), Re-Orient: Global Economy in the Asian Age, Vistaar Publications, New Delhi.

Freeman Chris and Soete Luc (1997), The Economics of Industrial Innovation, 3rd Edition, A Cassell Imprint, London.

Furtado Celso (1963), The Economic Growth of Brazil, University of California Press, Berkley and Los Angeles.

Friedman Milton and Schwartz A.J. (1970), Monetary Statistics of the United States, Columbia University Press.

Galbraith J.K. (1955), The Great Crash 1929, Hamish Hamilton.

Galbraith J.K. (1973), Economics and the Public Purpose, Published in Pelican Books.

Gallagher John and Robinson Ronald (1953), The Imperialism of Free Trade, Published in Louis W.M. Roger Imperialism.

Gernet Jacques (1996), A History of Chinese Civilization, Combridge University Press.

Gide Charles (1913), Cours D' Economie Politique, Authorised translation by Constance H.M. Archibold (1914), Political Economy, George G. Harrap & Company, London.

Government of India, Ministry of Finance, Economic Survey, 1989-90, 1990-91, 1991-92, 2001-02, 2002-03.

Hayek Friedrich A. (1988), The Fatal Conceit: The Errors of Socialism, University of Chicago Press.

Headrick Daniel R. (1981), Tools of Empire: Technology and European Imperialism in the Nineteenth Century, Oxford, Oxford University Press.

Headrick Daniel R. (1988), The Tentacles of Progress: Technology Transfer in the Age of Imperialism (1850-1940), Oxford, Oxford University Press.

Heil Brad (1978), Sunbelt Migration, Published in the *U.S. Capitalism Crisis* by The Union for Radical Political Economics.

Heilbroner Robert and Thurow Lester (1998), Economics Explained, Simon and Schuster.

Helleiner Eric (1994), From Bretton Woods to Global Finance: A World Turned Upside Down in Stubbs and Underhill.

Hicks J.R. (1967), Critical Essays in Monetary Theory, Oxford, Clarendon Press.

Hobsbawm Eric (1962), The Age of Capital (1848-1875), Viking, Penguin Books India (P) Ltd.

Hobsbawm Eric (1975), The Age of Revolution (1789-1848), Viking, Penguin Books India (P) Ltd.

Hobsbawm Eric (1987), The Age of Empire (1875-1914), Viking, Penguin Books India (P) Ltd.

Hobsbawm Eric (1994), The Age of Extremes, The Short Twentieth Century (1914-1991), Viking, Penguin Books India (P) Ltd.

Huntington Samuel P. (1996), The Clash of Civilizations and the Remaking of World Order, Penguin Books, India.

Inglis Brian (1975), The Forbidden Game, A Social History of Drugs, Hodder and Stoughton, London.

India: Reducing Poverty, Accelerating Development, 2000, The World Bank, Oxford University Press.

India Development Report, 2002, Edited by Kirit S. Parikh and R. Radha Krishna, Oxford University Press.

Jack J.C. (1916), The Economic Life of a Bengal District, Oxford.

Jalan Bimal (1991), India's Economic Crisis, The Way Ahead, Oxford University Press.

Kahn Herman (1979), World Economic Development, Vikas Publishing House Pvt. Ltd., New Delhi.

Kaldor Nicholas (1980), Essays on Value and Distribution,

Duckworth, London.

Kaldor Nicholas (1980), Essays on Economic Policy I, Duckworth, London.

Kaldor Nicholas (1980), Essays on Economic Policy II, Duckworth, London.

Kaldor Nicholas (1978), Further Essays on Applied Economics, Duckworth, London.

Kaldor Nicholas (1980), Reports on Taxation II, Duckworth, London.

Kaldor Nicholas (1980), Essays on Economic Stability and Growth, Duckworth, London.

Kennedy Paul (1993), Preparing for the Twenty-first Century, Indus, an imprint of Harper Collins Publishers, India.

Keynes John Maynard (1936), The General Theory of Employment, Interest and Money. Macmillan and Co. Ltd., London.

Korten David C. (1995), When Corporations Rule the World, Kumarian Press, U.S.A., Indian Reprint Published in 2000 by Other India Press, Goa, India.

Kriedte Peter, Medick Hans, Schlumbohm Jurgen (1981), Industrialisation Before Industrialisation, Cambridge University Press.

Landes David (2000), The Wealth and Poverty of Nations, Abacus, London.

Lareau William (1992), American Samurai, Warner Books.

Lenin V.I. (1917), Imperialism, The Highest Stage of Capitalism, Published in Selected Works of V.I. Lenin, Vol. I, Foreign Language Publishing House, Moscow.

Little I.M.D. (1957), A Critique of Welfare Economics, Oxford University Press, Oxford.

Louis W.M. Roger (1976), Edited, The Robinson and Gallagher Controversy, New View Points, New York.

Malecki Edward J. (1997), Technology and Economic Development, Longman.

Marx Karl, The Future Results of the British Rule in India, Published in the *New York Daily Tribune*, Aug. 8, 1853, Reprinted K. Marx and F. Engels on Colonialism, Foreign Languages Publishing House, Moscow.

Marx Karl, The British Rule in India, Published in *New York Daily Tribune*, 25th June 1853, Reprinted K. Max and F.

Engels on Colonialism, Foreign Languages Publishing House, Moscow.

Marx Karl, Lord Canning Proclamation and Land Tenure in India. Published in the New York Daily Tribune 7th June 1858, Reprinted K. Marx and F. Engels on Colonialism, Foreign Languages Publishing Houses, Moscow.

Marx Karl (1887), Capital, Vols. I, II, and III, Foreign Languages Publishing House, Moscow.

Marz Edward, Joseph Schumpeter (1992), Scholar, Teacher and Politician, Oxford University Press.

Mason Edward S. (1967), Comment on Planning in India in Max F. Millikan Edited, National Economic Planning, National Bureau of Economic Research, Columbia University Press, New York. Reprinted in Edward S. Mason *et. al.*, Leading Issues in Economic Development.

Meier Gerald M. (1975), Leading Issues in Economic Development, Oxford University Press.

Meszaros Istvan (1995), Beyond Capital, Towards a Theory of Transition, 2 Volumes, The Merlin Press; First Indian Edition (2000), K.P. Bagchi and Co., Calculta.

Minhas B.S. (1974), Planning and the Poor, S. Chand and Co. (Pvt. Ltd.), Delhi.

Moggridge D.E., Maynard Keynes (1992), An Economists Biography. Routledge, London and New York.

Mokyr Joel (1985), Edited, The Economics of the Industrial Revolution, Rowman and Allanheld.

Naoroji Dadabhai (1901), Poverty and Un-British Rule in India, Publication Division, Ministry of Information and Broadcasting, Government of India, First Published in 1901 by Swan Sonnenschein and Co. Ltd. London.

Nurkse Ragnar (1953), Problems of Capital Formation in Underdeveloped Countries, Oxford University Press.

Oppenheim Phillip (1992), Trade Wars, Weidenfeld and Nicolson, London.

Oye Kenneth A., Leiber Robert J., Rothchild Donald (1983), Edited, Eagle Defiant, United States Foreign Policy in the 1980s, Little Brown and Co.

Packard Vance (1957), The Hidden Persuaders, Langmans Green.

Parkinson C. Northcote (1977), The Rise of Big Business, Weidenfeld and Nicolson, London.

Patel I.G. (2002), Glimpses of Indian Economic Policy, An Insider's View, Oxford University Press, New Delhi.

Pillai P. Padmanabha (1928), Economic Conditions in India, With an Introductory Note by Gilbert Slater, George Routledge and Sons Ltd., London.

Pollard Sidney (1981), Peaceful Conquest, The Industrialisation of Europe 1760-1970. Oxford University Press, New York.

Porter Michael E. (1990), The Competitive Advantage of Nations, The Free Press.

Ray Parimal (1934), India's Foreign Trade Since 1870, George Routledge and Sons Ltd., London.

Ray Kalyan (1984), A Search for Demand, The Missing Link in Economic Development, Archana Press, Cuttack.

Robinson R.E. (1986), The Excentric Idea of Imperialism, with or without Empire, in Cain P.J. *et. al.*, edited *Imperialism* (Vol. 2).

Robinson Ronald (1972), Non-European Foundation of European Imperialism, in Peter J. Cain and Harrison Mark Edited *Imperialism* (Vol. 2).

Robertson D.H. (1937), Money, Cambridge University Press.

Roll Eric (1953), A History of Economic Thought, Faber and Faber Ltd., London.

Roorbach George B. (1933), Problems of Foreign Trade, MacGraw Hill Book Company, New York.

Root Hilton L., Asia's Bad Old Ways, *Foreign Affairs*, Vol. 80, No. 2, March/April (2001).

Ritortus, The Imperialism of British Trade, Contemporary Review LXXVI (1899), Reprinted in Peter J. Cain *et. al.*, edited *Imperialism* (Vol. 1).

Sampson Anthony (1977), The Arms Bazaar, Hodder and Stoughton, London.

Schumpeter Joseph A. (1954), History of Economic Analysis. Allan and Unwin (Puhlishers), Ltd., Reprinted by Routledge in 1997.

Seitz John L., Global Issues—An Introduction.

Sen Amartya (1984), Resources, Values and Development, Oxford University Press.

Smith Adam (1776), An Inquiry Into the Nature and Causes of the Wealth of Nations, Published by Encyclopaedia Britannica, INC.

Southgate George W. (1960), English Economic History, J.M. Dent and Sons Limited, London.

Soros George (1998), The Crisis of Global Capitalism, Little, Brown and Company, London.

Stiglitz Joseph (2002), Globalisation and its Discontents, Penguin Books, India.

Stubbs Richard and Underhill Geoffrey R.D. (1994), Edited, Political Economy and The Changing Global Order, The Macmillan Press Limited, London.

Speeches of Gopal Krishna Gokhale (1920), G.A. Natesan and Company, Madras.

Tawney R.H. (1979), Equality with an Introduction by Richard M. Titmuss, George Allen & Unwin, London.

Teich Mikulas and Porter Roy (1996), Edited, The Industrial Revolution in National Context, Europe and the U.S.A., Cambridge University Press.

Toynbee Arnold (1884), Lectures on the Industrial Revolution of the 18th Century in England, (Newton Abbot, 1969),

Tyson Kirk W.M. (1997), Competition in the 21st Century, St. Lucie Press, Florida.

Trade and Development Report 2001, United Nations, Book Well, Delhi.

The Reality of Aid 1997/8, Earthscan Publication Limited, London.

UNDP (2001), Human Development Report, 2001, Making New Technologies Work for Human Development, Oxford University Press.

UNDP (2002), Human Development Report, 2002, Deepening Democracy in a Fragmental World, Oxford University Press.

U.S. Capitalism in Crisis (1978), The Union for Radical Political Economics, New York.

Veblen Thorstein (1974), The Theory of the Leisure Class, with an Introduction by J.K. Galbraith. Vikas Publishing House Pvt. Ltd.

Waters Malcom (1995), Globalisation, Routledge, London.

Withers Hartley (1937), The Meaning of Money, Published by

John Murray, London.
World Economic Outlook (1985), International Monetary Fund, Washington D.C.
World Bank (1993), The East Asian Miracle: Economic Growth and Public Policy, New York, Oxford University Press.
World Bank (2000), Entering the 21st Century, World Development Report, 1999/2000, Oxford University Press.
World Bank (2000), World Development Report 2000/2001, Attacking Poverty, Oxford University Press.
World Bank (2003), World Development Report 2003, Sustainable Development in a Dynamic World, Transforming Institutions, Growth, and Quality of Life, Oxford University Press.

Index